Victor Charlie

Victor Charlie

THE FACE OF WAR IN VIET-NAM

Kuno Knoebl

INTRODUCTION BY BERNARD B. FALL

TRANSLATED BY ABE FARBSTEIN

FREDERICK A. PRAEGER, *Publishers*

New York · Washington · London

FREDERICK A. PRAEGER, *Publishers*
111 Fourth Avenue, New York, N.Y. 10003, U.S.A.
77–79 Charlotte Street, London W.1, England

Published in the United States of America in 1967
by Frederick A. Praeger, Inc., Publishers

Title of original German edition:
Kuno Knoebl, *Victor Charlie: Viet Cong der unheimliche Feind*
© 1966 by Verlag Fritz Molden, Wien-München

Library of Congress Catalog Card Number: 67-18835

Printed in the United States of America

Editor's Note: Quotations from English-language sources in the book
have generally been translated directly from the German.

Foreword

"Know the enemy and know yourself, and you will be victorious in a hundred battles," the Chinese thinker Sun Tzu wrote more than 2,000 years ago. His teachings can be found again today in Viet-Cong training manuals.

Viet-Nam offers a rare opportunity to study closely the political and military intentions of a new breed of revolutionaries. The purpose of this book is to contribute to the knowledge about an enigmatic enemy capable of defying the strongest military power on earth. If it does, it will have fulfilled its aim.

I dedicate this work to all the journalists in Viet-Nam who are engaged in their difficult calling. Their responsibility is great and so are their perils. Fifteen of them have already died in this war, more than forty have been wounded.

KUNO KNOEBL

Vienna
Summer, 1966

Contents

Introduction

One of the less unfortunate by-products of the protracted Second Indochina War* is the fact that now there is time to learn about the character of the enemy while the war is still going on. In the case of short-lived or low-level insurgencies—such as those in Greece and the Philippines—the outcome had pretty well been decided by the time serious research could be undertaken about the character and structure of the insurgent forces. In other cases, such as the Mau Mau, the war seemed so remote and the adversary so esoteric that solid research did not even begin until after the end of the conflict.

Initially, the Americans approached the Viet-Cong as if the movement did not exist as a separate entity and was nothing more than an emanation of the North Vietnamese political-military structure. This viewpoint is still officially espoused in Washington. Afterward, the Viet-Cong came into focus as a separate combat force ("assassins striking by night"); but still, it remained in official thinking an adjunct to North Vietnamese regulars "streaming" across the boundaries of South Viet-Nam rather than a main factor in the struggle. Between late 1965 and mid-1966, as the arriving U.S. units began to inflict serious setbacks upon enemy

---

* Since North and South Viet-Nam, all of Laos, the border areas of Cambodia, and Thailand (through the use of its airfields by American bombers operating in Viet-Nam) are involved in the war, the term "Second Indochina War" is both accurate and historically appropriate.

regulars—Viet-Cong as well as North Vietnamese—a wave of highly premature optimism rolled across the reporting from Viet-Nam, both official and unofficial. It said, in effect, that with the gradual destruction of the enemy regulars, an early collapse of the whole Viet-Cong structure in South Viet-Nam could be expected in the near future. One of the most respected American weekly news magazines, not previously known for its overly sanguine views of the situation, quoted a highly competent journalistic observer and retired general as saying that he was returning to Viet-Nam in November, 1966, to watch the total disintegration of the Viet-Cong insurgency and, presumably, the victorious end of the Second Indochina War. As events have since shown, all announcements of the demise of the Vietnamese insurgents have been somewhat premature, and the pendulum of opinion seems to swing back to the long-war concept again. Conceivably, the war might end through negotiation before the warmaking potential of either side is decisively damaged. But the brutal facts of early 1967 point to a protracted conflict, and one in which the estimated 240,000 *South* Vietnamese Viet-Cong insurgents might be far more difficult to deal with, in the long run, than the 50,000 or so North Vietnamese regulars identified by American intelligence as operating inside the country.

This is why books such as Kuno Knoebl's are of such significance. Not that his book is the only one thus far dealing with the Viet-Cong. There have been the Department of State White Papers, which, for all their obvious (and, regrettably, needless) errors, give a valuable documentary glance at one phase of the insurgency; Wilfred Burchett's *Inside Story of the Guerrilla War* and the more recent *Vietnam North,* though heavily weighted in favor of the

National Liberation Front (NLF), provide deep insights into the everyday life of the other side; and, most recently, Douglas Pike's admirable *Vietcong*, offers a scholarly appraisal of the techniques and organization of the movement. But in every case, authors have seen only one side of the war: the State Department and Pike—who is a U.S. Government official in Saigon, though his book often disagrees with the official viewpoint—from the American vantage; and Burchett, from the other.

French authors, myself included, have perhaps come a step closer to looking at, or into, both camps. The American reader is entitled to ask whether past French involvement in the area does not leave French observers with emotional blocks of their own that detract from detached observation. There still exists an American black-white belief that "the French want to see *us* lose because *they* couldn't win in Indochina," a belief which, in more or less sophisticated form, one can hear from cabinet secretaries down to GI's in the mud. However, French writers on Indochina and French news media run the gamut from those who wholly approve the American stand and strongly criticize Charles de Gaulle—such as *Le Figaro*—to those who disagree with some, or all, American policies.

In the case of Kuno Knoebl, we need not be concerned with any of these caveats or stereotypes. An Austrian, born in 1936, Knoebl was not old enough to be influenced by Nazism or, for that matter, by an undying love for the Allies, of East or West, who occupied his country until 1955. What we have here is the firsthand testimony, from direct observation in both camps, by a European neutral who is more concerned with people and what war does to them than with the grand strategy which, of late—to paraphrase Samuel Johnson—seems to have become the last refuge of all scoundrels. He is capable of telling his Viet-Cong escorts that antiwar demonstrations in the United States mean little in the face of American governmental resolve to prosecute the war; he describes in detail the death by torture at Viet-Cong hands of a South Vietnamese Government informer; and he reports that plain hatred among the Viet-Cong for the white man extended to him, the neutral. But Knoebl, firsthand observer, can also write that the South Vietnamese, and the American diplomats who advised them, "failed miserably" in rising to the Viet-Cong challenge, and were prisoners of their own self-delusions.

The initial American description of the Battle of Ap Bac appears in David Halberstam's *Making of a Quagmire*. It is interesting to see once more, through the eyes of a non-committed observer, the story of this disastrous battle in which freshly constituted Viet-Cong units inflicted a humiliating defeat upon a strong American-advised Vietnamese armored force. It is particularly interesting to imagine the effect upon European eyes and ears of a senior American general attempting to deny the obvious. Knoebl grew up in an Austria whose elders—because of their experiences in World War II—must have known a lot about official prevarication and instilled in their young a healthy distrust for military reports. The subsequent statements about Ap Bac, in all likelihood, were more damaging to American standing than the defeat itself.

In a perceptive passage, Knoebl quotes an American officer as saying that "many prisoners first learn what Communism really is from us during interrogation, in prison camps, and in re-education courses. And quite a few of them go for it." Knoebl's observations are most meaningful too when he is faced with acts committed by friendly troops (mostly South Vietnamese, but also South Korean and American) that would normally be considered violations of international law. This is a difficulty which, despite official denials, has simply not been tackled in a serious and consistent manner by the American field commanders in Viet-Nam. The plain reason is that nobody of any influence in Washington seems to be aware that this *is* a problem, and that it is likely to kill all chances of a meaningful pacification program. One official who deals with this problem in Washington once told me bluntly: "The trouble is, the Viet-Cong prisoners don't have any recourse." But the fact is, they do. It is that of the *American* prisoners whom the Viet-Cong hold and whom they can execute in reprisal for the ill-treatment or death of their comrades captured by the "Free World" side in Viet-Nam. The level of barbarity to which this war has sunk—it is far below that of the French Indochina War or the preceding war in the Pacific, but very close to that of the German-Russian front—gets a close and critical look by Knoebl. Its implications must be faced up to by the American reader and, with him, his policy-makers.

There are some errors in this book that could have been avoided by somewhat more digging than is usually feasible for a journalist under fire. But it is really irrelevant whether the author is fully accurate in every detail. Knoebl became a journalist after the Russians crushed the Hungarian freedom fighters, across the borders from his own country, in 1956. He is as ideally suited as any European can be to understand the struggle between freedom and Communism. What really counts is that he has apparently remained unconvinced that the Viet-Nam war is truly nothing else but a part of that struggle. This cannot be the fault of the hard-working information officers in Saigon, or of the rather primitive propaganda of the other side: After all, the Korean War, although its tactical aspects were objects of criticism, did not meet such sales resistance. A close examination of the differences between the two wars would make an interesting study in itself.

Here again, the author provides the beginnings of an answer when he attempts to describe what is perhaps the least "describable" of all the problems of the conflict—the incredible ability of the South Vietnamese Liberation Front thus far to continue to find replacements for its losses. To be sure, there is impressment; no doubt, it is the equivalent of the draft on the other side, and, from personal observation, it often operates in the same manner. Yet, remarkably, the Viet-Cong's desertion rate (though, in late 1966, twice what it was the previous year) is eight times lower than that of the government forces: 14,000 against 117,600. What makes the Viet-Cong "tick," in Knoebl's view, is their belief in the strength of the common idea and the hatred of the other side's might, rather than fear of it. They become, according to Knoebl, powerful mainsprings that compel the village guerrillas to stay in the fight. The whole war is being fought to prove that this mainspring can be broken under the sheer weight of the military power of the world's mightiest nation; or at least bent sufficiently so as not openly to resist its will.

This is the first major book on the Second Indochina War written by a national whose country is not an interested party to the conflict. Kuno Knoebl's book and his news reporting in German have already contributed to shaping the views on Viet-Nam of 100 million German-speaking Europeans. His reporting deserves an attentive hearing by the English-speaking public as well.

BERNARD B. FALL

Saigon, South Viet-Nam
January, 1967

Victor Charlie

Across the Border

A partisan commander leading his units into action is like a fisherman casting his net. He must spread it wide and then draw it firmly together. When he casts his net, the fisherman must take into account the depth of the clear water, the swiftness of the current, and possible snags. If partisan groups are scattered widely, their leaders must have a clear grasp of the situation and avoid blunders that will produce casualties. The fisherman must have a solid grip on the lines of his net in order to pull it in. When partisan detachments go into action, their leaders must keep in constant touch with them . . . and, in addition, hold strong combat groups in reserve. Fishermen often have to shift location; so do partisan units. The methods of flexible leadership in partisan warfare include the use of dispersed and closed formations, constant change of position, and the most precise planning.

MAO TSE-TUNG, *Guerrilla Warfare*

THE CHU PHONG MOUNTAINS are blue silhouettes on Viet-Nam's border. Crooked trees rise on their ridges like bearded phantoms in the damp heat of the highlands. Dry brushwood, scorched blue-green elephant grass, and dark palms cover the slopes that descend to the valley of the Ia Drang River, which flows down from the Annamite highlands and disappears into southern Cambodia.

The bamboo huts of the *montagnards* stand clustered in narrow clearings. The short men of Jaraï and Rhadé (Edé), two nomadic tribes, hunt small game with crossbows and waylay tigers in the forest with large bows. Overhead, American jet fighters thunder by, searching the impenetrable jungle to destroy an invisible enemy.

From the border, on clear days, you can see the red dust blown upward by the hot wind over the American military camps in Plei Me or Duc Co, western outposts at the end of the Ho Chi Minh Trail. It forms thick clouds and, merging with the smoke from brush fires, hangs over the earth like a blanketing fog.

Here, near the mountains, in the northernmost corner of Cambodia, the Ho Chi Minh Trail ends; it has run its 500-mile-long course through the mountains and jungles of eastern Laos and vanishes now in a spider web of narrow paths, trenches, tunnels, and roads. It is an artery built of blood, along which new forces flow incessantly into South Viet-Nam's tortured body.

We crouched behind a row of bushes at the edge of a wide field of withered grass and watched a jeep slowly approach and then disappear quickly behind the brush and thick clumps of trees. We were alone: a Vietnamese of about thirty, my interpreter and guide; an older, stocky man with a pale moon face; and I. My companions were members of the South Vietnamese National Liberation Front (NLF), the revolutionary movement that for years has been fighting American troops and the Saigon government and has maneuvered the world's most powerful nation to the brink of political defeat.

We waited about half an hour—then, one of the two jeep drivers suddenly appeared in the clearing in front of us. Two other men followed cautiously behind. They looked us over and came toward us. They were young, perhaps twenty, even younger. They moved warily through the grass, bodies bent and tense, ready to drop to the ground at the slightest sign of danger. Both wore black shorts and black, collarless shirts, with white buttons, open at the chest. One had an old nylon stocking filled with glutinous rice wrapped around his waist—his rations for many days. Small rubber bags of water hung from their wide cloth belts. Each carried two short-fused hand grenades in a small net. One wore a broad-brimmed hat with a red strip of cloth in front and the word "Viet-Nam" sewn on it. Hats like these can be bought in the souvenir shops of Saigon and the large coastal cities. GI's buy them to wear when they go on a few days' leave or to send home.

Both youths carried long-barreled rifles, Chinese carbines modeled on the Soviet 7.62-mm. Simonov. The bayonets at the end of the glistening, oily black barrels were folded back like the blades of oversized jackknives.

They stood waiting in front of us silently. One of my escorts rose, approached the strange pair, and waved his hand vigorously as if to show me how comrades-in-arms greet one another in this region. His exaggerated gestures seemed inappropriate. The two armed men responded like automatons, without a word, their faces impassive. My companion turned to me and said: "These are our guides, soldiers of the Liberation Army." There was a proud note in his voice, and he patted one of them on the shoulder. The two youngsters now registered my presence, stared at me, sized me up, and then turned away. One addressed my escort briefly in a soft, surprisingly high-pitched voice. "Let's go," my interpreter translated. The soldiers turned sharply and started across the field with quick steps.

I had thought my first meeting with the Viet-Cong, the soldiers of the NLF, would be different and not so matter-of-fact. I had thought of these guerrillas as shadowy jungle fighters who moved on the edge of reality, springing from some exotic jungle thicket, attacking and then vanishing, leaving barely a trace behind. I had thought of them as men who knew how to die mutely and unhesitatingly. So little was known about how they lived. You only saw them when they were dead—rows of corpses in front of American positions; small, shattered bodies with empty faces no different from those of Saigon cab drivers or of peasants in the rice fields.

I buckled my knapsack and followed the small column along a path whose end I did not know. I had started along that path just a few days before, coming from life in a well-organized European society. Those days now seemed remote.

My trip to this point had started in Stung Treng, the last big Cambodian settlement near the Laos border. It was a replica of all the other settlements along the Mekong River. Near Stung Treng, the Sekong and So San rivers flow into the wide, brown bed of the Mekong, which begins in Tibet, runs 2,200 miles down into the great delta near Saigon, and flows into the South China Sea.

Where these three rivers converge, the old French colonial Route 19 (often mentioned in French Army reports during the Indochina War) begins, running eastward straight across Viet-Nam, past Pleiku and An Khe, reaching the coast near Binh Dinh. Today, Route 19 is a line of communication—exactly as it was fifteen years ago—to South Viet-Nam's battlefields in the jungles, mountains, and swamps.

Friends in Phnom Penh, Cambodia's capital, had put me in touch with the widespread organization that supports the South Vietnamese rebels in the neighboring countries. I was lucky enough to be able to attach myself to this tightly run apparatus and use it. It is a minor front in the Viet-Nam War, but those in charge of it examine every plan in minute detail; not one step is taken before the next one is known. Yet, my trip to the highlands was improvised and accidental. I did not know its purpose or destination.

We had changed vehicles in Stung Treng. A jeep had been waiting for us; I did not know where it had suddenly come from or how the two men sitting in it knew of our arrival. It was an old, battered jeep and undoubtedly had traveled these highways during the Indochina War occupied, perhaps, by Frenchmen or Foreign Legionnaires on long patrols through lonely jungles. Now two wiry young men sat up front, peasants or workers or small shopkeepers. Their bearing marked the confident attitude of people with military training, soldiers, members of the clandestine army that was challenging the Western world

Everyone in Phnom Penh knew Route 19 was unsafe and closely watched by the Cambodian Army. Yet we did not run into any roadblocks or meet a single patrol. Our drive into the mountains ended near the jungle villages of Bo Kheo and La Bang. We were told to get out, and the jeep disappeared. I was informed that my two escorts and I would have to march a few more hours and then pitch camp for the night.

The area we were in is crosshatched in red patches, as I later saw, on the maps of both the American Army Command in Saigon and the South Vietnamese General Staff. It is an area controlled or infiltrated by the Viet-Cong or North Vietnamese Army units. The Vietnamese city of Pleiku is about fifty miles to the east. From army outposts there, the Americans try to check North Vietnamese units that steadily slip down through this border region into South Viet-Nam. By now the area has become both a staging ground and a sanctuary for the Communist rebels, a fact that keeps relations strained between the Saigon and United States governments and the Cambodian chief of state, Prince Sihanouk.

Sihanouk denies there are Communist troops on his territory and tries hard to convince the world that this is so. He invited American correspondents to visit Cambodia; accompanied by high-ranking Cambodian officers, they flew by helicopter over the border area. Trained American reconnaissance pilots frequently see nothing, and the reporters did not fare any better. They did not spot a sign of North Vietnamese troops or Viet-Cong soldiers beneath the thick cover of the jungle.

The prince's policy, he says, is designed to stave off the destruction of neutral Cambodia. He does not appear too anxious to know exactly what is happening on his country's frontier. Instead of defending the border provinces, he has withdrawn the troops stationed there and prudently concentrated them in a few small garrisons where they are not tempted to join the battles. Thus, the border strip between South Viet-Nam and Cambodia, several hundred miles long, is a no-man's-land, where American, South Vietnamese, and Communist troops move about without much hindrance from Sihanouk's soldiers.

One of my escorts first told me that Cambodia's northeast provinces and eastern Laos were minor theaters of war in the Viet-Nam conflict. He said that the only real danger we might run into in the area was from American commando troops, Special Forces units, which operate in the region. "Earlier," he said, "civilian armies, mercenary bands, were active here too, fighting for the side that paid most. They were made up of mounted tribesmen or southerners who came here to fight and pillage."

I asked, "What became of these bands?"

"The tigers got them," was the terse reply.

It would have been unpleasant to have stumbled on an American unit in this area. From what I later saw of their methods, their Special Forces would not have treated me gently had they caught me with this strange Viet-Cong patrol.

We made up a curious group. There were five men with me: Bui Van Dieu, about thirty, a member of the NLF Association of Journalists, who had traveled with me from Phnom Penh; Phan Lieu, a small, stocky, taciturn man, the group's real leader and probably a middle-echelon Viet-Cong official; one of the two jeep drivers who had brought us from Stung Treng to the edge of the border; and the two tight-lipped young guerrillas who acted as our guides and would, if necessary, defend us.

Bui Van Dieu was always the one who answered my questions. That is not the name he used; in any event, I doubt that he told me his real one. (Nor, since it might harm them, do I use the real names of any of the men who traveled with me.) He was born in Haiphong, he told me, came to Saigon in 1950, and joined the NLF in 1962. Since then he has been living "between the borders," as he put it. He had recently been in the capital for a meeting of local NLF cadres. "Then I traveled quite legally to Bangkok, and from there to Phnom Penh," he once said, laughing. "It's really not very hard. High officials of the Liberation Front often fly from Tan Son Nhut [Saigon's airport] to conferences abroad. The police are on the hunt for all of them, but not one has ever been picked up."

Bui Van Dieu was supposed to bring me as far as the "south of Pleiku Province" and there pass me along to another functionary who would supervise the rest of my journey. "I hope we'll reach the frontier tomorrow afternoon," he said. He spoke excellent French; he probably had been educated in one of the country's many French schools. When we discussed France, he could barely conceal a certain sympathy for his former colonial masters. I was to meet this reaction later in Saigon and other South Vietnamese cities. As the Viet-Nam War expanded, relations between the French and Vietnamese seemed to improve—whether the latter were NLF members or not. Probably, one reason was President de Gaulle's policy. Members of the Vietnamese middle class—to the degree that the small number of government officials, academicians, and intellectuals can be so described—draw a sharp line between "civilized France" and "rich Americans."

We had to cross rolling hills and broad strips of brush before reaching the jungle. The brush was exhausting. Our guides did not follow the worn paths but trudged six feet higher and broke a new trail through tangled thickets. Heads down, hats covering our faces, we practically crawled. Thorns scratched my face and hands, and the branches snapped back hard at my body.

There were nests of huge red ants in the thickets, often hanging six feet high. Clusters of ants fell on my back and neck; their bites were painful, and it took a long while to shake them out of my clothing. The first time a nest fell on me I began a devil's dance to get rid of the ants. My companions shook with laughter, and even our silent guides grinned broadly at my predicament. Both young men cut a path through the brush effortlessly, at a pace that soon left me gasping. But what I most admired about them was their ability to avoid the ant nests. I later asked them how they did it, but they only smiled and kept their secret.

We waded into a shallow river and proceeded a few hundred feet along its bed until one of the guides signaled us to stop. "Fill your water bottles now. We won't come across any more water today," Bui Van Dieu said, letting the muddy current run into his canteen. I had not expected water to be a problem in the tropics, but he explained: "Many rivers are completely dried up in this season. We have to go easy on our water."

We stopped, after another hour's march, at the edge of a cleared slope. Nothing was on it but two tumble-down huts; beyond it lay the jungle. We pitched camp for the night in the brush; we would reach our destination the next day.

Our young guides sat apart from us, their calm indicating we were in no danger. The man who had driven the jeep sat down beside me and told me his name. I gathered that he was personally responsible for my safety, my body-guard. But it was not clear whether he was supposed to be looking after me or keeping watch on me. My escorts were determined to avoid all danger, and I believe that they would have sacrificed their lives for my sake. At the same time, they distrusted me. I knew that as long as nothing happened that could be misinterpreted, I could count on them completely. I was equally sure they would not have hesitated to kill me had I acted suspiciously. Bui Van Dieu had said: "There are many agents and enemies here, and we know how to defend ourselves against them." Had I been suspected of being an enemy agent or—even worse— an American, the friendly man sitting beside me and telling me about Saigon and his family would have had no scruples in ordering me shot. And the two youths, squatting nearby and talking softly, their long carbines resting easily on their knees, would have executed his command immediately.

These men were used to living in constant danger; they knew exactly the risks they were taking and had carried out similar missions before. Traveling with them through the border jungles and no-man's-land, I had come to understand that guerrillas must be better disciplined, more strictly organized, and often braver than soldiers enjoying the relative security of a large regular army.

It took the Americans a long time to realize how tightly the Communist guerrilla troops were organized; that everything they did was minutely planned and directed; and that even their mute deaths seemed subject to a higher order of things. This organization alone has made it possible for the Communists to wage the war so long and so successfully.

The notion that American troops face murderous, bloodthirsty bands of jungle fighters is a fairy tale. Not just wildly imaginative comic-strip artists indulge in this fantasy; American officers and soldiers sometimes believe it too. *Smilin' Jack* and *Steve Canyon* in the army newspaper *Stars and Stripes* distort the image of the invisible jungle enemy just as much as the reports from American soldiers about the "dirty Charlies" and "those lousy pajama boys we could crush if they'd only let us."

There has been just one kind of war since Korea, and

Western armies and their leaders, trained in the school of Clausewitz, have difficulty in coping with it. It has no clearly defined fronts, and traditional strategies are useless. No matter where they drop the bombs, fire the shells, deploy the troops, the enemy is not there.

Guerrilla fighters, tracking down their prey singly or in groups, have become the decisive factor in the war. They would go right on fighting even if all supply routes were destroyed, all means of transportation blown up. Modern warfare belongs to those versatile soldiers who are self-sufficient and fearless, who can handle the most modern machine gun or use a knife, who can manufacture their own weapons.

The Viet-Cong elite troops undergo training comparable to that given the West's special units. They have learned to obey unconditionally and to wage a war that shatters the concepts and strategic plans of the most brilliant general staff. They live in the forest and mountains, scattered to avoid concentration of troops. They unite shortly before battle, and afterward break up into small groups often made up of two or three men. And there are times when a single guerrilla holds up an entire enemy detachment or at least keeps it on edge.

This is one example: The guerrillas controlled a small highway running from Cambodia's frontier mountains to Pleiku. They would ambush the trucks and jeeps that their mines failed to blow up. Finally, in December, 1965, an American Special Forces company from Pleiku set out to secure the road. The operation lasted several days, but the Americans drew a blank: no enemy. The only traces of enemy activity they found were scraps of metal, junked trucks that had hit mines, and shreds of uniform ripped off by the explosions. At last they stumbled on a small, abandoned dugout in the brush. It contained mines, a nylon sack with small-arms ammunition, and an earthen pitcher filled with rice. This was obviously the camp of the guerrillas who had made the road unsafe. The Special Forces men set a trap and caught a Viet-Cong guerrilla a few days later. He had been trained in North Viet-Nam, was a member of the Rhadé mountain tribe, and knew the area around Pleiku thoroughly. They questioned him, trying to learn the hiding place of his comrades. The small *montagnard* was not very talkative, but he did reveal that he had been terrorizing traffic on the road by himself for months. He had been living in the brush and had constructed his own mines. He had picked up his food –rice and fruit—at nearby mountain villages. Whenever his ammunition and explosives gave out, he replenished his stocks at designated mountain hideouts. When captured, he had been at his post four months, without any expectation of relief. During interrogation he said that he had always believed he would be caught sooner or later and shot.

The American forces in Viet-Nam keep coming up against such situations. The guerrillas almost always succeed in creeping up on their objective unobserved, attacking, and then vanishing. Very rarely can the GI's block the withdrawal or destroy the retreating guerrillas. It is a maxim of guerrilla strategy to avoid troop concentrations. This tactic is being followed very closely now that the U.S. command is using bombers and fighter planes on an ever-increasing scale.

One has to know the Vietnamese jungle, brush, mountains, and swamps to understand what precise planning and magnificent organization are required to unite these troops, on the march for days, into a combat-ready unit at the right time and place. These clashes do not last long, seldom more than half an hour, so that the guerrilla troops must unite and disperse in order to meet elsewhere in the jungle.

My own trip demonstrated the astonishing planning and organization. We had linked up with our guides in the heart of the brush as if it were the most ordinary thing in the world. I did not know how the two guides had learned we were coming; yet, they had expected us. Possibly they belonged to a special unit assigned to accompany visitors, officials, or agents of the NLF who wanted to reach guerrilla-controlled South Vietnamese territory from Cambodia. Very likely it was a regular wartime service.

We struck camp at 4:00 A.M., leaving Shom Nhai—a small hamlet on Route 19—behind us. At about 10:00 A.M. we crossed a second river, probably the Ia Kri. The water came up to our shoulders, so that we swam rather than waded across it. One of the guides stopped suddenly and made a quick sign; the men beside me dropped to the ground, and I did too. The scout slid away from us like a snake, disappearing into a dense thicket. A few minutes later, we heard screams and then the young guerrilla, grinning broadly, reappeared. He was prodding two women toward us with his rifle. They were Jaraï tribeswomen returning to their village. They were young and wore black cloths, embroidered at the hem, wrapped around their hips. In the jungle twilight the naked upper parts of their bodies, with full high breasts, shimmered dully. They were chattering as they sat down; their long black hair hung loosely over their shoulders.

They looked at us and laughed in embarrassment. Our

two guides stood grinning in front of the women and even my "bodyguard," whom I had not seen laugh once, smilingly eyed their slender bodies. The young women were carrying small hand-woven baskets on their backs. Now, they placed the baskets on the ground and squatted alongside them. Their gestures indicated they were prepared to serve their new masters; they did not seem in the least averse to having a good time with the two armed youths. But Bui Van Dieu, who at first had been amused by the scene, barked a few words and the soldiers' faces changed immediately. They raised their guns and motioned to the women to stand up. The tribeswomen, equally surprised, did so, hitched on their baskets and disappeared into the underbrush. The now sullen guides took the lead again, obviously unhappy that they had been denied their fun.

We rested a fourth time at 2:00 P.M. We were progressing slowly, and our group had stopped repeatedly while the guides scouted the way ahead. We found ourselves at the edge of a *ray*, an area that the mountain peasants had cleared for rice by burning down trees. One of the guides disappeared and returned in a few minutes, but not alone. Four armed men were with him. The youngest may have been about sixteen, the oldest thirty-five years old. They wore coarse gray-green uniforms. They appeared exhausted, their uniforms and equipment filthy, their faces creased, gray, and tired. The four soldiers belonged to a South Vietnamese NLF group of about forty men. They had set up camp near us, having just emerged, as Phan Lieu, the quiet head of our group said, from a "victorious battle against the imperialists." Phan Lieu added: "These soldiers will accompany us as extra guards." But he seemed disturbed by their presence. I did not understand why at

first. I knew, of course, that the closer we came to the frontier the greater the danger. But for the time being—so it
seemed to me—things were going well and we were moving forward safely.

I approached Bui Van Dieu, who had spoken briefly
with Phan Lieu and was now talking to the soldiers, and
asked him what fight they had been in. The newspapers
in Phnom Penh had reported clashes between Americans
and the Viet-Cong near the Cambodian border. But the
accounts had been vague—and tailored, as usual, to the
official line—so that it had been hard to make out what was
actually happening. Sihanouk's papers had written about
"shameless encroachments" by American troops on sover-
eign Cambodian territory and threatened that every American who in the future violated the border—and Cambodia's sovereignty—would be "crushed."

Later, in Stung Treng, we were told the NLF Army
had won "great and decisive victories over the aggressors"
near Plei Me and in the provinces of Cong Tum, Gia Lai,
and Dac Lac* (Kontum, Pleiku, and Darlac). Evidently,
the engagements had been battles fought around the Special Forces camp of Plei Me, and Communist casualties
were heavy. Four Viet-Cong battalions and North Viet-
Nam units had besieged the strongly fortified camp for a
whole week. The U.S. Air Force had shattered them, and
then units of the 1st U.S. Air Cavalry Division routed the
survivors.

We had heard something else in the Mekong town;
there had been another battle recently, close to Plei Me,

* The names cited are those the NLF has given to these provinces.
Beside creating its own administrative system, the NLF has drawn
new district and provincial boundaries, which often vary greatly from
existing borders of provinces in South Viet-Nam.

near the Ia Drang River. A picture of the actual events slowly began to emerge from conversations with these four weary men.

Bui Van Dieu and Phan Lieu talked with the four soldiers for a long time. I saw how they pressed their questions and how reluctantly, and often distrustingly, the guerrillas answered in the fewest words possible. At last Bui Van Dieu called me over: "I will tell you frankly what our problem is," he began. "These men are members of our regular army. They have told us of an encounter with the imperialists. We still don't know exactly what happened, but it appears the fighting was very savage, and"—he paused to give special weight to his next sentence—"it seems the Americans took a terrible beating." Then he laughed briefly to himself, lowered his head and looked up at me, partly in amusement, partly to watch my reactions. "And another thing, you remember the river we crossed today and our near-amorous episode?" I remembered, of course. "Well, about two miles beyond the river we crossed the frontier, about the time we met the Jaraï."

Surprised, I asked, "Then we're now in Viet-Nam?"

"Yes." Then, as if to apologize, he added: "We couldn't tell you sooner. You understand." I understood.

"Now we have to wait a while for news, and possibly we'll stay here longer than was planned," Bui Van Dieu began again. "I've asked my comrade," pointing to Phan Lieu, "and he has given permission for you to talk to the soldiers. They will tell you everything. Just go easy with the questions. I'll serve as interpreter."

The soldiers were squatting on the ground and I crouched facing them. They looked at me suspiciously, and none of Bui Van Dieu's attempts to present me as a friend dissipated their distrust. I asked some trivial questions, which my companion translated; I'm sure he embroidered them with flowery propaganda, because in each case he seemed to be making a small speech to the soldiers. They barely answered my questions, and when I wanted the oldest member of the group to tell me whether he was married and where his wife lived, he merely shrugged his shoulders.

The soldier Le Tu was sitting near us. He was twenty-four years old and came, I finally learned, from a village in the frontier province of Quang Duc. He had two years of service in the Liberation Army behind him and had been wounded twice in combat with South Vietnamese troops. At the beginning of October, 1965, his platoon had been shifted to Pleiku and ended up operating north of Duc Co, one of the most heavily fortified camps of the U.S. Special Forces along the Cambodian border, an important check point at the end of the Ho Chi Minh Trail.

Le Tu's group had not taken a direct part in the Camp Plei Me battle that began on October 19, but it had been involved in many fights with American units. Apparently, casualties had been heavy in these actions since Le Tu said he had lost "many comrades and friends." Along with about thirty-five other men, he had been assigned to a new platoon. At the beginning of November, this unit had spent a few days on the wooded slopes of Chu Goungot—a mountain north of Duc Co—and then had marched south to the old French colonial Route 19.

The soldier answered my questions very hesitantly. Then he fell silent and looked questioningly from me to Bui Van Dieu, who spoke a few words to Le Tu and explained: "I told him he could speak freely to you. We have no secrets either from you or the world. Let everybody learn about our struggle for freedom."

The soldier continued: "I believe we crossed the highway on November 2 and kept moving south till we hit a camp in the jungle. There were other units in the camp and this was very dangerous."

"Why?" I asked.

"The Americans were very much on the alert at this time, and it is easier to discover a lot of people than a few. The tiger also hunts alone. Our platoon commander . . ."

"What was his name?"

Again he looked uncertainly at Bui Van Dieu, who nodded to the soldier. He went on in a faltering voice: "Our platoon commander, Phan Van Hung, explained to us that it had been necessary to join the other units for an important briefing."

Phan Lieu interrupted at this point to deliver a short lecture to me on the importance of political education for the soldiers. "The soldiers with the better morale will ultimately conquer," the NLF official declared. I wanted to know what he meant by morale. "Every soldier in our army knows what he is fighting for," he answered in a condescending tone, a tone I would hear often in Saigon when high Vietnamese officials spoke to low-ranking Americans or when Vietnamese talked in general about whites. "Every soldier is also told exactly why he must follow his orders. He has a goal: the liberation of his people. The Americans have worse morale because their soldiers do not know what they are fighting for. They have been sent to a country where everything is against them: the earth, the air, the climate, and the people. They are supposed to fight and die here. Why? That's the reason they are poorer fighters than the soldiers of the Liberation Army."

Still, I interrupted, the Americans can throw in an enormous army and have an overwhelming military-technical superiority. His answer: "We have the better weapons because the people are our weapon. If the imperialists want to win here, they will have to destroy a whole people. But they can't do that. Who will cultivate the plantations, who will they sell their weapons to if they exterminate the people? Besides, they would lose face before the entire world. They must give the appearance, at least, of supporting part of the people."

"You mean the government?"

"Yes. But this government no longer exists. It is a minority, American puppets. The government commands an army of more than half a million men. Yet, if the Americans hadn't intervened we would already have wiped out this army. We would have destroyed it even if it had been a million strong. And I'll tell you why. The government soldiers don't want to fight. They don't want war; they don't want to shoot at us because they fear our revenge and because they are afraid they might be shooting at their own brothers. Every month hundreds of government soldiers desert to us. They come with their uniforms, weapons, and important information. They no longer want to fight against the people but for their own freedom and that of their people." Phan Lieu suddenly ended his brief speech and allowed the soldier to continue.

"We had already heard something big lay ahead. As in the past, we did not learn the exact details until after the operation had been thoroughly discussed and every man knew what his job would be," Le Tu went on. "We usually aren't told the name of the spot where the action is to take place, and there are times we discover where we fought only after the battle is over. But this seldom happens because almost always a ·few comrades are from the area and know it intimately.

"This time all we learned was that we would attack two American camps. We were told there would be reinforcements when we reached the objective and that it was a ten days' march from the camp. You must understand," Le Tu repeated slowly, almost in the tone of a lecturer, "that we seldom begin an operation until every soldier has been assigned a specific task. Yet here we were marching through the night of the third day and not all our questions had been answered."

"It is customary," Bui Van Dieu interjected, "for all operations to be discussed. Sometimes an attack is even put to a vote, and if the majority is opposed, the action may not be carried out or completely new plans are drawn up."

"That surely doesn't happen often," I objected.

"Of course, the discussions are limited, since the basic task of our Liberation Army is to fight. That's why the major topic is how best to attain our objective," Bui Van Dieu said.

Soldier Le Tu's group crossed the Ia Drang River and the Chu Phong Mountains; then, it was ordered to turn around and set up camp on the northern bank of the river. That was on November 12, 1965, two days before the battle in the Ia Drang Valley started.

In the same period, the men of the 3rd Brigade of the U.S. 1st Air Cavalry Division were preparing for a big search-and-destroy operation in the Cambodian border region. American intelligence assumed that strong North

Vietnamese units had infiltrated South Viet-Nam in the latitude of Duc Co and Plei Me. Never before in the history of the Second Viet-Nam War had so many North Vietnamese People's Army (VPA) soldiers entered South Viet-Nam. In Washington, Secretary of Defense Mc-Namara announced that the monthly infiltration rate had risen to 4,500 men (it is now more than 5,500); that since September, 1965, 15,000 members of the VPA had infiltrated down the Ho Chi Minh Trail, across Laos, into South Viet-Nam. The South Vietnamese Government stated that there were already "more than 30,000 members" of the VPA in South Viet-Nam.

The Red military road running through the east Laotian jungle was now being bombed on an unprecedented scale; American jet bombers, taking off from the air fields of Ubon, Nakhon Phanom, Udorn, and Korat, in Thailand, attacked the trail day after day; the Royal Laotian and South Vietnamese air forces flew missions endlessly against the jungle trail. Yet, men and matériel kept flowing without a hitch.

From the beginning, the NLF guerrillas had been able to count on some support from Hanoi, although on a much smaller scale in the first war years than Saigon and Washington indicated. The situation changed as 1965 came to a close. The Viet-Cong began steadily losing previously won terrain to American troops; the U.S. Air Force was mauling them and, for the first time since the struggle had started, the fortunes of war had slowly turned against the Communist guerrillas. The Central Committee of the Lao-Dong (Communist) Party in Hanoi now decided to provide massive help for its beleaguered comrades in the South.

Thousands of peasants, both from North Viet-Nam and the regions in eastern Laos controlled by the Communist Pathet Lao movement, were organized as labor commandos in Dan Congs, labor brigades,* and brought to the mountain jungles of Laos. The coolies of the Communist revolution began to extend the Ho Chi Minh Trail with picks and shovels. The American spotter pilots and commando troops in Laos soon discovered that this army of coolies had wrought a technical miracle in the jungle: There now existed a new stretch of road about 150 miles long. It began east of the Laotian Mekong town of Thakekh and ended close to the jungle village of Chavane, near the South Vietnamese border, in about the same latitude as Quang Nai. I later flew with a bombing mission against this section of the Ho Chi Minh Trail and saw the amazing jungle road, fifteen feet wide at some points, along which trucks, and even tanks, now roll. Every night North Vietnamese regiments marched down this route to vanish into the mountain provinces of Pleiku, Kontum, and Darlac in South Viet-Nam. U.S. Secretary of Defense Robert McNamara had said in Saigon: "We are no longer losing this war." But later he admitted in Washington: "If we do not succeed in halting the flow of men and supplies from North Viet-Nam, the Communists will be able to continue the war unhindered. In that case there will be no end of the war in sight."

In the first days of November, 1965, the helicopters of

* Dan Congs, in the main, are made up of peasant men and women—frequently also teen-agers—who work on the construction of roads, trenches, tunnels, fortifications, etc. on a more or less voluntary basis for a few days or weeks. Peasants can buy exemption from service, for example, through larger deliveries of rice. In many South Vietnamese districts, it is customary for the peasants to set aside one or two days a week for "community work" on behalf of the NLF.

the U.S. 1st Air Cavalry Division stationed at An Khe began intense patrol flights along the infiltration routes. On November 4, two OV-1 Mohawks flew night reconnaissance missions, since it was almost impossible to check the Communist movement by day; Ho Chi Minh's armies march by night. The gray-green camouflaged helicopters were equipped with special cameras capable of photographing the enemy in the dark. They contained highly sensitive instruments that recorded the body temperatures of men or animals from a height of 900 feet. The lenses could take several dozen separate pictures of an object in a minute.

The Mohawks flew west from Plei Me over the valley of the Ia Drang River and photographed an area of more than twenty-five square miles. They returned to An Khe four hours later, and in another four hours, 1,500 feet of film had been developed. In another ten minutes, the film was being run off for Major General Henry Kinnard, commander of the 1st Air Cavalry Division, and his staff. What the U.S. officers saw was hardly gratifying. There were at least 5,000 enemy soldiers, more than two regiments, in the Plei Me, Duc Co, and Ia Drang Valley area, and it could be assumed that most of them were of the VPA. The commander of the 3rd Brigade of the 1st Air Cavalry, Colonel Thomas Brown, was ordered to prepare a large-scale action in the Ia Drang Valley region.

Le Tu squatted next to me, smoking interminably. "The spotter planes and helicopters kept circling over us," he continued. "That is always a sign the Americans are planning something. We had often shot down helicopters that flew low over our hideouts, but we had strict orders this time not to shoot. Nothing was to betray our presence.

We were to take the enemy by surprise. We are always cautious, but now we took special pains not to be discovered. Large flocks of helicopters came whirling over the valley and we knew we would soon be fighting. Our platoon was still concealed, and we hadn't received any order to advance, so we remained where we were."

The NLF official interrupted: "You must understand," he said to me, "that it is often hard to keep our soldiers from fighting. They all want to be in on it when we are crushing the imperialists."

"Right after the Americans landed we heard heavy fire. Now we knew the battle had started, but we had no idea where our comrades-in-arms were located, how many of them there were, and when the shooting would reach us." The young soldier looked at me with his dark, tired eyes, and I felt I could read in them something of the fear and tension he must have felt.

"Then the planes came and we also heard artillery fire. It lasted for three days. For three days the planes bombed our positions on the other side of the Chu Phong Mountains. Finally, the first of our comrades arrived from the battle area. We didn't see many, since they were under orders to move in very small groups and withdraw as inconspicuously as possible. Many were wounded and told of savage fighting. The day before, we learned, a whole platoon had been destroyed by fire [napalm] bombs—but the Americans had also lost many soldiers. A platoon commanded by Nguyen Yuan Giang had set an ambush 500 yards south of the peak of Chu Phong, and two American companies had fallen into the trap. Our comrades did not fire until the Americans were right in front of their machine guns. It couldn't have been easy for them to wait so long because they were very angry—especially furious about the bombings—but they had adopted the right tactic."

According to Le Tu, the American companies were totally wiped out in a few minutes. "They told us about one of our comrades who had shot twenty-five Americans with one burst of his machine gun. They tried to take cover, but they were so hemmed in that almost all were killed. Our comrades felt no pity; they knew they had to kill as many Americans as possible. We had been told to slaughter as many imperialist soldiers as we could since, if the number of American dead mounted, the American people—who dislike this war—would overthrow their government. We have also heard that there have been uprisings in the United States against the warmongers."

Bui Van Dieu chimed in, "That's right," looking to me for confirmation. I said nothing, but decided to explain to him later that foreign Communists consistently misinterpret anti–Viet-Nam War demonstrations in the West and in the United States. They see them colored by Communist revolutionary theory and do not understand the demonstrations for what they really are: free expressions of opinion in a democratic society in opposition to a specific policy.

"The planes returned but missed our comrades' positions and bombed their own people, killing those who had survived our attacks. Our troops had taken cover in time, but not one man was wounded," the soldier went on. "When we got this news we felt very good—we were saddened by the sight of the many wounded passing by and the dead being buried near the river. We knew there was trouble ahead for us. At last the order came to get ready, and we cheered up at the prospect of battle. We had been ashamed of hiding in the jungle so long.

"With twenty comrades, I was ordered to cross the river and wait on the southern bank. We—Cham Boa was with us . . ." Le Tu pointed to one of his companions squatting nearby, staring emptily, who did not even look up when his name was mentioned. "We crossed the river and soon met many friends who had been well concealed. I don't remember any longer just what happened then. Probably, I wasn't too alert, because suddenly in front of us were a lot of American soldiers." The man began pressing the knuckles of both hands against each other, and the sallow skin over his jaw muscles tightened. He was agitated by the memory and began talking rapidly in short sentences. "There were many of them. They came out of the woods and through the short grass. We saw them plainly—the cautious way they approached the river. I felt like my friends; I wanted to shoot, but couldn't. I had my gun ready and had drawn a bead on the man I wanted to kill, but I couldn't fire until the order was given."

"What would have happened had you fired anyway?" I asked.

"I would have been punished severely."

"What are the penalties in your army?"

The soldier fell silent and Bui Van Dieu answered instead: "Most soldiers who have made a mistake or disobeyed an order are assigned to labor in Dan Congs. Often, they are just given a warning. A man's mistakes are discussed by the members of his unit who then vote on the penalty. Frequently a soldier who has committed a grave error volunteers for an exceptionally dangerous action. Sometimes his weapon is taken away—this is a terrible disgrace." He added: "We very rarely have to impose such penalties."

"What happens if a soldier is captured?" I asked.

"That depends on the circumstances. Our soldiers are under orders to surrender to the imperialists only when there is no other way out: if they no longer have weapons or ammunition, can no longer fight, and can't escape, or if they have been wounded. But if somebody just surrenders, it is possible that he will be condemned by the people as a traitor."

"I've heard that soldiers of the North Vietnamese Army who are members of the Communist Party are automatically expelled if they are captured."

"True. But we don't do that," Bui Van Dieu replied. Le Tu had listened to us without understanding and haltingly resumed his report only after a command from my escort.

"The Americans had thrown in too many men, and we got the order to withdraw. We left our hiding place reluctantly. In an hour, we heard violent firing on the other side of the river; it lasted a long time, half an hour, or longer. We started off again on the same paths the Americans had taken into the brush. There were signs of the imperialists everywhere. One of our comrades passed by holding the head of an American soldier. He had knifed the enemy from behind and thrown his corpse into the brush after he had cut off the head—so great was his fury against the Americans. He showed us the head and then flung it far into the jungle."

In Viet-Nam, beheading is considered the most shameful death and indicates contempt for the victim. In fact, it is frequently used by Communist terrorists for executing government officials, police, or any enemy sympathizer before an assembled village community. Le Tu continued:

"There were some enemy units ahead of us; we were to attack them from the rear. We were probably too careless, because they discovered us and fired. We lost a few comrades but kept going. Suddenly, we were right in the middle of the American positions. We killed as many of them as we could find, but most of them had taken such good cover that it was impossible to catch them. We lay facing each other—the Americans were probably sixty feet away—and we yelled, 'GI's, GI's!' That was all the English we knew; and every time we shouted they shot wildly into the air. They must have been very frightened. They were even afraid of our wounded and killed those they found. Naturally, this made us even angrier, and when we spotted an American, we tried to kill him."

"The wounded as well?"

"The wounded too—and we would certainly have killed all of them if we hadn't been ordered to retreat. We marched east and an hour later heard planes approaching and the sound of bombs exploding exactly at the positions we had left. Then the planes reached our path of retreat and started bombing again. We weren't afraid, but it was dangerous because the brush around us was on fire. Some comrades couldn't escape the flames. We couldn't advance, so we dug in and waited. We didn't move until the next day. We met a few fellow soldiers coming from the battle area who said the Americans were right behind us and that a big trap was being laid for them and they would never escape. I doubted this because an effective ambush requires time, preparation, and patience.

"Then we were ordered to find the wounded and dead and bring them to a nearby rendezvous. We were given long wire hooks to drag off the dead. We worked four days because so many of our comrades had died, and there were many seriously wounded. Some field hospitals had been built at great distances from each other and were well concealed. We moved the wounded from the rendezvous to the hospitals—a hard job—and some wounded died while being transferred.

"Then we received the command to flush out the Americans—but we didn't find them. They had fled. We came here two days ago; we were allowed to rest yesterday, the first time in many days."

My escorts and I listened intently to his report. It would largely decide whether we could proceed or not. Phan Lieu and Bui Van Dieu seemed disturbed.

While we were listening to the exhausted Viet-Cong soldier in the jungle, teletypes and radios were flashing news of the biggest and bloodiest battle of the Second Viet-Nam War to all parts of the world. Helicopters were flying American soldiers—survivors, wounded, and dead—from the battlefield to Pleiku and An Khe. South Vietnamese paratroops had been dropped into the area to mop up retreating Viet-Cong units. Heavily armed Special Forces troops, *montagnards,* and smaller air cavalry units were pursuing the beaten enemy. But it had become clear, finally, to the West that the adversary was a real soldier. Now, people could no longer talk of scattered partisans and guerrillas but of an army in the jungle whose fighting power had been consistently underrated.

From the soldier's account, we realized that a far greater

battle had taken place than we had at first assumed. Later, I learned what actually had occurred in the Ia Drang Valley. The headquarters of the 1st Air Cavalry Division had decided to launch a big action along the Cambodian-Vietnamese border after reconnaissance planes and commando troops had confirmed the presence of strong Communist formations in the Duc Co and Plei Me area. Major General Kinnard, division commander, ordered Colonel Thomas Brown, head of the 3rd Brigade, to start the operation on November 14. There had been minor skirmishes on the preceding days with Viet-Cong troops supported by North Vietnamese units.

On the morning of November 14, the 1st Battalion of the 7th Air Cavalry Regiment landed in LZ X-ray, a zone near the Ia Drang River. "The 2nd Platoon of B-Company and two platoons of C-Company ran straight into Viet-Cong ambushes on the very first day," I was told by Major Frank Henry, second in command of the 2nd Battalion of the 5th Cavalry Regiment. The platoons had been sent out to secure the area around the zone. The Communists were waiting for them half a mile south or west of LZ X-ray. B-Company platoon was hit the hardest, the major reported. "The men ran straight into the machine-gun fire of the Charlies. Fourteen were hit in a few minutes. They didn't see the guns until the muzzles flashed in front of their noses. The VC didn't give them a chance and mowed them down like ducks in a shooting gallery. Those still alive tried to retreat or take cover. They dragged as many wounded as they could find with them. For hours on end the men heard the wounded out in the open yelling as the Charlies slowly helped them into the next world. You must realize," the major rasped, "that the VC have invented very special methods of embellishing a man's death."

The platoon lay ringed by the Viet-Cong for fifty-six hours and did not break out of the trap until the napalm bombs from the fighter bombers began hitting the Viet-Cong positions, forcing the Communists to retreat. The same thing happened to the two platoons of C-Company, south of the landing zone, where they put up a bloody fight against the NLF soldiers.

The Communist pressure eased up on the third day of fighting. On November 17, strong units of the 2nd Battalion of the 5th Cavalry Regiment, thrown into the battle as reinforcements, moved north to block the enemy on the other side of the Ia Drang Valley.

"We ran into a damned beautiful Communist ambush," Major Henry told me. "We had been saddled with a lousy job. The Communists were in back of us, and the bombs and shells of our own air force and artillery were hitting us instead of Charlie."

The Communists drove a wedge between the advancing American troops and split their units. The fighting was exceptionally savage. Colonel Harald Moore later told me that the GI's had to stop shooting because the pile of Viet-Cong and North Vietnamese bodies blocked the line of fire. "The Communists built us a bunker with their bodies."

Finally, on November 20, the battle-weary men of the air cavalry were flown out by helicopters and replaced by South Vietnamese paratroopers. On that day there were 1,238 Communist dead and over 2,000 wounded on the battlefield, in the hospitals on the Cambodian border, and at the rendezvous camps. The Americans had "more than

240 dead and 358 wounded." The American casualty rate had reached the same level as in the heaviest fighting of the Korean War.

October and November, 1965, were the bloodiest months of the Second Viet-Nam War. The Communists had hoped for a prestige victory over the Americans to make up for earlier defeats in 1965; American diplomacy vainly tried to negotiate an end to a war that was escaping the control of those who had let it start. The dimensions the war reached in the autumn of 1965 were plainly evident in the statistics of the battle in the highlands. Between 19,000 and 20,000 soldiers faced each other in an area of about thirty square miles around the fortified camp of Plei Me and in the Ia Drang Valley. This comes to more than two divisions. The Communists had deployed more than four North Vietnamese regiments and two regiments of the NLF Army; the allies had thrown about 8,000 men into the fight. A total of 2,293 men had been killed, over 4,200 wounded; 138 Communists had been captured, 34 Americans were missing. The South Vietnamese tally included "more than 300 men" taken prisoner, of whom at least half had deserted or gone over to the enemy. All together, the combat units had lost around 7,000 men—that is, more than three regiments had bled to death in the highlands. Casualties on a comparable scale had not been reported during the Indochina War until the battle of Dien Bien Phu. Both American and Communist soldiers reported afterward that they had killed whenever they could. It did not matter whether the enemy was wounded or wanted to surrender.

As in Pleiku, Kontum, and Darlac provinces, the fighting in other Vietnamese theaters of war had been more vicious than in preceding months. In all, American casualties amounted to 632 dead and 2,246 wounded; every day 10 American soldiers died and 38 were wounded. "More than 2,000 government men" had been killed and 4,400 wounded. The official figures of the Military Assistance Command, Viet-Nam (MACV), in Saigon, showed 8,611 Communists, Viet-Cong, and troops of the VPA dead. But the real figure was probably lower, while government casualties had undoubtedly been higher than announced.*

Despite the heavy fighting in the highlands, the allies did not succeed in stopping the infiltration of North Vietnamese troops. The operation had failed, though the Communists had suffered large casualties.

* Casualty figures released by the U.S. Department of Defense for selected months indicate the mounting intensity of the Vietnamese conflict:

	Killed	Wounded	Captured/ Missing
March, 1965			
U.S.	15	79	26
ARVN (South Vietnamese Government Army)	751	1,585	665
Viet-Cong	2,022	—	394
November, 1965			
U.S.	469	1,470	141
ARVN	1,034	2,182	425
VC and North Vietnamese troops	5,516	—	592
December, 1966			
U.S.	432	2,200	972
ARVN	815	—	—
VC and North Vietnamese troops	3,864	—	701
Total for War to January, 1967			
U.S.	6,711	38,217	474
ARVN	44,638	—	27,353
VC and North Vietnamese troops	167,900	—	44,614

All this I was to find out later. Back in the jungle, the soldier's report had deeply affected Bui Van Dieu. He withdrew for a brief consultation with Phan Lieu. When he returned, he said to me: "Stay here, you will be taken care of. We are not in danger, and we will be helped by friends. I'll be back soon." When he reappeared, I could tell that things were not as good as the soldier's account suggested. Bui Van Dieu began in an unusually loud voice: "The peace-loving forces have won a great victory." He was talking in propaganda clichés, something he had refrained from doing up to this point. "But the battle has not yet ended. We must wait until we receive reinforcements from our comrades and brothers."

I asked, "You mean troops from North Viet-Nam?" There was no answer.

Strong units of the VPA that had fought in the Ia Drang Valley were in the province at the time. In October and November, the 18th, 25th, and 101st regiments of the 325th North Vietnamese Infantry Division and two independent regiments, the 32nd and 250th, had reached South Viet-Nam via the Ho Chi Minh Trail. American intelligence also believed that elements of the 304th and 308th North Vietnamese Infantry divisions—units that had distinguished themselves in the battle of Dien Bien Phu— were marching south.

Bui Van Dieu told me they could no longer vouch for my safety and that we probably would have to return unless we found another way of reaching the southern provinces. Phan Lieu, who had listened silently, rose and disappeared. He returned in half an hour. His round face, so friendly at first, on closer examination appeared frighteningly harsh. He exchanged a few words with Bui Van

Dieu, pointed to me, called over one of the young guides, and disappeared with him into the brush.

Bui Van Dieu approached. He looked at me for a moment and then said wearily: "Now we can't guarantee anything." He made an apologetic gesture. "You are not only in danger from the aggressor, you are also a white man." I could not tell whether he was being contemptuous or sympathetic. "Our comrades are angry, they might even kill you." I was stunned and said so. He replied: "Sometimes even Vietnamese who look too European are excluded from our activities to save them from 'accidents.' They might be confused with whites."

It was growing dark when a group of about thirty soldiers emerged from the woods. In the twilight I saw their gray, torn uniforms, the dirty, blood-stained bandages on the small figures staggering past us in exhaustion. Weapons hung on their backs, empty rice bags dangled from their hips. Slightly built, they seemed too weak to lift their long black carbines; their hands seemed too tiny to hold them. The soft hum of conversation surrounded them; perhaps they were talking of the last battle, of lost friends, of pain.

What strength enabled these men to plunge screaming into the line of machine-gun fire, to defy the pounding of bombs and the inferno of napalm? In their minds, it was the dream of freedom to be achieved and the honor of belonging to the select few privileged to fight for that freedom.

The crickets were loud, and night had fallen when Phan Lieu returned again. I could see his face, but could not make out its features. His voice rang out shrill and hard. Bui Van Dieu, who had not moved from my side, took my arm and said softly but urgently: "We must go!" We could hear the sound of branches snapping, of grass rustling in the brush and jungle. The night seemed crowded with a thousand bleeding shadows, groping through the darkness back to the border.

2

The Invisible Enemy

The partisan movement must spread among the people like a drop of oil on water.

MAO TSE-TUNG

THE WAR had moved indoors.

It was one of those official but informal meetings political parties all over the world seem compelled to stage. The topic was the struggle in Viet-Nam. First, a member of the NLF Association of Journalists spoke, then came slides and a film showing starving peasants cheering the return of Viet-Cong soldiers to their destroyed villages. It was a propaganda film that could have served, with some variations, all the revolutions of our time.

I sat next to Mrs. Nguyen Thi Binh, chairwoman of the Women's Committee of the NLF, who had just arrived from a Viet-Cong jungle district. Her hair was combed straight back, her angular face was hard and unfeminine, and she seemed ill at ease in her wide, white silk dress. Probably, she would have been more comfortable in a uniform or the loose trousers her countrywomen wear. She sat in an armchair and puffed deeply on a cigarette. She spoke with the cold mechanical friendliness of a trained bureaucrat.

Mrs. Binh was supposed to speak on peace, but talked war. She spoke of the enemy in a proud, arrogant, and sometimes jeering tone, and afterward, appeared to submit to the embraces and congratulations of the people on the platform—Communists from other Asian states—coldly and reluctantly.

One of her escorts, a Vietnamese in a gray-green linen suit, told me that Nguyen Thi Binh had been fighting for the revolution from the start of the war. "When did the war begin?" I asked.

"It never began. Our struggle today is a continuation of the first revolutionary struggle to liberate our country," Nguyen Thi Binh answered. Two functionaries broke in. The wife of Nguyen Van Hieu had arrived. Her husband is one of the highest officials of the NLF, foreign minister in the shadow government, and an ideological leader of the Liberation Front. She was accompanied by several NLF functionaries.

I had expected revolutionaries, but the men I met displayed all the Byzantine formality of Communist bureaucrats. They seemed bored by the unrestrained enthusiasm of some younger Communists. There was no talk of revolution here. These men were introduced as the rulers of a movement that would soon control the state. A wide gulf divided this bureaucratic elite, which glowed in the aura of a revolutionary war almost won, and the lower cadres and Viet-Cong soldiers, the peasant guerrillas I would meet later in South Vietnamese villages. Inside the hall, the war had already been won, but outside, they were still fighting for victory. Yet these men must once have been minor officials, chiefs of village communities, or leaders of small guerrilla bands that raided military posts to capture weapons and ammunition. Perhaps they had been heads of small party cells in Saigon, Hué, or Danang and had been sustained only by the faith that some day they would conquer and reunite their country.

"How did the war begin?" I asked one Vietnamese.

His face was furrowed and wrinkled. "The people began to revolt against the dictator Diem. The many separate uprisings finally merged into one great rebellion." Could he name any particular battles or military actions as the real start of the Second Viet-Nam War? "There were many clashes, one so much like the other that it is impossible to say the war started at any given point," he said. Then the name of Tua Hai came up. Other officials had also described the battle of Tua Hai as the start of the war, as the first big action, typical of many armed conflicts to come.

The first revolts against Ngo Dinh Diem's government had one thing in common: They seldom seemed the product of Communist agitation. The guerrillas were poorly armed and badly led in small operations. Obviously, no central organization was guiding them.

I was told: "You mustn't forget we were an underground movement. There were no ways of linking up with other groups. We held our meetings in the strictest secrecy. It took weeks and months for delegates from other provinces to reach us in time for crucial conferences. Many of our leaders were jailed or executed."

By the beginning of 1959, the clandestine Communist movement in South Viet-Nam had tightened its organization. As soon as the Lao-Dong Party in Hanoi gave the signal, the first better-led and equipped guerrillas moved into action. There were surprise attacks in the provinces of

Tay Ninh, Hau Nghia, Binh Long, Binh Duong; sabotage and terrorist acts in Saigon and other large cities. The aim of these tactics was to smash government installations, drive out government officials, and undermine the regime's authority.

On May 1, 1959, more than 210,000 people marched on Saigon to protest against Diem, who answered by decreeing the infamous Law 10/59. This controversial law was enacted on May 6, 1959. Under it, any Vietnamese who committed a crime against the security of the state or "had the intention" of doing so faced either death or life imprisonment. It was one of the reasons the Communist revolutionary movement grew so quickly.

The government believed the delta had been swept clean of guerrillas, but well-armed partisan groups reappeared, and in January, 1960, the battle was fought that the NLF considers the beginning of the Second Viet-Nam War.

Tua Hai had been a French fort on the Cambodian border in Tay Ninh province. It was protected by earthen ramparts half a mile long and dense barbed wire. The fortifications were in poor condition because there seemed to be no reason to maintain them after the Indochina War, and the barbed-wire entanglements had collapsed in many places. Yet, the fortress still represented a formidable government outpost. A regiment of 2,500 men had been stationed there, a few miles from the provincial capital of Tay Ninh, to keep the northwestern part of the province under control. The government feared attacks and knew that former Viet-Minh fighters had formed new guerrilla groups in this traditionally rebellious province.

The garrison, the 32nd Regiment of the 21st Vietnamese

Infantry Division, had been sent to the frontier fort in August, 1959. The day before the battle the men were happy; they expected to be relieved in six days. Scouts had reported all quiet in the area around the fort. The peasants had been terrorized by the government forces and did not dare air their grievances. Government flags flew over the villages around Tua Hai.

On January 7, 1960, a patrol had driven a group of armed Cambodians back across the border. The commander was decorated for this exploit. These Cambodian bands gave the soldiers a lot of trouble, repeatedly slipping across the border to attack villages and rob the peasants.

A few days earlier two companies had swept through the surrounding villages and arrested peasants suspected of having cooperated with the Communists. The soldiers did not care whom they seized; what mattered was the number of arrests. The better the reports the province chief sent to Saigon, the better his standing with Diem; the more secure his position, the pleasanter the life of the officers and, in turn, of the soldiers.

There had been attacks by guerrilla bands in July, 1959, but their real strength remained a mystery. Had Saigon, Tay Ninh, or Tua Hai known the number and plans of the guerrillas, they would not have felt so complaisant about the months ahead.

There were about 1,000 armed guerrillas in Tay Ninh. The largest group numbered 300 men and was led by a Viet-Minh veteran, Queyt Thang. A native of the province, he had held minor commands in the Viet-Minh Army. He had been trying to train guerrillas for two years, without much success. The bloody government mopping-up actions and the control exercised by strongly entrenched garrisons had at least one result: Many experienced Viet-Minh cadres were flushed out, taken prisoner, and executed. This intimidated the population, and few dared join the rebels. Not until the government blundered did the peasants start going over to the guerrillas despite the threat of reprisals.

One factor favored Queyt Thang and the other partisan chiefs in the province. The headquarters of the Cao-Dai sect were located in the capital of Tay Ninh. The sect had been represented in one of the Diem government's cabinets, although earlier, it had attempted to overthrow Diem with the help of the Binh-Xuyen sect, whose chief, a former convict who called himself "General" Le Van Vien, controlled virtually all organized gangs in and around Saigon. He had proposed that the Cao-Daists join him in ousting Diem and forming a coalition government, but the plot failed.

Cao-Dai is a broadly based faith combining Catholic, Buddhist, Taoist, and Confucian religious ideas with an organization similar to that of a political party. Particularly strong in the South, it had its own pope and clergy. The Cao-Daists first clashed with the French authorities when their supreme being began levying taxes on his followers—numbering about 1 million. When the Japanese occupied Indochina, the sect participated in the rebellion against the French. Later, it formed an alliance with the Viet-Minh, but bowed to the French again when they conquered Tay Ninh. It collaborated with French troops against the Communists. The Cao-Daists had a well-equipped army of 20,000 men that fought bitterly and mercilessly against the enemy. The more disbelievers the faithful sped into the next world, the greater bliss they were promised after death.

When the Indochina War ended, the sect tried to take power in Tay Ninh and the neighboring provinces; finally, it made an alliance with Diem. But he soon dropped the Cao-Daists and started persecuting them. They went over to the side of the gathering Communist revolt and placed their soldiers under the command of the guerrilla leaders. The Viet-Cong promptly paid its debt of gratitude. The NLF acclaimed the sect as a "patriotic force" and gave it representation in its official bodies. In 1959, the number of armed Cao-Daists was estimated at 4,000. One group joined the veteran Viet-Minh partisan Queyt Thang.

Fort Tua Hai was a problem to the guerrillas for many reasons. Government forces stationed there could control over half the province. They made it difficult for the guerrillas to cross the nearby Cambodian border. Cambodia was a favored sanctuary for the South Vietnamese rebels even then, and they could usually count on help from Prince Sihanouk. Even then, as the revolt took shape, the most direct and swiftest lines of communication with Hanoi and other Communist centers in East Asia ran through Cambodia.

The government had stocked supplies of weapons and ammunition in Tua Hai for future large-scale conflicts— and the rebels needed these desperately in the opening days of the revolt. They launched their first attacks with the most primitive types of weapons, in many instances with bows and arrows modeled after those of the highlanders (crossbows were very effective) or with homemade guns. A Viet-Cong soldier told me that at the outset of the fighting, one company, consisting of 120 to 140 men, had only ten to fifteen carbines and a few hundred rounds of ammunition.

Queyt Thang commanded a force of 300 men; yet, only half the battalion had guns. The Cao-Dai sect had furnished 100 soldiers. The veteran guerrilla hoped to attack and take Fort Tua Hai with this unit. A number of government soldiers inside the fortress sympathized with the rebels and supplied them with valuable information. A few days before the assault the rebels captured some members of the fort's garrison, a practice the guerrillas had followed during the Indochina War in order to obtain the latest intelligence. Before each attack the guerrillas tried to learn all they could of the enemy's intentions so that they could plan their action thoroughly. Every guerrilla knew all the details of the objective he was to take, and for days the attack was rehearsed in sandboxes and full-scale mock-ups.

The guerrillas rounded up several hundred peasants from the villages around Fort Tua Hai. They were to help the attackers carry off captured weapons and to impress the garrison with the size of the attacking force. The peasants were completely unarmed. If the attack was to fail, they would have to defend themselves with their bare hands.

Tua Hai was rectangular, its earthen ramparts about seven and a half feet high, and the barbed-wire entanglements twelve to fifteen feet high. There were machine-gun emplacements at each corner of the fortress, and bunkers ran along the ramparts.

Two days before the attack several guerrillas slipped into the fort and informed their sympathizers within of the time of the assault. These men were ordered to place mines in the installations and barracks. The mines would explode at zero hour on January 10. The day before the operation Queyt Thang assembled his partisans and had them advance toward the fort in small groups. The first were only a few hundred yards from the walls by late afternoon. They dug into the jungle and waited for nightfall.

The fort's commander had been warned of the coming attack. He radioed Tay Ninh for help, but the province chief considered the fortress impregnable and refused to send reinforcements. The commander of Tua Hai then decided on his own to risk a sortie in order to forestall the attackers. At about 11:00 P.M. he marched out at the head of a battalion in search of the rebels.

The attackers were well concealed near Tua Hai's ramparts. Queyt was worried when he saw the troops emerge. He knew he had been betrayed, but he did not know to what extent and decided to continue with his original plan. He had hidden about 500 peasants on the north side of the fort, and he left a platoon—called a "section" after French usage and having from 50 to 100 men—on the Tay Ninh road. These guerrillas were to set an ambush in the event that combat troops came from the provincial capital.

The mines exploded at 1:00 A.M. Some of the barracks and munition depots immediately burst into flames. The garrison streamed out and ran directly into the attackers' fire. The rebels quickly poured into the fort, occupied the machine-gun towers and the bunkers along the ramparts. The soldiers were strafed from their own fortifications.

A guerrilla commando unit found some army trucks and quickly began loading them with arms and ammunition that they carried out of the burning storehouses. The fighting was furious, but less than ten minutes after the first shots had been fired, the trucks—loaded with the most modern weapons—raced out of the fort. It was a ride to death.

The commander's battalion had turned back when it heard the firing and prepared an ambush on an exit road. The guerrilla truck column drove right into the trap. It was stopped and the rebels shot down to the last man.

By now the guerrillas and peasants had penetrated the fort and cleaned out the undamaged storehouses. The fighting was still savage, but the garrison surrendered because, in the dark, it greatly overestimated rebel strength and considered further resistance useless.

The guerrillas had captured 400 soldiers; the rest had escaped or lay dead. The prisoners were loaded with boxes of weapons and ammunition and marched out of the fort. A half hour after the attack the first column of men bearing munitions had started out for the rendezvous.

In the meantime, Queyt Thang had been warned of the ambush set by the troops who had gone out on the search mission and had learned that the truck column was lost. He decided to abandon the fort as quickly as possible. He detoured around the ambush and at dawn safely reached his troops' defense positions in a thick jungle about eight miles away.

Some of the prisoners voluntarily joined the guerrillas, the rest were escorted halfway back to the fort. The frightened soldiers were told they would not get off so lightly the next time.

The NLF claims that more than 1,000 weapons, including recoilless rifles, 40 machine guns, and over 100,000 rounds of ammunition were captured in the attack on Tua

Hai. The booty also included two mortars and mortar shells. The number of rebel casualties, it is said, was small: 11 dead and over 20 wounded. It was also alleged that more than 100 soldiers of the "puppet government" had died defending the fortress, and that more than 200 had been wounded.

Official Saigon reacted wildly to the Tua Hai battle. First, rebellious Cao-Daists were blamed; then, Cambodian bands. Finally, it admitted the assault had been the work of former Viet-Minh soldiers. The government mounted a tremendous propaganda campaign. Mobile loudspeaker units drove through the province reporting the attack and the atrocities committed by the Communists. The publicity, meant to fill the population with fear and terror of the rebels, often had the opposite effect. In some places, where posters had been put up describing guerrilla atrocities, the people applauded the rebels and openly sided with them. Many peasants first learned that a powerful rebel movement existed from government propaganda and then sought to contact and join it.

The attack had a devastating effect on the already low morale of troops stationed in Tay Ninh. Two hundred men deserted from Fort Tua Hai that same January, and an entire infantry company went over to the guerrillas. Queyt Thang's forces grew rapidly and by March, 1960, had more than 350 well-equipped soldiers, with a far better fighting spirit than that of the government troops. In May and June more units sprang up in the province; by the end of July, 1960, there were 1,500 insurgents. Since then the government has never been able to exercise effective control over this border province.

There are now several Viet-Cong headquarters in Tay

Ninh, and not one South Vietnamese or American soldier has been able to enter its northwestern sector. In the past six years, the rebels have fortified the province so effectively, and created such an elaborate network of tunnels, trenches, and bunkers in the jungle, that every operation in this area is like a "ghastly descent into hell," to quote an American officer who headed commando units in Tay Ninh.

Queyt Thang had seized a larger amount of booty than expected. The surplus arms were hidden in the jungle or carried by porters along hidden trails to other provinces. There, other guerrilla groups were armed and the old weapons handed over to the peasants. Suddenly Saigon faced larger, well-equipped rebel units not only in Tay Ninh, but in adjacent provinces. Attacks of the Tua Hai type took place elsewhere against government bases, forward garrisons, outposts, ammunition or arms depots. Officials, civil servants, teachers, and police were kidnaped, blackmailed, tortured, or murdered.

The population in the delta and highlands soon revolted as well. Communist agents reaped the harvest of many years of propaganda. The uprising spread as quickly as "a drop of oil in water," and the many small, slashing guerrilla actions, even more than large-scale attacks on government bases, systematically wore down the army and finally undermined Diem's regime.

A small partisan group would ambush a company of government troops; small combat units, often made up of less than ten men would challenge far superior Saigon forces. The guerrillas rarely engaged in large, set battles, for these generally turned out badly for them. Guerrilla warfare, with troops excellently trained and armed for such operations, was the Viet-Cong's true domain—and has remained so till now.

On April 20, 1962, a guerrilla force, led by Nguyen Hien, attacked a government base in the Danang area. The outposts were overrun and destroyed. The guerrillas then withdrew to a nearby village. A week later a big government force surrounded the village, and the guerrillas began retreating, they said later, to save the villagers from trouble.* They came under heavy fire and pulled back to the ruins of Cong Bo, another outpost the Viet-Cong had razed some time earlier. There they were cornered by a company of South Viet-Nam militia (Dan Ve) and raked with heavy machine-gun fire. In spite of this, Hien ordered his men to hold the position if at all possible. Two guerrillas were sent to the left flank to harass the enemy. Hien, a man of about thirty, huddled with his NCO, Hung. "We've got to move out before they have us completely surrounded," Hung yelled. There were machine-gun blasts on the left flank.

"All right," Hien decided, "let's go." The guerrillas crossed a small sand field, a dune, and another sand field without any cover. While they were racing through the second field, their pursuers had reached the top of the dune. A company of Nungs, a Vietnamese minority group of Chinese origin, joined the militiamen and tried to cut off the retreat. Hien and his men threw themselves behind a narrow rise of sand at the end of the field as their pursuers approached fast, firing sporadically. The troops had obviously been ordered to take the rebels alive.

Nguyen Hien had seven guerrillas under his command

* See *Arts et Litterature au Sud-Vietnam,* Vol. I (n.p.: Edition Liberation, 1964) and *Etudes Vietnamiennes* (Hanoi, 1964).

and two village officials armed with pistols. He ordered the unit to separate into two groups. "Wait till they're very close," he said.

The attackers stopped, realizing they could not overrun the guerrilla position without suffering heavy casualties. They set up two machine guns and began strafing the hill behind which Hien's group lay. "Don't fire unless you're sure you'll hit your mark," Hien shouted. Each guerrilla soldier had about seventy rounds of ammunition for his carbine.

The militia crept up on the left flank. Hien had posted Si and Tho, two of his best men, there. A sharp exchange followed. Si silently tumbled over the top of the sand strip. A bullet had shattered his skull. Tho was badly wounded. Hien noticed that the defensive firing on the flank had suddenly stopped.

"Hung and Nghia, get over there and help Si and Tho," he ordered. His NCO, a small, sturdy peasant's son from Quang Nam Province, and Nghia crawled over to their comrades. They arrived in time to repulse a group of soldiers who had come within thirty yards of the guerrilla position. Tho had been shot in the left armpit. His arm was practically severed, and he was bleeding to death. He died a few minutes after Hung and Nghia reached him. They dragged both corpses back to Hien on a cloth hammock.

Only five guerrillas were left. The two village officials were not seasoned fighters. One knew how to use his pistol, but was afraid to raise his head; the other had no military training at all. The attackers began bearing down again with heavy fire. About 11:00 A.M. the Nungs tried to storm the guerrilla position and were barely beaten off. During this exchange Hien was hit by a machine-gun volley and wounded in his throat and upper right arm; both wounds were bleeding badly. "Leave me here and try to save yourselves," he ordered. But Hung, his NCO, refused to leave him.

"We have to get out of here. We can't hold out any longer," he said. Two guerrillas, Thac and Tam, were ordered to cover the withdrawal, and while the pursuers were preparing for a new advance, Hien, Hung, Nghia, and the two village functionaries fled across a cactus field to a neighboring village.

Hien's wounds were bandaged there. Then, he gave the order: "We're going to move eastward and shake off our pursuers." The partisans fled through some small hamlets, doubled back sharply in their tracks, and turned coastward. They soon reached sand dunes near the sea. The guerrillas had thrown away their sandals when they began their flight, and now every step in the sand burned, cactus thorns tore at their feet.

Again they turned westward and came upon peasants working in rice paddies. Hien asked them for something to eat. "Keep going," one of the peasants replied. "We saw a company from Dien Dang searching for you along the shore." Hien thanked him after he and his companions had drunk the dirty water from the rice field.

The guerrillas traveled inland. Suddenly, shots came whistling from behind a clump of palms outside the village of Dien Ngoc. They had almost run into an ambush set by two companies from Hoi An. "Into the rice field," Hien ordered, and threw himself behind one of the small earthen dikes that separate the water-covered fields. The guerrillas lay in the water up to their necks—only their heads and weapons showed above the dirty gray slop. The Nungs and militia were right behind them. Within half an hour the guerrillas in the rice paddy were completely surrounded. Near the village Hung had spied a small temple in the middle of a cluster of palm trees. "We have to get there," he said to Hien. "We'll be able to defend ourselves there until nightfall."

"Impossible, the moment we move they'll shoot us," Hien answered. He had lost much blood and was very weak.

"We can't defend ourselves here any longer. Let Thac and Tam cover us," Hung said. Hien hesitated, then agreed.

The group slowly crawled along the low embankment. Thac and Tam followed, trying to draw the attention of the attackers. A few yards in front of the temple, Hung discovered a deep bomb crater. "Into it—We can defend ourselves better here," he called out. The exhausted guerrillas slid into their new shelter. Thac and Tam were still in the rice paddy, their chances of survival small. Thac was caught in the cross fire of two machine guns as the soldiers moved cautiously toward them. "Watch out," Hung shouted. At that moment Thac saw his pursuers, only ten yards away, crawling up the other side of the dike. He rose—and a burst of machine-gun fire ripped his chest to shreds. Tam succeeded in reaching the shelter. Hien, Nghia, and Hung were blazing away at the enemy. The two village officials tried to help, but no sooner did one of them get off a shot than he was wounded.

The pursuers spread out and surrounded the guerrilla position, but did not attack. They set up mortars and began lobbing shells. It took them a long time to find the range, since the bomb crater was only four yards across, a small target. But soon the shells were exploding close to the hole, every detonation covering the defenders with a cloud of dirt and dust.

It was 7:25 P.M. and growing dark. The guerrillas hoped to escape in the night. Hien still had some packages of plastic explosive that he had brought for the attack on the government post. He placed the explosives on the crater's rim, believing they would be able to escape in the confusion after the explosives blew up.

The soldiers expecting that the guerrillas would try to slip away under cover of darkness, intensified their fire. A shell exploded at the edge of the crater. Nghia and one of the village officials were torn to shreds. A little later a shell killed Tam and another one Hung.

Hien decided to flee no matter what the risk. He lit the explosives and called to Hoa, the remaining village official: "Let's go, we have exactly twenty seconds!" The two leaped up, raced to a nearby tobacco field, and dropped between some dense shrubs as the bomb exploded. A black cloud rose from the crater.

Hien and Hoa escaped. That was in 1962, the second year of the war. A guerrilla unit had been wiped out; but to defeat it, the government had been forced to use more than 400 men. Four years later both the government and the Viet-Cong had increased their military operations tenfold. Saigon's troops were now equipped with America's superior military hardware—including tanks, helicopters, and planes—on a scale unknown before. The technical superiority of the American and the government forces posed a serious problem for the Viet-Cong. It would take it a long time to adapt its tactics to the new situation. The report, given to me by an NLF journalist, of a Viet-Cong soldier on a battle between guerrillas and a Vietnamese marine infantry battalion reveals some of the methods employed to beat a technically superior enemy.

A mobile column of the 4th Marine Rifle Battalion is on its way to Luc Tanh [near Binh Gia]. The partisans are still five miles from the chosen battlefield. It has been decided to fight. The plan of attack is quickly discussed among the commanders, cadres, and rank-and-file. The following instructions are given: "We begin by attacking the M113 tanks.* The foot soldiers of the Liberation Army are going to defeat the mobile enemy. The heavy weapons are to back up the light ones, just as the light-armed units must aid those that are heavily armed." The troops repeat the orders in chorus.

The unit advances on the double. The explosions of rockets and bombs, laying down a protective barrage for the attack on the mobile government forces, boom through the woods. Route 2 comes into sight. Fourteen M113 tanks approach at full speed. There is no longer time to cross the road ditches. The unit prepares for battle. The branches every soldier had set up as camouflage suddenly stop moving. Silence on the highway. The enemy tanks are nearing the field of battle. The commander confirms this with a quick glance.

Firing. The woods come alive. A partisan plunges onto the highway, leaps up on the first tank, supports himself on the barrel of the tank's gun, and unfurls the NFL flag. A blast of the trumpet signals the attack. We must conquer quickly and retreat quickly; that was impressed on us before battle.

A soldier jumps from cover in order to take better aim at the enemy; another, wounded, his camouflage already

---

* The M113 of the U.S. Army is not a tank but a "personnel carrier, full-tracked, armored."—Ed.

stained with blood, races onto the road. A group advances forward swiftly, and the soldiers scramble up like cats onto the tanks. Quickly, they pull the pins from their hand grenades and hurl them into the vehicles. The grenades explode with a muffled roar inside the tanks.

The enemy rolls back a little way and bunches his undamaged vehicles. He lets go with all the weapons he has. Then the planes come: fighter bombers, bombers, and helicopters. We had taken too much time in destroying the tank unit.

Bombs, rockets, and napalm explode in front of our positions. Some of the M113's are still undamaged and are firing at us. A few detachments with mines and hand grenades are sent forward. Again the sound of muffled explosions inside the tanks. But one group has succeeded in capturing two undamaged tanks. Our men are now seated in them, blasting the enemy with his own weapons. They concentrate on the planes and helicopters and shoot down three planes. In another half hour the battle is over. Thirteen M113's have been destroyed, the fourteenth tried to flee and foundered in a rice paddy. We break off the fight and withdraw in perfect order.

Surprise attack on a government base, small guerrilla groups engaging the superior enemy, and the ambush had been the Viet-Cong's preferred tactics from the first. They remain such today and probably will continue to remain so.

But in the autumn of 1965 and the first four months of 1966, the guerrillas committed an error that cost them almost as many lives as all the fighting in the preceding years. They sent large forces into open battle with the Americans and South Vietnamese.

The reasons are not completely clear. Possibly the Viet-Cong ideologists considered the time ripe to begin the third phase of guerrilla warfare—open combat; possibly, a prestige victory was needed; or, perhaps, they had overestimated their military potential and underestimated that of the American forces. Probably each of these factors influenced the Viet-Cong to adopt a tactic it was soon to regret. Some time in April, 1966, it switched back to the old, tested fighting methods. And since then the Americans are once more confronted by an enemy they cannot find or smash with the weight of their military apparatus. It hides in the jungle until it is ready, then strikes from secret bases with lightning speed—and again disappears.

"What wears us down is that we can't come to grips with them. The French wanted one big battle and they lost when the enemy finally met them head-on. We want this battle too," Colonel Hal Moore said to me. "We seek a decisive battle in order to end the war. But the Viet-Cong knows that there can be no Dien Bien Phu for us. That's why it fears this battle more than anything else."

3

The Other Side

The United States of America is joined with the people and Government of Viet-Nam to prevent aggression. This is the purpose of the determined effort of the American armed forces now engaged in Viet-Nam. The United States seeks no bases. It seeks no colonial presence. It seeks to impose no alliance or alignment. It seeks only to prevent aggression, and its pledge to that purpose is firm. It aims simply to help a people and government who are determined to help themselves . . .

The purpose of the United States remains a purpose of peace. The United States Government and the Government of Viet-Nam will continue in the future, as they have in the past, to press for a peaceful settlement in every forum. The world knows the harsh and negative response these efforts have thus far received.

From the "Declaration of Honolulu"
February 8, 1966

A DEAD MAN lay at the end of a row of bushes where a thin bamboo fence began. His wax fingers still clawed the earth, the scratched ground evidence of his death agony. Another corpse lay a little further away, legs protruding over an embankment, head and shoulders submerged in the slimy water of a rice paddy. The wet uniform clung to the twisted body like matted fur to a filthy cat.

I was lying with two American soldiers behind the corpses. It was drizzling. The dull gray surface of the rice field spread out in front of us, beyond it a line of trees, brush, and thorns. The VC was there. Each time we raised our heads a bullet whistled by. A machine gun chattered occasionally.

Behind us a Negro GI crouched, his back against a small earthen wall. With both hands he pressed hard against the sides of his upper right thigh to staunch an open wound that bled in short, dark spurts. His face was a study in surprise. He was too busy with his wound to care about the shots from across the paddy.

A patrol had crossed the rice field twenty minutes ago. Now it lay on the other shore, also pressed to the ground, waiting for the snipers to end their shooting.

I had been marching with the Americans for two days through jungle and brush in search of the Charlies. I was crammed with theories about this war and felt more relaxed now that I was with the stronger side. In traveling with NLF soldiers, I had sometimes been overwhelmed by a feeling of abandonment. Now helicopters would no longer suddenly appear and shower us with rockets. The drone of motors would no longer drive me to take cover in the jungle from napalm bombs and shells. I felt safe, protected by the most powerful military nation in the world.

My companions were well armed. We knew we could call for artillery or air support if we ran into trouble. If I were wounded, a superb medical organization would tend to my needs. A helicopter would ferry me straight from the battlefield to the hospital. I remembered how I feared being wounded while crossing the Vietnamese border with a Viet-Cong patrol. No one could have helped me. Even a small wound would probably have meant death or at least a few days' journey through the jungle to the nearest field hospital.

My pack was jammed with first-class canned food; I had

wrapped a sleeping bag on top and a waterproof poncho. At camp, I had been given a small field medical kit and an emergency ration. "You certainly won't need it, but you can take it home as a souvenir," a friendly staff sergeant in a trim uniform said.

We had spent the previous night in a small camp. Helicopters had dropped food and ammunition at evening and in the morning. A GI with a sprained foot was flown to an evacuation hospital. The company commander had personally ordered the helicopter for this man. "We want the men to know we're doing everything to make this miserable war easier for them." In Saigon, I had heard how pilots of planes shot down in North Viet-Nam were picked up and even how a helicopter crew had been rescued right in the middle of a Viet-Cong battalion.

An L-19 observation plane buzzed overhead, its presence enough of a guarantee that big, strong brother was waiting somewhere to help us if we ran into danger. I remembered a Liberation Army soldier, seventeen years old, who had been fighting with the guerrillas for two years. He had been wounded in the highlands and dragged himself through the jungle for four weeks. A VC patrol picked him up. He had two wounds on both arms, and gangrene had set in. It would take him several days to reach the next camp, and the patrol left him behind because he could scarcely walk. He promised to follow, although he didn't have a chance in the world. His corpse is probably now rotting somewhere in the mountains.

A machine gun began raking us on the right. A lieutenant crawled forward and motioned us back. The Viet-Cong had attacked the company's left flank, and we learned that at least 300 guerrillas—a battalion—lay in wait for us. "The Charlies have dug in in a village behind the trees," the lieutenant growled. He was a very young man with a smooth face.

We crawled back, guerrilla bullets slapping into the rain-soft earth. We left the dead men where they were. It would have been dangerous to drag them out of the rice paddy. Besides, a helicopter would soon be there to carry off the corpses. "It will take some time till we smoke the bastards out," a sergeant said to me.

I had come to Viet-Nam from Laos five days earlier. I had landed at Tan Son Nhut, Saigon's airport and the busiest in the world when its civil and military traffic are combined. I had seen long rows of American jet fighters, giant Hercules cargo planes standing side by side, Globemasters, radar and small transport planes, bombers. A mighty armada organized by the United States to smash the enemy in the impenetrable jungle.

Saigon was a dirty city stamped by years of crimes and war. By the time I met a U.S. Embassy official for lunch, my initial depression had lifted. And before long I did not have the slightest doubt that my host was right when he said: "Of course we'll win this war against the pajama boys. It's not even so much a question of time as it is of method." The air conditioning kept us cool. The waiters in white scurried softly around the tables. Music floated toward us from a roof terrace, a tune from *My Fair Lady*. A Vietnamese girl at the next table laughed throatily as her companion, a tanned American in a white dinner jacket, whispered in her ear.

The next day I was given statistics at the Rex building located in the center of Saigon. Businesslike officials drew up a sober balance for the newly arrived journalist: the amount of bombs dropped, the number of enemy killed. The press officer in the impeccable gray suit said: "Their casualties are five to ten times greater than ours." At times the cool precision of American officials seems unreal. They act as if events were naturally under control, that everything is operating smoothly, on a sound basis. They swamped me with documents, figures, reports, and analyses in incredible detail. I found a brochure describing the best way of meeting a Vietnamese woman; and there was the ten-point program for GI's who had just landed, beginning with the sentence: "You are a guest here."

A press officer invited me to dine with him at the topfloor restaurant of the Rex building. A credential card was pressed into my hand with a flight schedule showing when, how, and where I could fly. My press card was a free plane ticket to the war.

The frictionless way in which the American machine functioned impressed me in those first days of my stay in Saigon. The men I met seemed to have shaken off all problems and doubts. Technicians were at work here—military and political executives, specialists in public relations.

An atmosphere of sober objectivity seemed to envelop the public information officers. They were friendly, displayed little personal feeling, and were cool, moderately optimistic, and self-confident.

Soon after I arrived I was told the situation had never looked better. Hanoi had lost prestige by reacting negatively to President Johnson's peace offensive. The Americans and their ally had not only been morally strengthened but now had greater freedom of action. The outcome of the war would probably be decided this year. No doubt more mistakes would be made, but none that counted. The Saigon government had never been as firmly entrenched as now, and with the current commitment of more American troops the rebellion would fizzle out, as in Greece, Malaya, and the Philippines.

"We'll force the Charlies to use up their reserves," a young major told me in the cafe of the Hotel Continental. "We'll isolate them." The major was thirty-one. He was brimming over with health and strength; he seemed to have been poured into his uniform, and the combat bars over his breast pocket appeared new and fresh. "If we have to, we'll kill so many that not one will be left." He believed the most sensible thing to do was to bomb Hanoi and Haiphong immediately. "That will soon finish off their hold here too. We'll pound them until not one damned pair of slant eyes is left."

It was a different story in the field. The "damned slant eyes" on the other side of the rice paddy were damned good shots. A sergeant had been hit in the forehead and blood was streaming down his face. Near me a bullet plopped wearily into the ground. About thirty Viet-Cong had managed to surprise us on the flanks. A young medic, whose blonde crewcut hair was stiff with mud, reached us, panting hard, and reported we would have to fix our bayonets for hand-to-hand fighting. Then bullets from a machine-gun blast whistled through the bushes. I asked the company commander why no one had called for air support. "Impossible, we're too close to the enemy," he replied. I suddenly realized I was not so safe on the winning side. What was taking place in this rice paddy scarcely resembled anything I had been told of in Saigon. I thought of the jet bombers in Tan Son Nhut. They could not be used here. Nor could artillery. My supplies and equipment suddenly seemed useless. Only the individual, the soldier, counted here. Not the one who was backed by greater power, not the one with better weapons, but the one who fought better. There was no victor here, just men defending their lives, who would kill or be killed.

An hour later the firing died out. The guerrillas had withdrawn to their fortified positions in the village that the company was going to attack. Perhaps they had disappeared completely. "They always stop firing, break off, and vanish, and you can't stop them," the company commander said. We started creeping forward again—to the edge of the paddy. The dead were still lying there. A sergeant bent over the man half-submerged in the rice field. He was fixed in the same position, as if he wanted to drink the dirty gray water—but his head was deep under the surface. The sergeant looked at me and I stared back. This was the first dead American soldier I had seen. I had somehow believed that Americans could not be killed, because the military machine they served was too massive. The sergeant moved his lips as if he wanted to say something. Then, the corners of his mouth tightened, and he turned around and moved off.

The dead man had been the first soldier of his company to try and cross the paddy. A machine gun had cut him down. The company moved forward slowly again. It was very quiet as the men crossed in single file on the rice field dikes. Once in a while we could hear some shooting, but it seemed far off. I stepped onto the slimy top of the dike and, with the others, safely reached the other side of the field. The wounded were carried behind us. There was a sandy stretch of ground in front of us. The company dropped into a trench the Viet-Cong had occupied. A helicopter was called for to fly out the wounded. Ten minutes later we heard the whirring blades overhead. The helicopter raced in about six feet above the tops of the palm trees, then descended and hovered just a few inches off the ground, the blades whipping sand in our faces.

A machine gun started up suddenly. The pilot zoomed high, turned his plane sharply, and disappeared behind the trees. The wounded were still with us. I squatted on the sandy soil of the trench. Four field radios blared away in front of me. Two very young medics ran around bandaging the wounded. A patrol returned, carrying a man whose foot had been torn off by a ricocheting bullet. The GI's near me didn't even look at him. They sat there tired, leaning on their guns, waiting. A red-faced soldier began opening a can of food. The company commander turned to me, "Nice job, huh?" I nodded. "Well, the helicopters won't be back today. The air is too full of lead."

The Americans fought hard and slowly forced the enemy back to his defensive positions. Three hundred guerrillas lay facing 160 Americans. It slowly began getting dark and a long, black night was ahead of us. The trench was full of wounded men. Four corpses lay on the sandy earth. The helicopters had not returned, and there was a good chance the guerrillas would encircle or overrun us during the night. The company commander sent a few patrols out into the open field, which was about 100 yards from where the Viet-Cong had dug in. Then the artillery came up, and shells roared over our heads. The sandy ground in our trench heaved every time the shells exploded in the enemy's positions. One wounded man wanted the artillery barrage called off because it kept him from sleeping. Two or three soldiers laughed.

It was still twilight as the colonel in command stood up in the trench to observe the enemy's positions. His lips spread in the hint of a smile, and he said to me that he had taken on a lousy job.

"Job." I often heard that word in Viet-Nam. I recalled a conversation with a major I met at An Khe, headquarters of the 1st Air Cavalry. We had discussed the combat strength of the American forces in Viet-Nam. "Our soldiers are very young," the major had said, a forty-five-year-old man who had fought in the Pacific and France during the World War II, then in Korea, and afterward served several years in West Germany. "They're good soldiers, but completely different from what we were like. We hated our enemy. How we fought in the Pacific! How angry we were when we landed in France to beat the Nazis!" The major was squatting on a small wooden box, a pair of torn, high, leather jungle boots, originally green, lying in front of him. He offered me a can of orange juice. A young soldier lolled on a cot, reading *Playboy* magazine and chewing on a ham sandwich.

"I don't mean that these kids are worse soldiers," he continued. "Korea symbolized something for us; we had a feeling about the Chinese, and it wasn't very nice. There's nothing like that here. I don't believe any of our boys hate the Charlies, unless they've knocked off a friend. My impression is that our men are fighting because they have to. In a matter-of-fact way. They're brave, they do what they're told to do, and yet this war means nothing to them —they're just doing a job, that's all."

Night came to the jungle. The palm trees were barely silhouetted against the blue-black tropical sky. The air, which usually carried the smells of fires, spices, flowers, and swamp, was filled with acrid powder smoke. Whenever an artillery salvo landed on enemy ground the flash of exploding shells lit up our positions like flares.

During the night the Charlies tried to reach the Americans, but their scouting patrols came no further than the defensive line of outposts. The next morning the bombers arrived and demolished the Viet-Cong positions with napalm and high explosives. When we advanced, we found a few charred corpses, a few caved-in trenches, two guns. The guerrillas had vanished into the jungle.

The company moved forward and reported its success to headquarters. We had some dead, even more wounded, were tired and filthy—yet we claimed victory. I began to doubt whether such actions, which occurred almost daily, could have even the slightest influence on the outcome of the war.

What had really happened? An American company had caught up with a Viet-Cong battalion. It had fought bravely for a rice paddy and a narrow, sandy strip of barren ground. A few huts had been shot to pieces, some Americans and guerrillas had been killed. The enemy had withdrawn, escaped the annihilating bombs and mortar fire—but they had not been defeated. Their battalion was probably just as ready for combat now as it had been before the thirty-six-hour battle.

United States troops ruled the battlefield, but they were not victors. It was part of the proven tactics of Communists to break off a skirmish early and disappear, a method carefully expounded in all textbooks on guerrilla warfare. However, this battle was presented later at the Saigon press information center as an American victory.

In the Plei Me Special Forces Camp, a red-haired sergeant from Boston was trying to pull a white sweat shirt over the head of a small brown-skinned boy. He finally succeeded with the help of the boy's mother. The sergeant, a medic, was surrounded by a yelling crowd of small children: Jaraï, members of a mountain tribe, who had come to get new clothing from the Americans.

"My mother sent these things here for the kids," he explained. "She and her friends made them. I wrote that the children don't have anything decent to eat or wear. She organized a sewing circle for poor Jaraï children. They made these things." He showed me a pile of boxes. All were full of dresses, pants, sweaters, and sweat shirts.

The sergeant was twenty-four and had come to Viet-Nam "to fight for freedom." "But that isn't very important," he said, rubbing disinfectant powder on the emaciated scab-covered body of a two-year-old girl. Was he fighting Communism? He stared at me in surprise: "Communism? No. I'm here to help these people live better and learn something so they'll be treated like human beings, not animals. Communism? I think there's a lot of phony talk about it. All we have to do is simply help these people, and we won't have to fight the Communists."

His superior was a North Carolina sergeant, head of a small clinic in Plei Me where he daily treated thirty to forty patients. He was ordered to lead a patrol on a visit to a *montagnard* village five miles from Plei Me. He was to examine its inhabitants and distribute leaflets. A propaganda specialist would make a short speech and then the patrol would return.

"We have to show the people we're here. They must get

used to us slowly and learn to trust us," I was told by the American camp commander, a tall, twenty-nine-year-old West Point graduate, and one of the best troop leaders I met in Viet-Nam. I was granted permission to go along with the patrol. They gave me an AR-15 Colt rifle. "You never know what will happen; we'll be passing through VC territory," the sergeant from North Carolina said. I buckled on a bandolier and filled my water canteen. Forty *montagnard* soldiers came with us.

We set out at 8:00 A.M. After a half-hour march we reached the jungle that rose steeply to the right and left of the narrow colonial highway. The wind blew up the red dust from the road. The patrol advanced in three groups. The vanguard, the main force—of which the sergeant and I were a part—and the rear guard, commanded by a small Rhadé officer.

The soldiers moved forward in single file on the right and left sides of the road, separated at wide intervals. "It's better this way," the sergeant said. "If the Charlies attack, it will be harder for them to catch us." I wanted to know if the highway was mined. "Maybe," came the answer. "It probably isn't. We'll soon know."

I asked him whether he had ever run into an ambush. "Thank God, no," he replied. "It would be pretty bad in these mountains because the Charlies hold back their attacks until they see the whites and shoot at them first. We've already lost men on patrols." I looked around. The sergeant and I towered over the mountain tribesmen by almost a foot. We could be singled out from a long distance. The terrain seemed ideal for an ambush, and I said so. "Right, but they aren't around," he growled.

A few minutes later they were. A grenade exploded at

the bottom of the hill. The *montagnards* dropped to the sides of the road. I fell into a thorn bush. Ten yards ahead of us a machine gun began rattling away. Bush and jungle cracked with fire, black shapes flashed in front of us. We heard them shouting *Xung phong,* which roughly means, "Forward, kill." For the first time in this war I was using a weapon. I was somewhat dazed as my bullets zipped into the underbrush. The sergeant cursed as he fired into the woods. The trees were only a yard away. All we could see were screaming black shadows that loomed up suddenly and then disappeared. Ten yards uphill the brush began burning and a *montagnard* fell forward with an animal roar, still firing his machine gun. He disappeared into the hedges.

The guerrillas set up a machine gun level with us. We heard the shouts of the gun crew. The bullets whistled above the ground and buzzed around our heads. It was impossible to stand up. I raised the barrel of my gun slightly and blindly fired in the direction of the enemy.

Five minutes later there was silence. The guerrillas broke off the fight because they did not expect such strong resistance. The sergeant worked his radio, vainly trying to get the nearby fort. We had time to care for the wounded. Our losses were light: two dead, one *montagnard* bleeding heavily from a flesh wound.

Our force advanced a little ways to the point where the jungle ended abruptly and a level field began. Two hundred yards away we saw the Viet-Cong racing across the bare ground. Our soldiers took pot shots without hitting anyone. Plei Me still did not answer our calls. It took half an hour before we established contact. No, we didn't need support. "Shall we continue on to the village or turn back?" the sergeant bellowed into the mouthpiece. A pause. "Okay, we're going on to the village. We'll be back at noon."

An hour later we resumed our march, and in another twenty minutes reached our destination. Our patrol was met by unfriendly, half-naked mountain natives. "Was the Viet-Cong here?" the sergeant had the interpreter ask the village elder. No, they had seen nothing. The shooting earlier? Hunters, they had thought. Had they been threatened by anyone? No, they hadn't seen any guerrillas for months.

These people were plainly afraid, and did not want to talk. The sergeant's medical supplies didn't impress them. Neither did the rice wine he had brought along, nor the colorful leaflets, whose crude drawings depicted the Viet-Cong's vicious behavior. They remained impassive. Only when I snapped some pictures did their wrinkled and haggard faces break into smiles.

I had been told in camp that the people around Plei Me were friendly and hated the guerrillas; that the mountain tribes could be counted on completely for support. Had the situation been misjudged, or was the assessment based on the desire to paint a rosy picture? I think both factors were involved. Not only in Viet-Nam, but in Laos and Cambodia as well, I observed how wrong even the most intelligent American officers and officials could be in judging the mood of people. One reason must be the overwhelming sense the Americans have of their mission. It leads them to ignore the subtleties which are so important in winning the friendship of a foreign people and race.

Shortly before leaving Viet-Nam I discussed the subject with a high-ranking American officer. He claimed contacts with the population had never been so good. "The people like our men. They cheer when we pass through the villages and towns." I had seen these welcomes often enough: small kids yelling "Okay," "Hello," and "Number one," happily skipping around the strange white men as they probably had done with the French. I rarely saw adults greet the Americans with the same enthusiasm.

"Brother, talk French and the world is yours. Don't ever let them catch on you're with the Americans," a young West Berliner employed by a construction firm in Chu Lai told me. Once, an unfriendly waiter in a Saigon restaurant asked me what I wanted to eat. He spoke pidgin English. I ordered in French. The waiter was startled and asked if I was French. I lied and said, "Yes." The man's attitude immediately changed. He cleaned off the tablecloth, brought a menu and apologized with many bows: "Please pardon, I thought you were American." The incident recurred a dozen times in one way or another.

The villagers were visibly relieved when the Special Forces patrol left. The trip back could have been more dangerous than the one to the village. "The Charlies know we're on our way, maybe they're waiting for us," the sergeant from North Carolina said. But nothing happened. We reached Fort Plei Me safely. Captain Willangby received us with a worried look, which changed when he saw I was all right. "It looks pretty bad when something happens to a journalist here." A young Danish correspondent had been shot in the head just outside Plei Me the year before.

"You were very lucky," the camp commander remarked to me later, after hearing the sergeant's report. "They either organized the ambush quickly or were only local guerrillas who are afraid of us. We usually don't get off so lightly. Most of the time a third or half of our men don't return."

Colonel Patch left the map room in a rage. Again, the commander of the 5th U.S. Special Forces in Pleiku had been unable to talk to the head of the Vietnamese Special Forces (Lu Luong Bac Biet), Colonel Phong. Colonel Patch had reason to be upset. Outlying forts had reported that new, strong North Vietnamese units had infiltrated south along the Ho Chi Minh Trail, and there had been increased activity by Viet-Cong forces around Plei Me. Through their excellent intelligence networks, the fort commanders had learned that Communist units—after the battles of Plei Me and the Ia Drang Valley, where they had suffered heavy casualties—intended attacking one of the American camps along the Cambodian border.

I had just arrived at Pleiku from Plei Me. Twenty-four hours had passed since the attack on the highway, which Colonel Patch viewed as the first warning signal. We soon received more bad news. A forty-man patrol had moved out of Plei Me to comb the surrounding area and had run into an ambush. A North Vietnamese company had been lying in wait. The patrol leader radioed for help and twenty minutes after the first shots had sounded the bombs of U.S. Skyraiders were crashing down on Communist positions. When a relief patrol reached the battlefield at midnight it found the shattered bodies of forty-four North Viet-Nam soldiers; the rest had withdrawn and disappeared. "A few months ago our patrol would have been lost," Colonel Patch explained. "We needed special permission then from the Vietnamese commander for every mission by our planes. It was usually too late to do anything by the time he had made up his mind."

In 1965, American camps in the highlands were repeatedly attacked or overrun. The assaults never lasted more than twenty minutes. But that is how long it took for a cry for help to reach Pleiku from the mountains, for the planes to take off and get to the battlefield. Later, the guerrillas took more time when attacking. They quickly noticed that the American planes showed up irregularly and sometimes not at all. And their intelligence service had informed them about the poor coordination between American and Vietnamese commanders.

"We often wasted hours contacting Vietnamese officers on duty, who were not where they were supposed to be, or who refused to wage war after hours. Frequently they wouldn't let the planes take off, without even offering an explanation. That's been changed since November, 1965. We can order them out when we wish. But then—it made me sick!"

A few hours later the colonel was sick all over again. He had learned why his Vietnamese colleague had not been able to come to the scheduled important staff meeting. The Vietnamese dispatched a courier to report that he had not been able to drive over to the American compound because no jeep was available. Yet, the Vietnamese camp was located right next to the American, and the command barracks of the two officers were about two hundred yards apart.

That evening Fort Duc Co reported catching a Viet-Cong spy. He belonged to one of the camp's defense units. He gave the names of twenty-eight others, working secretly for the Communists. I recalled a conversation with

Captain Willangby at Plei Me. The fort had 400 soldiers, Vietnamese and mountain tribesmen. The captain estimated that at least 10 per cent of the men had secret ties with the Viet-Cong.

The next day a patrol from Duc Co occupied a radio station. Its equipment was Chinese and belonged to a North Vietnamese regiment that had entered South Viet-Nam in December via the Ho Chi Minh Trail. The Americans were able to monitor Communist communications for two days and learned two important facts: A plan was afoot to attack one of the U.S. camps, and the rebel army had a secret intelligence school north of Pleiku where it was training agents for work in South Viet-Nam's northern provinces. Pleiku had long been aware that such a school existed, but had never turned up any evidence.

Ten days later I left Pleiku. I "commandeered" a Hercules cargo plane on the airfield. It had come from Danang and would pass over Saigon on its flight to Manila. Hitchhiking by plane is sometimes the only way for soldiers, civilians, and newspapermen to get anywhere in Viet-Nam. We landed in Saigon at 9:00 P.M. I stayed at a hotel on the Hai Bu Trung* in the center of the city. The hotel owner was friendly. He was a stout Vietnamese who spoke English and French. He was now riding the crest of the wave of prosperity that had inundated Saigon. "I have news for you," he laughed. "They found a time bomb today under a taxi outside my hotel."

I had an appointment with Rick Merron, a photogra-

* One of Saigon's main thoroughfares, named after the "heroic [terrible] sisters"; in the ninth century, the sisters led the Viets in the struggle against the Chinese and are now being used by South Vietnamese propagandists as symbols of resistance to Chinese aggression.

pher. He had been a paratrooper in the 101st Division when General Maxwell Taylor commanded it. His colleagues called him "Mr. Cool" because he kept clicking away in the most dangerous situations.

Rick showed up at the Cafe Grival with a tall American captain, an adviser to a Vietnamese regiment in the delta. His face was sunburned and he looked exhausted and discouraged. He had volunteered for Viet-Nam, had been in the country for two years, and that very day had decided not to extend his tour of duty. He had had it. Rick told me why while the captain gulped down one whiskey after another, without showing any signs of drunkenness.

The captain was stationed in the delta. In My Tho he met a Vietnamese girl named Mai. She was very pretty. He had known her for a year and intended to take her back to the States and marry her. Mai had to provide for two younger brothers and her parents. The family took to the American, an experience common to occupation troops in all wars. He brought them canned food, cigarettes, clothes, as well as the things he could buy cheaply at the PX.

The girl's house soon became a rendezvous for a few Americans stationed in My Tho. "They wanted to make contact with the people, get to know them," said Rick. The girl, who spoke excellent English, gave some of the captain's friends lessons in Vietnamese. The South Vietnamese secret service began to pay attention to the family and put it under surveillance—a usual practice when Vietnamese became too intimate with Americans. One day his superior called in the captain and told him his girl friend was strongly suspected of serving the Viet-Cong; in any case, her older brother was a high rebel official. The captain made the mistake of telling this to the girl, whom he trusted fully.

Of course, she denied the accusations. Two weeks passed. One day a young man appeared at the captain's quarters and asked him to come to Mai's house because she wanted to talk to him right away. The captain appealed to a friend, a helicopter pilot stationed in Tan Hiep, to drive him to Mai's in a jeep. The girl was waiting. She begged the pilot to be patient and went off with the captain. She returned in half an hour and told the pilot his friend would be back in another hour. The pilot, believing he had enough time to drive into the city, got into his jeep and switched on the motor. Then it happened. The vehicle blew up, and all they found later of the young American pilot were blood-stained scraps of uniform stuck to the cracked wall of the house.

The police came and questioned the girl and her family. The captain vouched for the family. He drove back to headquarters. When he returned the following day to the house, it was empty. He learned that the girl's parents and two brothers had been arrested; Mai had disappeared. The next day the two boys—eight and ten years old, whom the captain had nicknamed "Tom" and "Jerry"—confessed they had placed a mine in the jeep. It had been meant for the captain; the pilot had been killed by mistake. The younger of the two boys was so badly tortured while being questioned that he died a few days later.

The captain sat opposite me mumbling into his whiskey glass. A Frenchman joined us, a newspaperman who, unlike many of his countrymen, passionately defended American policy in Viet-Nam. I would be returning to Europe in a few days so we decided to have dinner that evening at the Club Nautique on the bank of the Saigon River. It was 10:00 P.M., and we took a taxi to the club.

Like almost all conversations in Saigon at that time, ours ended in a debate about America's involvement in Viet-Nam. It was dark. Jet fighters from Tan Son Nhut thundered overhead on the way to their nightly attacks. Small houseboat lanterns flickered on the river, and on the other shore we could see lights almost drowned in the glare of a big sign advertising sewing machines. The darkness on the other side covered Gia Dinh, a wretched shanty-town district of Saigon. It was Viet-Cong territory, and they ruled it when night fell. We were within range of their guns.

Three hundred yards behind us stood the massive white concrete building of the U.S. Embassy, the nerve center of America's military strategy and policy in Southeast Asia. The guerrilla outposts in the heart of the capital were a bare 600 yards away from it. The rebels could have shelled the embassy easily with mortars, but had never done so.

Gunfire flashed on the horizon. American artillery boomed all night long. Ten miles north of us the Viet-Cong held a strongly fortified position. The detonations lit up the sky over us like the northern lights.

The Frenchman began talking about Paris; a breath of Europe suddenly struck me. At the next table a brawny, open-shirted American was propositioning a Chinese girl no older than fourteen. They looked as if they had been forced on each other. Two Frenchmen were talking about sailboat voyages around Cape St. Jacques, and an elderly, married Vietnamese couple silently spooned up their food.

A column of tanks rattled along the shoreside road. The stooped, shabbily dressed taxi drivers, waiting in front of the club, eyed the wheezing monsters.

By now the captain was drunk.

4

From Rebellion to War

The battle of Ap Bac, which ended in a victory for the Liberation Army and local guerrillas of My Tho, throws a glorious light on the heroic struggle of the South Vietnamese people. It created new courage to pursue the enemy mercilessly and kill him.

> GENERAL VO NGUYEN GIAP,
> in the North Vietnamese Party newspaper,
> *Nhan Dan,* July 19, 1964

It was a victory that laid the foundation for our success against Communist subversion. Ap Bac is a symbol of the South Vietnamese people's will to resist.

> MAJOR GENERAL HUYNH VAN CAO,
> Commander of the 3rd Army Corps of the South Vietnamese
> Government troops after the battle on January 3, 1963

THE GUERRILLAS ruled the delta region in the first phase of the war. Eighty per cent of all fighting took place there in a 11,500-square-mile area inhabited by 5,000,000 people. Most battles ended in defeat for the government forces. Yet, President Ngo Dinh Diem paid less attention to the densely populated delta than to the narrow coastal strips of central Viet-Nam. His actions were not based on strategic considerations. Diem, a native of central Viet-Nam, believed its population was able to resist Communist subversion. He distrusted the rest of the people, especially the delta peasants.

Only two of the seven Vietnamese divisions were stationed in the delta. They were unable to suppress guerrilla activities and almost never left the cities they occupied. The Viet-Cong extended its rule in the countryside undisturbed. The people soon realized who had the strength to defend them, who had the military advantage, and who exercised power. They openly sympathized with the Viet-Cong. Even today, when the allies have slowly gained a foothold in some delta areas, and the U.S. Air Force, troops, and weapons have furnished the Saigon government with new fighting strength, the guerrillas still retain political ascendancy in the delta.

People there never refer to the Viet-Cong but to the "Front," and NLF flags fly in this no-man's-land. Woven Soviet stars have been set up in the rice paddies, and hand-drawn guerrilla posters cover primitive billboards on the muddy roads. The peasants respect them as symbols of a political force on the road to power. The government and the U.S. have been unable to regain the terrain lost in the first years of war; the guerrillas continue to move freely within sight of Saigon's gates. So far, only one effective means against the guerrillas has been found: bombs. But these hurt the population more than they do the invisible enemy.

The guerrillas hardened their grip on the provinces around Saigon between 1960 and 1962. No one could challenge their rule, and they established a smooth-running administration. The regular army of the NLF operated without hindrance, while Communist guerrillas controlled the villages.

Many government officials were murdered; others were intimidated into collaborating with the Communists. The

power of the district and province chiefs reached no further than their headquarters. They knew that if they left
their houses, they could be shot down on their doorsteps.
This was the period in which "the NLF laid the foundation for victory in the delta," a Central Committee member of the NLF told me in Phnom Penh.

While the political cadres of the NLF carried on their
propaganda undisturbed, the strategists exploited all the
natural advantages offered by the swampy delta landscape.
The Mekong Delta, a region crisscrossed by canals, rice
fields, swamps, dense brush, and concealed paths, is ideal
terrain for guerrilla warfare and has traditionally been a
hide-out for Vietnamese rebels and gangs. The Binh-
Xuyen and Cao-Dai sects had ruled there, and during the
Indochina War, the Viet-Minh found refuge there too.
While the government troops, operating along traditional
lines, floundered in the swamps, the small guerrilla forces
moved about without difficulty.

The Americans made their first stabs at the military situation in the delta in 1962 and succeeded in gaining some
ground. They hoped to drive the guerrillas back with new
weapons, particularly with helicopters and the amphibious
tank constructed especially for swamp warfare.

The 514th Battalion of the Liberation Army operated at
that time in the provinces of Dinh Tuong, Vinh Long, and
Kien Hoa. It was an elite unit, which had inflicted defeats
on the government forces, advanced to the gates of Saigon,
and represented a permanent threat to government-held
cities. For U.S. military advisers, crushing this battalion
was a hopeless task; for Vietnamese commanders, meeting
the 514th Battalion in battle was a nightmare. In October,
1962, the battalion operated between My Tho and Saigon.

In November, it was seen in the northwestern part of Dinh Tuong Province. In December, the NLF soldiers encamped near the village of Babeo. Finally, on December 28, one of the battalion's camps was spotted a mile and a half west of the village of Ap Bac, forty miles southwest of Saigon.

Under strong pressure from his American adviser, the commander of the 7th Vietnamese Infantry Division, Coloned Bui Dinh Dam, decided to attack the battalion and set January 2 as the date. The commander of the 514th Battalion, Duyen, had reached Ap Bac on December 27. Three days later, he learned the attack was imminent. The Viet-Cong intelligence service had monitored the government's radio messages and knew all details of the planned action. At 2:00 A.M. on January 1, Duyen moved his unit into the village; his soldiers immediately dug trenches and fortified them.

Battalion Commander Duyen, with only two companies (slightly less than 240 men) under him, radioed for reinforcements against the oncoming attack. New Year's Day, at 3:45 A.M., fifty guerrillas from neighboring villages joined the combat-ready battalion. Half an hour later Duyen shifted his troops again. The guerrillas dug in along a row of trees in front of Ap Bac. The battalion was relatively well armed. It had four 37-mm. machine guns, automatic weapons, and carbines, but not enough ammunition for a prolonged battle.

At 6:00 A.M. on January 2, the government artillery began its shelling. Half an hour later the 11th Battalion of the 11th Regiment landed north of the Viet-Cong trenches. Both the Vietnamese and Americans had counted on surprising the enemy. They now realized they were up against well-defended positions. The crack units A and B led by the province commander, Major Lam Quang To, landed south of the village. A number of M113's moved in west of the village. By 7:00 A.M. the enemy was completely surrounded. The government troops attacked four times—and were thrown back each time. The Viet-Cong battalion withdrew to the south and ran into elements of the crack A and B units. There were brief skirmishes, all of them ending in heavy losses for the government troops. The Viet-Cong had its first losses: one man dead and four wounded.

Colonel Dam decided to have helicopters bring in reserves west of Ap Bac. Twelve helicopters whirled toward the battlefield, but came under fierce fire when they tried to set down. Five were destroyed, another eight damaged. The troops suffered heavy casualties as they tried to disembark from the helicopters. The survivors lay in the middle of a rice field, defenseless, with the sharp-shooting enemy in front of them, the burning wrecks of their helicopters behind.

At 9:00 A.M. the artillery began a new bombardment of the 514th Battalion. It lasted twenty minutes. Battalion Commander Duyen said later, "We were concealed. We didn't lose a single man during this or later shellings."

The attackers had encountered a situation that was to unnerve them repeatedly in the succeeding years of war. Hours of bombardment had failed to undermine the ability of the guerrillas to defend themselves. (Once I was present when a village north of Bong Song was bombarded for two days with napalm and demolition bombs; not a house was left standing—yet the Viet-Cong continued to fight back. When an American unit finally reached the enemy's positions, it found them abandoned; some dead had been left behind but no wounded. The network of tunnels and trenches was practically undamaged. The ground above had been devastated, but the defense installations beneath were intact.)

Shortly after 10:00 A.M. Colonel Dam ordered the commander of the M113's to bring the tanks up. It took them four hours to cover the mile to the battlefield. Captain Ly Tong Ba, commander of the tanks, had initially refused to advance. One of his lieutenants even stopped his tank, destroyed its radio, and later explained he had not moved forward because he had not received any command. The tanks rumbled up behind the wrecked helicopters. Captain Ba put an ex-sergeant in command of the unit and left the dangerous area.

The M113's had been built for the kind of situation and terrain that lay ahead: a swampy rice field under enemy fire, which the infantry could not cross. The enemy, hiding on the other side of the rice field, could be overrun by the armored amphibious vehicles. But the weapon that superb technicians had dreamed up became a joke in the hands of men who refused to attack. The tanks, with their heavy, rapid-fire guns and their 12.7-mm. machine guns, stood motionless in the exposed rice field.

At this point Commander Duyen sent out a special squad of fifteen volunteers to knock the tanks out of commission. Hand grenades and daggers were their only weapons. Slowly they crawled toward the steel monsters and blew up four and damaged two. Only one member of the special squad returned safely to the trenches around Ap Bac, dragging with him a badly wounded comrade who died a few minutes later.

The government troops, abandoned by their officers, were firing blindly around the M113 armored carriers, because they were afraid to raise their heads and take aim. To the south, Major Lam Quang Tho was ordered to advance and attack the enemy from the rear. Tho had prudently taken a stand some seven miles southeast of Ap Bac and knew nothing of what was happening on the battlefield. He was commanded to move forward four times; four times he refused to obey. He had squandered the chance to fall upon the enemy's rear and flanks; and the outcome of the battle was virtually decided. (Reports that Major Tho later faced a court-martial are not true.) By 6:00 P.M. it was clear the battle could no longer be won, that the enemy battalion could not be driven from its positions. Duyen said: "The fight was over at 7 o'clock."

The Vietnamese commander, however, still hoped for a victory. At 4:00 P.M. the commander of the 3rd Army Corps, Major General Huynh Van Cao, had ordered reserves ferried by helicopters west of Ap Bac to dislodge the Viet-Cong. A paratroop battalion finally landed behind its own lines at 6:20 P.M. and immediately ran into a blistering fire in the twilight. Four paratroopers were killed on the spot, eleven wounded. The paratroopers had been shelled by their own troops who had taken them for guerrillas.

Colonel Daniel Porter, American adviser to the corps commander, realizing that the battle could not be decided that day, asked that Ap Bac be shelled during the approaching night. He also asked that the open terrain around the village be cordoned off with the light of flare bombs so that the guerrillas could not withdraw under cover of darkness. The colonel's proposals were rejected on the grounds that the American flare bombs had to be used sparingly.

Duyen, the 514th Battalion commander, had anticipated that the enemy would block any night retreat, and he ordered his unit to strengthen its defense positions in the village for the next day's fighting. A scouting patrol reported at 11:00 P.M. that government forces had not occupied the terrain east of Ap Bac. The battalion left its position and proceeded to Binh Phong Thanh, a village about three miles from Ap Bac. All twenty-one dead and seventeen wounded were taken along. Some of the men had been badly wounded, but Duyen comments, "The villagers took such good care of them that none died."

The government troops had far greater casualties: 61 dead and 123 wounded. Three American military advisers had been killed. Next morning, U.S. General Paul Harkins visited the command post and as *The New York Times* correspondent David Halberstam reported it, declared to the American advisers: "Now we've got them in a trap, and we're going to spring it." The Americans were bewildered by their superior's estimate of the situation. They knew the Viet-Cong had left Ap Bac hours ago. But the Vietnamese commanders knew nothing or were poorly informed about the situation. While the dead were being ferried from the battlefield by helicopter, Major Tho suddenly opened artillery fire on what he thought were enemy positions—exactly twelve hours after the 514th Battalion had withdrawn. The senseless barrage cost the government forces another five dead and fourteen wounded. Even when the Americans promptly flashed word to Major Tho that the partisans were no longer in Ap Bac, he refused to stop the shelling. As for Major General Cao, while his men were being slaughtered by their own artillery, he was preparing a victory celebration to proclaim his military triumph to the world.

A company of the 514th Battalion returned to Ap Bac on January 4. But this time the Vietnamese officers absolutely refused to attack. American advisers mobilized personnel, mechanics, and cooks in an attempt to blockade and trap enemy patrols. The entire battalion returned to Ap Bac on January 9 and raised the NLF flag over the wrecked village. Cao refused to attack. Not until April did he advance on Ap Bac with 5,000 men to smash the 514th Battalion, which had been reinforced by two more companies and numbered 550 men. On the eve of the operation, Cao sent out a militia company to secure the way to Ap Bac. It ran into a Viet-Cong ambush and was wiped out. Major General Cao finally entered Ap Bac the next day only to find the 514th Battalion gone. Nevertheless, Cao announced he had won an "important and great victory."

In fact, the Ap Bac battle was an important turning point in the Vietnamese war. It laid bare all the shortcomings of South Viet-Nam's political and military system. It also demonstrated the plight of the American advisers. Trapped in the confusing mechanism of Vietnamese domestic politics, without power of command, they had to look on helplessly as Viet-Nam was slowly being lost to the Communists.

United States policy was another crippling factor. It still hoped Diem would be able to stabilize South Viet-Nam to the point where it could deal with Communist subversion on its own. American representatives, diplomatic and military, had to accept the president's line, even when they knew it was wrong, and approve his measures and support him.

Ap Bac proved, in addition, that not money nor first-rate equipment nor modern weapons could replace training, fighting spirit, initiative, and courage. It had offered the government troops an opportunity to stop a weak enemy with superior forces. Some 3,500 government soldiers had faced less than 250 insurgents, who lacked artillery, helicopters, bombers, and tanks. All the possibilities had existed for completely destroying an elite enemy unit that had kept half the delta in turmoil for months. But an incompetent South Vietnamese military leadership could not beat even an inferior enemy.

There was one more crucial factor. Most South Vietnamese officers still had a feudal mentality. Rank represented a chance to rise above the men placed under them. They reluctantly accepted the unpleasant side effects of war as a necessary evil. As at Ap Bac, the Vietnamese officer corps, the army leadership, failed on hundreds of other occasions. The attitude of many officers toward war has hardly changed even today. When Diem was overthrown, the United States had to pull the reins tighter in Viet-Nam. Yet, it had to leave the Diem officer corps untouched to keep the structure of the army from total collapse. I will cite just two examples of the failure of South Vietnamese officers. In Quang Nai, a South Vietnamese captain had four bar girls brought to his quarters just as his unit was moving out for a dangerous action along Route 1. A worse example: A company of the 1st U.S. Air Cavalry was encircled by a Viet-Cong battalion near Bong Son. A Vietnamese platoon commanded by a young lieutenant was with the company. For two days I watched the lieutenant desperately work his radio. He crouched in a trench and tried, his voice hoarse, to reach his superior officer, a major, in Bong Son. It was a waste of time. The day after the operation began—one that had been planned as the biggest military action ever undertaken in South Viet-Nam—the major had sped off to Saigon "to visit relatives." This happened not in 1962 or 1963, but in the spring of 1966.

The American military advisers had learned a bitter lesson at Ap Bac: All their efforts to search out and beat the enemy would remain useless as long as the Vietnamese Army leadership distrusted them and ignored their suggestions. The Americans serving with the troops could not expect support either from President Diem, who distrusted American officers on principle, or from their own superiors in Saigon, who had no choice but to play along with Diem. Washington had laid down the law: "Don't cross our touchy ally."

General Paul Harkins, then head of the U.S. Military Command, proclaimed the battle of Ap Bac a victory "for our ally," although he was an experienced officer from whom the facts could not possibly have been hidden. The day after the battle, Admiral Harry Felt arrived in Saigon and said: "As I understand it, it was a victory." At a subsequent press conference, he commented: "It was a victory —we took the objective." Yet, the American advisers who had taken part in the battle knew that it was not a victory, that even if the South Vietnamese military system had not experienced a shattering defeat, its morale had been dealt a serious blow. According to Admiral Felt, the only purpose of the mission had been to drive the guerrillas out of the village, that is, win some real estate. In conventional warfare, taking a village may be an important military victory —but it means nothing in guerrilla warfare. It is not territory that has to be conquered but an enemy who must be ferreted out and defeated. It is a supreme maxim of guerrilla strategy never to defend a position at all costs and risk huge casualties, but to remain mobile, evade the enemy, and attack at the right moment. The guerrillas stick to hit-and-run tactics and return to the battlefield only after the enemy has left. This is precisely what happened at Ap Bac. As Admiral Felt was announcing that the action had been a success, Communist flags were again flying over the shattered village.

The Ap Bac battle was quickly picked up and used in Communist propaganda. For the first time since American intervention in Viet-Nam, a relatively small guerrilla unit had repulsed government troops equipped with the most modern weapons. The appearance of specialized American weapons had troubled the Viet-Cong leadership. They feared they would be unable to cope with the superior weapons, above all with helicopters and armored vehicles. Ap Bac proved to the Communists they could. The guerrillas destroyed five helicopters and a column of M113's. These accomplishments strengthened their self-confidence and proved an extremely important psychological factor in the war.

After the battle the victorious Battalion Commander Duyen commented: "It proved to us that the terrifying helicopters were vulnerable. It showed we could defeat a much stronger enemy." Victories demonstrate strength and success, and the South Vietnamese Army practically handed these to the Communists at Ap Bac and on many other occasions.

David Halbertstam wrote about the delta situation in 1963:

> In a fluctuating military and political situation there is sometimes a crucial moment which even fairly knowledge-able observers overlook: the moment when the population knows which side is winning. Although we recognized that things were not going well, we . . . did not fully compre-hend just how badly things were going. We often talked in terms of a stalemate, but I now believe there is no such thing in a guerrilla war. One side has the momentum, the other doesn't. It's a simple as that. And the first people to be aware of this are the peasants.

An article in a Viet-Cong propaganda pamphlet reads like a supplement to Halberstam's analysis: "At Ap Bac, An Lao, Phu My, and Binh Gia we became aware of our military strength and knew we would triumph. The proof was not as necessary for us as it was for the people whom we could now convince and win over."

The inhabitants of Ap Bac themselves provided a tragi-comic sequel to the drama of the battle. After the 514th Battalion reoccupied Ap Bac on January 9, Commander Duyen sent a delegation of villagers, accompanied by two of his NCO's, to the province chief. The delegation de-manded compensation for damage inflicted by government troops during the battle.

It was American advisers who agreed to pay them, since a psychological and political struggle was also being waged. But neither this nor other generous American gestures could hide one fact: The rebellion had turned into a war. In the future the South Vietnamese, and later the American troops, would not face small guerrilla groups but a real army. Two years later this army succeeded in driving the United States close to the brink of military defeat.

5

Liberation Front
or Just Viet-Cong

Our policy is to strengthen North Viet-Nam and do everything conceivable to unify the country. A solid foundation must be laid for a good house. North Viet-Nam is the basis of the struggle for national freedom and unification of the entire country.

Ho Chi Minh, June 19, 1956,
in an open letter to South Vietnamese Communist
officials evacuated to the North

A YOUNG WOMAN strained against the ropes binding her to the trunk of a coconut tree. A dozen peasants stared at her as a short man in a faded gray uniform paced back and forth, his mincing steps contrasting sharply with his sweeping gestures. Hoarsely he roared his accusations against the woman. A few armed men stood behind the tree, listening without expression. The man ended his tirade in a raging staccato, then he bent to the ground and brought up, cradled in his hands, a broad, long-handled knife with a curved point, the kind used by peasants to open a coconut. He slowly turned toward the woman, who was struggling vainly to break loose. Her long black hair fell loosely over her anguished face.

The uniformed man signaled, and two armed men stepped forward and kneeled on each side of the trunk. With a jerk they separated the woman's legs. The small man plunged his arm forward; a piercing scream filled the village square. The peasants still stared impassively. Again the man's arm plunged forward. Again a cry of torment rose from the prisoner. The uniformed man turned around and took two steps to the side. The woman drooped, gasping, against the rope. The lower part of her body was in shreds, and reddish-gray entrails seeped out of a gaping belly wound.

The man pulled out a yellow paper and read loudly: "Death to traitors of the people. The same will happen to all who betray the just cause of our liberation struggle." He put the paper on a small bamboo spear and stuck it into the entrails slowly dripping to the ground. The woman had thrown her head back and was breathing with a soft, rattling sound.

It was 10:00 A.M. in February, 1966, in a village in the coastal province of Binh Dinh. At 2:00 P.M. a company of American soldiers entered the village and found her corpse between the abandoned huts.

The woman had been a government agent. She had been told by her superiors that the village would soon be occupied by U.S. troops and had, on her own, urged the peasants not to resist. That was the reason she had to die.

She had been sent into the province six months earlier. Her primary job was to collect information on the political structure of the insurgent organization. Her work had just begun. In December, 1965, the Viet-Cong had started to transform its organization in the province because of growing American involvement in the war. Guerrilla losses had risen rapidly, and the leaders assumed at the beginning of 1966 that U.S. troops would sweep into the province with concentrated fighting power, an assumption that was soon proved right.

In this strategically important coastal province the Communists were testing new ways of adapting their administration and political and military organization to new circumstances. The experience acquired here would later be applied in other regions.

Both the Saigon government and U.S. officials in Viet-Nam wanted to learn the forms and laws of this reorganization, and had planted agents in Viet-Cong–controlled areas for this purpose. One of their spies now lay dead in front of us.

"Some comrades have displayed nervousness and indecision in the past months. They have been confused by the powerful military machine the American imperialists have set into motion to strangle our people's struggle for freedom," said a leaflet distributed by the NLF to its middle-level officials in November, 1965. "This is not the first time we have faced dangerous situations. We will master them now and in the future. We must be more alert, more courageous, and we need ideas on how to adapt our struggle to the new circumstances." This was the signal for a series of reforms and reorganizational steps that began in December, 1965, and are still going on.

Just what is the National Liberation Front? It was founded "somewhere in South Viet-Nam" on December 20, 1960, the day after the anniversary of the start of the war against the French in 1946, probably at a meeting near the village of Suoi Dai in the province of Tay Ninh. The NLF closely resembles the organization Ho Chi Minh established to struggle against the Japanese and later, the French. Ho Chi Minh had summoned the Vietnamese Communist leaders to the Eighth Plenum of the Indochinese Communist Party, held between May 10 and 18, 1941, in the village of Pac Bo near the Vienamese-Chinese border. This conference has been described as the jumping-off point for the Communist effort to seize power in Viet-Nam. Ho Chi Minh proclaimed his patriotic war and decided to create an all-inclusive front organization. The "League for Viet-Nam Independence" was founded shortly afterward. It was to win fame as the Viet-Minh. The Viet-Minh followed faithfully in the footsteps of the Chinese Communists, departing only slightly from the united front Mao Tse-tung had organized for the struggle against the Japanese. At the Sixth Plenum of the Chinese Communist Party, on November 5, 1938, Mao defined the tasks of his organization: "During the struggle for national liberation, the class struggle appears as a form of the national struggle. . . . Within the united front, the national patriotic struggle and the class struggle are welded into a unified whole."

In 1941, Ho Chi Minh wrote a "Letter to the Homeland" calling for national solidarity in the struggle against the Japanese and French. It appealed to: "rich people, soldiers, workers, peasants, intellectuals, white-collar employees, merchants, the youth and women—all who love the homeland selflessly. The cause of the National Liberation Front is sacred. Let us unite . . . to save our nation from destruction."

The ICP seemed ready to come to terms with all social classes. It shifted its activity from the cities to the countryside; the "peasant revolution" took priority over the "proletarian revolution." The "struggle against imperialism" continued, but the old demands—such as the establishment of workers, soldiers, and peasant soviets, and nationalization —were renounced to offset the widespread dislike of Communism. The South Vietnamese Communists adopted the same tactic later in different form.

The most varied groups soon joined the Viet-Minh: nationalistic students, intellectuals, the petite bourgeoisie, peasants, and idealists who wanted nothing to do with Communism but dreamed of creating a united, free, and independent Viet-Nam. Once the French had been defeated, Ho Chi Minh—like Mao Tse-tung before him— knew how to get rid of all needless fellow travelers quickly.

After 1954, Communist propaganda in North Viet-Nam raised its sights on a new objective: reunification with the South. The struggle for reunification became as decisive an element in North Viet-Nam policy as the ambitious industrial plans of the Lao-Dong Party (Vietnamese Workers' [Communist] Party). It still seemed Ho Chi Minh would be able to extend his political power southward by peaceful means. But in 1955, Ngo Dinh Diem replaced the weak South Vietnamese emperor, Bao-Dai. Diem was a fierce anti-Communist—a Catholic and ascetic who had lived a cloistered life in Catholic seminaries. Ho Chi Minh had invited him to join the Viet-Minh in the struggle against the French, but he had refused and been condemned to death. He was later pardoned by Ho Chi Minh and released.

Diem described the 1954 Geneva Treaty as "unrealistic" and refused to sign it. He was not interested in coming to terms with the Communists. The new ruler of the South had the support of a powerful ally. The United States had also refused to sign the Geneva Treaty, but had stated that it would regard any violation of the treaty as a "serious threat to world peace." That was in July, 1955. Two months later, on September 8, SEATO was formed and Washington issued statements guaranteeing the security of South Viet-Nam, as well as Laos and Cambodia. Fearful of armed conflict with the United States in the South, Ho Chi Minh and his comrades limited themselves to peaceful probes. They proposed the neutralization of South Viet-Nam, demanded Saigon renounce all American aid, and called on it to legalize the Communist Party. Had Diem acceded to Hanoi's wishes at the time, it probably would have meant he was ready to hand South Viet-Nam over to Hanoi.

Instead, the president, ruling in autocratic mandarin style, began ramming through a hard anti-Communist policy. Hanoi quickly recognized its dream of peaceful reunification was at an end and reacted promptly. A "Fatherland Front" was founded in September, 1955, a catch-all national movement intended to initiate a new phase in the Communist policy of reunification. In April, 1959, the Fifteenth Plenum of the Central Committee of the Lao-Dong Party decided to step up the struggle, after Diem, with American help, consolidated his rule and systematically began to smash existing underground Communist organizations. Hanoi decided to form a guerrilla army and, in the fall of the same year, Saigon's troops suddenly came face to face with well-trained insurgent forces, which dealt them one defeat after another.

The sharpening Sino-Soviet conflict at that time changed Peking's attitude toward South Viet-Nam—and Hanoi's as well. Ho Chi Minh knew he could not count on direct help from Moscow in the coming struggle, but the Chinese leaders expressed their eagerness to "support unconditionally the just struggle of our Vietnamese brothers." For Peking, the expanding civil war in South Viet-Nam and Laos became a testing ground in its conflict with Moscow, a practical demonstration of its thesis that revolutionary advances were possible without unleashing an atomic world war and that guerrilla warfare in the jungle, where no fixed fronts existed, excluded the use of atomic weapons.

The theses on national wars of liberation laid down by Mao Tse-tung, Ho Chi Minh, Vo Nguyen Giap, and Che Guevara became an essential part of Communist propaganda in South Viet-Nam. First-rate field commanders were ready to apply them. In almost every conversation with Liberation Front officials, I was lectured at length on the superiority of the people, the masses, over the imperialist army, the United States, the paper tiger. I met a Communist about twenty-five years old in Saigon who described himself as a "convinced Viet-Cong." It was his task to familiarize students with Communist theories of revolution and, above all, with the concept of the war of liberation. To do so he quoted Mao Tse-tung by the page.

In March, 1966, I visited a village in Viet-Cong territory northeast of Saigon. I was taken to the hut occupied by the chief of the local guerrillas. My escort, a Party official from Saigon-Cholon, asked the guerrilla leader to explain the village organization of the Liberation Front.

Twenty families lived in the village and all were integrated in the Front apparatus. The hamlet had a women's organization, a youth group, a guerrilla organization, a political school, a peasant organization, an administrative organization, a propaganda team. The Communist Party was organized along parallel lines, and some of the committees were the same.

The village was part of a group in which several smaller hamlets were combined. The chief of this group was a man in his forties, named An Thuan, who told me he had fought against the French and, right after the cease-fire agreement, had been sent into this village. He has lived there ever since: "My task was to educate the peasants politically and—as it became necessary—militarily as well." After a long talk I learned he was a member of the South Vietnamese Communist Party, and therefore the top Party leader of these villages.

"What is the real difference between the Liberation Front and the Communist Party?" I asked him.

My escort immediately corrected me: "There is no Communist Party in South Viet-Nam, only a People's Revolutionary Party."

An Thuan explained, "The People's Revolutionary Party is part of the Liberation Front. It is combined with other organizations in the Liberation Front."

"Are the goals of the Front identical with the Party's?"

"The NLF fights for independence, democracy, peace, neutrality, and a peaceful reunification of our fatherland. The People's Revolutionary Party has the same goal. Naturally, it seeks to attain a degree of independence and autonomy within the Liberation Front—as do all the other progressive forces within the NLF."

I had read almost precisely the same definition of the functions of a revolutionary party in one of Ho Chi Minh's essays, a definition I found again in a speech by Mao Tse-tung. Both Thuan and my escort spoke reluctantly on the subject and repeatedly guided the discussion back to the Liberation Front, "which is carrying on the struggle for the just cause."

I asked Thuan whether he would describe himself as a Communist. The official looked at me in confusion, stared at my escort and only slowly regained his composure when he realized I was not a Communist. He later told me that at the beginning of our conversation he had assumed I was a delegate from some European Communist organization. He answered my question cautiously: "I am a member of a party that subscribes to Marxist-Leninist theories." But he immediately emphasized that political debates on this subject were pointless in South Viet-Nam at the moment. "We will find time later to discuss everything," he said hastily. I asked if he had ever received Communist indoctrination. The former Viet-Minh soldier replied evasively: "The necessity of the anti-colonial and revolutionary war was explained to us during the war against the French."

"What tasks have you had to fulfill recently?"

"When Diem began to persecute all the patriots who had fought against the French, and as the terror steadily increased, I came here to teach the people how to defend themselves," Thuan said. "We formed self-defense units, and today not one government soldier dares come near our villages."

"When did Diem's terror begin?"

"Very soon after the signing of the Geneva Treaty. We had to defend ourselves, and many peasants helped us when they began to hate the government, which persecuted them, imposed new taxes on them, and whose soldiers treated them cruelly," he answered.

In South Viet-Nam, veterans of the Viet-Minh and

members of a wide range of political groups slowly prepared for massive resistance to Diem's government. At the
same time, the Lao-Dong Party, holding its Third Congress in Hanoi in September, 1960, decided not only to
struggle for the "liberation of the country," but also
stressed the importance of the political, military, and propa-
gandistic actions of the revolutionaries in the South. The
final resolution of the congress stated that "The greatest
efforts must be made to gather all national and democratic
forces together and to expand the bloc of national unity
. . . to isolate the Americans and their lackeys and ac-
celerate the struggle for reunification."

A South Vietnamese national front modeled on the
Viet-Minh was prepared, in which all kinds of political
groups could join the common struggle "against the neo-
colonial war of the American imperialists." No sooner did
the NLF come into existence than it launched an astonishing number of activities. Like the Viet-Minh, it em-
braced political groups of the most varied make-up, including peasants, students, workers, petite bourgeoisie,
businessmen, women, and youth. Extensive political activity abroad is typical of the NLF. It affiliated with international Communist organizations and sent delegates to
the Afro-Asian conference, to meetings of the World
Peace Council, to international student organizations. It
established permanent offices abroad: first in Peking, then
in Havana, Cairo, Algeria; later in East Berlin, Prague,
Budapest, and Moscow. Today there are NLF representatives not only in Paris, London, and Rome but in Stock-
holm, Zurich, and Vienna as well.

The NLF today has a regular press service and agency.
Its publishing organization, Editions Liberation, issues

books and propaganda pamphlets, some of them produced in printing shops in South Viet-Nam's jungles. The presses come from U.S. supplies and are bought easily on the Saigon black market.

Radio stations have been set up in Tay Ninh and Phuoc Long provinces; part of the equipment also consists of U.S. Army supplies. The Liberation transmitter broadcasts in Vietnamese, Cambodian, Chinese, French, English and in the different tribal languages. A press service publishes regular bulletins in Vietnamese, Spanish, French, English, and German. A film and photo service distributes films from the "liberated regions" of South Viet-Nam. NLF officials told me that the Front intended in the near future to set up more missions in Africa, Latin America, and Europe, and that the international propaganda campaign was to be intensified. In 1961, only one delegation of NLF representatives visited East Europe, but in 1965 twenty-seven delegations covered all conti nents. In 1962, the NLF was represented in seven international Communist or pro-Communist organizations. In 1963, the number was fourteen; in 1964, twenty-one. Today the figure is more than twenty-three.

In South Viet-Nam itself, the Front's primary concern is to build a powerful army and also, simultaneously, to consolidate its power in regions it controls and to expand into other areas. When the "Army for Propaganda and Liberation" was set up in December, 1944, under the command of Vo Nguyen Giap in North Viet-Nam, the future conqueror of Dien Bien Phu wrote: "Political activity is more important than military action, and fighting less important than propaganda."

The Viet-Cong worked hard to win over the peasants

by using primitive but effective propaganda. The peasants were given land whose owners had fled. This simple measure cost the Communists nothing more than the paper used for the deed. The tactic was explained to me: "The peasants were liberated from the degradation of tenancy. They received the land from us; naturally, they now had to defend it. They knew that they would lose it as soon as the government was fully restored to power."

When Diem took over the government, the state was totally disorganized. The army was demoralized, the police corrupt, the country dominated by feudal landlords, bandit chiefs, and sect leaders. The Geneva agreements stipulated that all Viet-Minh members were to return to the North, but Ho Chi Minh's men still controlled several southern provinces. Diem was probably sincere in his desire to establish the southern state as a viable structure—but he lacked the power and means to enforce his will. He began a policy of repression against unruly regions, but his measures backfired because he lacked authority and because the army was weak, the civil service corrupt. Diem had difficulty in holding his state together, and later he had to use violence to do so. Soon his "pacification campaigns" were punishing more innocent than guilty people. The peasants, who had rebelled against the landlords for a better life, against the bondage of rent and interest payments, were gradually driven into the arms of the Communists. The youth in the cities, who sympathized with the Liberation movement, also turned against Diem; so did the middle class, against which he discriminated, and the small number of Vietnamese intellectuals.

The social democracy the president had promised was soon nothing but a façade to mask dictatorship. "South

Viet-Nam is the only Communist state in the free world. All you have to do is change flags and you won't know whether you're in the North or South," a Vatican representative said of Diem's methods in 1959. In the last analysis, Diem had to lose the struggle against Communist subversion. Despite his ambitious social programs and pacification campaigns, all his anti-Communist measures—terror, punitive expeditions, and mass arrests—inevitably isolated him from the people.

The Communists moved warily. They knew time was on their side. They began to infiltrate the villages. Communist subversion undermined rule in increasingly larger regions of the country—until government control collapsed totally in those areas.

NLF cadres work hardest at slow indoctrination in their districts. In doing so, they are faithful to Mao Tse-tung's "three unities": "The cadre should live with the peasants, work with them, eat with them," says an NLF hand-printed manual. "He must not accept payment for his work; he must pay for his food. If need be, he will stay in a village for several years. He must not reveal he is a member of the Liberation Front. He should explain the necessity of the Liberation struggle to the peasants very slowly."

Years before the NLF was founded, the Viet-Cong had infiltrated the highland tribes with trained agitprop officials. These men adopted tribal customs, and sometimes even went so far as to be tattooed or have their teeth filed down, which many tribes believe to be beautifying. They did not begin their political work until much later, after they had won the confidence of the mountaineers. Most of the time a village falls under Viet-Cong influence without being aware of it. The agitprop officials come to a village, perform small services; they have a health worker with them who distributes medicines or bandages wounds; they demonstrate easier ways of cultivating rice. They leave the village, return, comment on how corrupt the government is and that no one really should pay taxes to it. The villagers soon agree. At a certain point, the villagers are asked for small services in return for what has been done for them, for some rice or for permission from the village chief to hold a political meeting. The NLF is talked about at the meeting and the peasants are told that when it forms the government, everything will belong to all. The peasants are asked to produce primitive weapons, to sharpen bamboo spikes or whittle bamboo spears. The women are asked to sew uniforms. Soon, villagers are found who want bigger things. In a short time, a new village council is elected, women's committees and youth groups formed. It doesn't take long before the entire village is firmly wedded to the Liberation Front organization.

Viet-Cong textbooks describe these and other methods in great detail. If a village balks at indoctrination, violence or other drastic means may be applied. For example, public trials are recommended: "The accused is someone who has shown he is an enemy of the people. These trials must be public and may end in a death sentence. Of course, the death penalty should be imposed only when the community approves. In that case, the execution is another bond that ties the village to our movement." But it is better "if the villagers attach themselves to our movement because they fear punishment or execution by the regime as 'enemies of the people.' "

At the outset, the guerrillas concentrated on breaking the government's power and undermining its authority.

Civil servants, officials, and soldiers were intimidated, kidnaped, or assassinated.* The activities grew so extensive that a transfer to the countryside was regarded by many civil servants as a death sentence. These methods paid off for the Viet-Cong, and it established its grip on the countryside in a short time. In general, the NLF still avoids harming women and children during its surprise attacks or razing of villages, unless it directly benefits from it.

Recently, to be sure, there have been more instances in which the Viet-Cong has indirectly terrorized the population by making it the target of American bombs and bullets. One day at noon, in a small village in An Lao Valley, the hum of a distant plane startled the peasants from their midday rest. Women scurried for shelter as the plane came closer and began circling the village.

Suddenly, a booming voice was heard: "Peasants, Vietnamese, fellow citizens. Tomorrow troops of the legitimate government will occupy your village. . . ."

The villagers looked at each other in wonder and dismay. Who was speaking? Where was the voice coming from? An old man began whispering about spirits and punishment. "Do not resist," thundered the voice in the sky. "We will not harm your friends, women, and children. Your cattle and fields will not be seized. But you must obey us. Do not resist. If there is any shooting, we will shoot back and then you and your families will suffer greatly. Do not resist; do not resist. . . ." The plane with the loudspeaker disappeared beyond a small chain of hills.

---

* South Vietnamese authorities report that 850 officials were kidnaped in 1960 and more than 1,500 murdered. Two years later, the murders rose to 1,900 and the kidnapings to more than 10,000. There were 2,200 murders in 1963; yet, in 1965 the rate declined, probably because of the changing character of the war.

The Viet-Cong had long had a firm grip on the village. The NLF District Committee and a party school for middle-echelon officials were located barely five miles away in An Lao, the capital of the district. For the Americans, An Lao Valley was "hard core" Viet-Cong territory and a center of resistance. The valley had been under bombardment for a year, its villages and hamlets pounded by American mortar shells and bombs. Now, a big operation had been started and the entire valley was to be "pacified."

The NLF District Committee in An Lao had decided on a weak defense of the valley since there was no point in risking fixed battle with superior American forces. The peasants were disturbed. They knew they could not be defended; they also knew that if the guerrillas fought the enemy here, the already devastated settlements would be razed to the ground.

The district cadres knew how the people felt. Indeed, the peasants' attitude had played an important part in shaping the Viet-Cong plan to leave the valley. At many meetings great stress was placed on the fact that the Liberation Army was the people's only real defender and that the Americans—if defied—would pay little heed to their problems. The rebel chiefs, soldiers, and local guerrillas withdrew into the mountains surrounding the valley to wait and see what happened when the Americans marched in. However, they left two armed youths behind. The two were ordered to open fire when the Americans arrived. "We must be warned," the district chief had said, before he fled to the mountains.

. The next morning a booming voice sounded again over the village. This time it did not come from the sky but from the nearby jungle: "Peasants," it thundered, "countrymen, your village is surrounded. Do not resist or we will shoot back. Do not resist."

The village was abandoned. The villagers had tied down their four water buffaloes in the bed of a small stream. The women and children had fled into the village bunker. The men had vanished into the jungle. They knew the habit the government troops and Americans had of seizing every man between fifteen and sixty-five in a Viet-Cong area and treating him as a guerrilla. Even if he actually was a government supporter, he would be put in a prison camp and questioned. And you did not get out of a camp so quickly—if you got out of it at all—without injury to body and soul. The peasants had learned this in twenty-six years of war.

Meanwhile, the camouflaged guerrillas crouched in their foxholes waiting for the first enemy. Hours passed. Then the first American soldiers appeared. They had crossed the rice paddy soundlessly. Now, arms at the ready, they approached. The village seemed empty; nothing moved in the great heat.

Suddenly, four shots rang out. A GI dropped his gun, grabbed his right upper arm, then dropped to the ground. Other Americans returned the fire. A machine-gun fusillade swept the dense foliage, followed by silence. Four soldiers lay hugging the ground in the manioc field just outside the village, hid behind the trunks of coconut trees. Every time one of the men in the manioc field tried to rise, a shot whistled across the level ground. The company commander gave the order to detour and close in on the village from the rear. But when a patrol tried crossing a rice field to the huts, it too met with a hail of bullets.

The American officers had not expected resistance. They called by radio for artillery support. Ten minutes later shells roared over the Americans and exploded among the huts. In another ten minutes they had destroyed the village. Flames, smoke, and ashes filled the air.

The Americans advanced again, and this time they met no resistance. The snipers had fled. Distraught women and children crept out of their foxholes and looked at the soldiers with hate. Their ruined dwellings smoldered all around them. A Vietnamese interpreter questioned an old peasant and learned how the Viet-Cong had evacuated the village, leaving the two guerrillas behind to "warn" them when the Americans arrived.

"They do this very often," Colonel Moore said to me later. "They shoot at us because they know we will return the fire. They provoke us into destroying the villages. After we leave, they return and tell the peasants: 'See, this happened because we weren't here. Only we can defend you from the imperialists.'"

Two days later, with U.S. troops ten miles to the south, the Viet-Cong returned to the village and built new fortifications for the next attack, knowing that next time the peasants would be fighting alongside them.

This form of terror is not new, but it is used only when it promises military and political gains. The guerrillas usually want to spare the villagers, but the relentless march of U.S. troops in South Viet-Nam since January, 1966, is forcing them to employ drastic methods to keep the allegiance of the population. "The imperialists can occupy our villages, they can take over entire provinces, but as long as the peasants remain with us, they cannot win," an NLF functionary said to me.

"Once a bus traveling to My Tho hit one of our mines and four children and seven women were killed in the explosion," a Saigon student, member of the People's Revolutionary Party, told me. "Because of this, meetings were held throughout the country in which we examined our underground activity in detail. Every Front member had to engage in self-criticism. We are not fighting against the people. We know how much we make the people hate us as a result of senseless devastation. The Americans have made a big issue out of this."

Not much propagandizing for the Communist Party is carried on. In the main, only the middle-level and top functionaries of the Front have had systematic party indoctrination. Communism is as vague a notion to the soldiers of the guerrilla army as it is to the peasants. In its propaganda speeches and crude, hand-drawn posters, the Viet-Cong calls on the people to struggle not for Communism but for the reunification of the country, to struggle for liberation, against the rich landlords, against the white man.

I witnessed the interrogation of a captured Viet-Cong soldier. The youngster, perhaps twenty, was squatting in front of an American military policeman and two Vietnamese. His feet were shod in "VC sandals," their soles cut from auto tires. His black shirt was torn and he was bleeding slightly from a small wound on his upper arm.

He had been dragged out of a bunker after he fired at approaching American soldiers. His bruised lips showed that he had not been treated gently. His arms were tied behind his back. One Vietnamese, acting as interpreter, questioned him. It soon became clear that the boy knew nothing. He may have been just an ordinary soldier, but now the war was over for him and all he feared—rightly, as it turned out—was that he would not survive the next few hours.

He readily named his commander, the number of his unit, its arms and strength. He told where he had come from, who he was, and what his comrades' names were. The Vietnamese began to question him about the Communist organization within the NLF. I don't believe the boy understood the question or that the word "Communism" had much meaning for him. His answers became uncertain, and a soldier began beating him with the butt of a rifle until he fainted. When he revived, he was asked again: Who are the officials of the People's Revolutionary Party? What is the structure of the village committees? What does he know about Marxism? With every question the rifle butt smashed into his back with a dull thud. The man tried hard to understand the questions, but he obviously could not. Just once—when he heard the name of Ho Chi Minh—did his face light up in recognition, and he began to talk. He knew the name of the man who had driven out the white colonial masters, but knew nothing about Communism and Communist organization. He was executed on the grounds that he had refused to supply information.

His ignorance about Communism was not unusual. The same thing could, conceivably, happen to thousands of Vietnamese peasants and soldiers of the Viet-Cong Army when questioned about the meaning of Communism or about NLF activities. A U.S. officer told me that "many prisoners first learn what Communism really is from us during interrogation, in prison camps, and in re-education courses. And quite a few of them go for it."

The interrogation of prisoners is usually rough in war, but in Viet-Nam it is often a matter of overwhelming cruelty. One method used to make a prisoner talk is to tie slip-knotted cords around his throat and feet, so that if he moves, the noose around his throat slowly tightens. Then he is laid in a rice paddy, where the water is no deeper than eight inches. The prisoner can keep from drowning by raising his head; but the noose around his throat draws tighter at every movement of his head. Within fifteen or twenty minutes he has strangled himself. Another method is to hang a captive by the feet over a rain barrel and slowly submerge him in it. He is not kept under long enough to drown at first; the process is repeated until the man talks or dies. In the delta, South Vietnamese soldiers use U.S. armored personnel carriers as instruments of torture. A Viet-Cong is tied to the vehicle by a rope and slowly dragged through the rice paddies. A victim may survive being pulled through one or two of the water-covered fields, but he is dead by the third.

How do the Viet-Cong keep the loyalty of the peasants in face of torture and threats of death? The activities of the Viet-Cong agitprop teams at first appear crude to American propaganda experts. But, on analysis, the simplicity and precision with which Communist propagandists treat problems of interest to peasants makes sense and is highly effective.

Another factor helps the Communists. The Vietnamese traditionally have a loose relationship with the state. The rulers in Saigon were always far away, their officials appeared only sporadically in the villages. Not the state or province, but the family or, at most, the village community has long been the dominant entity affecting the villagers' lives. Nothing comparable to European nationalism has ever existed; only now are the people beginning to concern themselves with national problems. And reunification may not be the major issue in the complex of national problems. More important are the many "antis": anti-imperialism, anti-Americanism, antirich, and above all, antiwhite.

The Liberation Front has accomplished many things while carrying on its propaganda work. It has built schools, hospitals, and administrative centers. It has established its own jurisdictional systems, organized agricultural advisory teams. In return, the peasants had to pay taxes—to the Liberation Front, not to the government. (If they were unlucky, they had to supply rice to both.) But the two most important tasks of the NLF agents were to indoctrinate the population politically and to create a strong army.

The Front made relatively quick progress within two years. In 1962, the revolutionaries went one step further: they organized their own Communist Party in South Viet-Nam under the name People's Revolutionary Party. American officials claim this party is just a branch of the Communist Lao-Dong Party in North Viet-Nam, even though it voices its solidarity with the goals of the Liberation Front—neutralization of South Viet-Nam, the right to own land, and free intellectual expression. And the fact is that the PRP did emerge from the Lao-Dong Party. Thus it is closer to the party than to other groups in the NLF and is also much more dependent on the North Vietnamese Communist Party. As early as 1959, a special department for South Viet-Nam was set up within the Central Committee of the Lao-Dong Party in Hanoi. The men who head this department are members of the Central Committee and Politburo. They were assigned to supervise, direct, and keep a check on military, propaganda, and organizational activities in South Viet-Nam in the two zones which were the first to be set up—central Viet-Nam, called Trung Bo by the Communists, and Nam Bo, the Communist designation for Cochinchina.

This special committee, which still exercises decisive influence on the internal affairs of the PRP and NLF, was the forerunner of the People's Revolutionary Party. In Phnom Penh I spoke to a member of the NLF Central Committee and learned why a South Viet-Nam Communist Party had been established: "Imperialist propaganda hammers away at the theme that the war in South Viet-Nam is a war of aggression by North Viet-Nam. Secretary of State Dean Rusk accuses North Viet-Nam of having attacked the South with guerrillas. In reality, the war has always been an affair of the South Vietnamese people. We finally decided to create our own organization to prove our independence. Naturally, it maintains very friendly relationships with our brothers in North Viet-Nam."

The name People's Revolutionary Party was first mentioned during a broadcast by Radio Hanoi on January 18, 1962. It was announced that a new party had been founded "at a Marxist-Leninist meeting under the guidance of leaders of the Vietnamese revolution." Besides all the chiefs of the South Vietnamese revolt, many leading North Vietnamese Communists were present. Held "somewhere" in rebel territory in December, 1961, the meeting included Politburo members of the Lao-Dong Party, Pham

Hung and Le Duc Tho; the head of the North Vietnamese Committee for Reunification, General Nguyen Van Vinh; and Central Committee member Tran Luong.

The PRP is a Communist party even though its proponents take great pains to keep the idea of "Communism" under wraps. It is the chief political as well as military organization of the war in South Viet-Nam. It—and not the Liberation Front—is destined to represent the rebels politically in the event of victory or of Communist participation in a government.

Almost all NLF leaders are members of the PRP, and those that are not belong to Communist-controlled fellow-traveling organizations. The chairman of the Central Committee of the PRP is Vo Chi Cong. The first general secretary of the party was Huynh Van Tam, who was replaced in 1964 by Tran Nam Trung. A number of lower party organizations are run by North Vietnamese Communists. The general secretary of the Lao-Dong Party, Le Duan, remained in South Viet-Nam during 1962, 1963, and 1964 to supervise and guide the building of the new Vietnamese party. Contacts between the South Vietnamese Communists and their northern comrades are close; a common party line is worked out at regular conferences and differences smoothed out.

In the fall of 1963, a force of Vietnamese Government soldiers accompanied by American advisers penetrated a Viet-Cong–controlled area in Binh Duong Province. The troops encountered little resistance and occupied a village on the edge of the "iron triangle," a strongly fortified rebel defense zone northwest of Saigon. In one hut they found two suitcases which had been stuffed—apparently in great haste—with papers and documents. The Americans soon discovered what a valuable catch they had made. The documents contained an extensive organizational plan of the PRP. For the first time they had an idea of the complex political apparatus the Communists had built.

Later, I tried to define the party organization from my conversations with PRP members. What emerged was a picture of a carefully conceived mechanism which, down to its smallest parts, seeks to penetrate every sphere of life in South Viet-Nam.

The PRP is organized on the basis of an ingenious cell system. "This is necessary because we must maintain secrecy about our political work," I was told. "Every member knows just as much as he must know about the party apparatus." The committees and suborganizations of the PRP run parallel to those of the Liberation Front or have replaced them. Often, their only function is to keep check on the respective organizations of the NLF; often, too, their work parallels that of the Liberation Front committees.

The PRP is directed by a Central Committee (Ban Chap Hanh Trung Uong Dang.) The organizational structure is a pyramid, and the Central Committee governs from the apex, while hundreds of village cadres form the base.

The second most important organization of the PRP are its interzonal committees (Su or Bo). These supervise three or four provinces and were created in order to keep party organizations in larger areas relatively independent. Thus, if U.S. troops mopped up the entire south or all the coastal provinces and the Communist Party organizations there collapsed, these organizations would still exist in other provinces, and if the Central Committee was captured or unable to function, the provinces would still be ruled by the interzonal committees.

The PRP uses different names for the provinces and a different system of dividing the country than the government. These provinces are supervised by zonal and provincial committees (Khu and Tinh Bo); the provincial committees, in turn, have authority over the district and city committees (Quan and Xa), while the latter supervise the village organizations.

Special committees were formed as a result of the military character of the entire Communist organization. These are responsible for checking on important roads and other channels of transportation, for certain cities and localities, for airfields, for workers employed by the U.S. Army, and even for Saigon's 7,000 bar girls. They engage in espionage and counterespionage, organize terrorist attacks, and collect road taxes. The smallest PRP organization is the village committee.

In addition, the PRP has formed a special apparatus that links individual party cells and synchronizes various military, political, and propaganda operations. These contact people (Dang Vien Don Tueyn), besides supervising the work of the committee, also act as secret couriers and party inspectors; they enjoy considerable authority. They serve as political commissars among the Viet-Cong troops. It is these men who train the guerrillas before battle and politically evaluate the results afterward.

The party had its headquarters in Binh Duong Province, in the notorious area Zone D. In January, 1966, an American strike force pushed deep into the jungle of Zone D and overran a strongly fortified Viet-Cong bunker network. The Americans captured about 6,000 documents. The bunker system had been part of the NLF and PRP head-quarters. It had housed the commissions for agriculture and education as well as a special commission for weapons. The bunkers were dynamited.

The documents revealed that both the PRP and the NLF maintained a headquarters in Saigon itself. The committee for the zone Saigon-Cholon–Gia Dinh had been located in a house in the center of the city. When the building was raided, it had already been abandoned.

I tried but failed to find out where the real headquarters of the revolutionary leaders were located. Certainly the heads of the PRP and NLF have quarters in Cambodia, and they are very close to the border province of Pleiku, as well as in the south of Hau Nghia. There are also Communist offices in Phnom Penh. A military suborganization and a commission for weapons and supplies exist in eastern Laos, very close to the jungle village of Chavane. The Americans believe that there is a Viet Cong command post in the "iron triangle" near Saigon. Probably most of the leaders of the PRP and the NLF live in Cambodia, close to the borders of Hau Nghia and Tay Ninh provinces. It is likely that the real headquarters of the rebels are located there. Due to the nature of the Viet-Nam War, the rebel leaders must constantly move from place to place. I was told that the NLF had several headquarters that alternated in directing operations.

The members of the PRP are today the true leaders of the rebellion in South Viet-Nam. As political commissars, they supervise the Viet-Cong Army; as officials of the NLF, they control the Liberation Front; as administrative heads, they rule practically all civilian organizations in the country. They are, so to speak, the gray eminences of the

Red revolution, and for that reason seldom play a conspicuous role. The struggle against the Saigon government and the United States must above all appear as the people's cause, not the Communists'.

The chairman of the Central Committee, Vo Chi Cong, is responsible for the party's over-all organizational work, as well as for agitprop and indoctrination. General Secretary Tran Nam Trung supervises the military, the NLF Army—the "Charlies." He must not only contend with the difficulties created by the greater American engagement, but with his comrades from the North who refuse to place Viet-Nam People's Army (VPA) units under the command of South Vietnamese troop leaders. In the last few months, serious disputes have broken out because the leaders of the Viet-Cong Army feared—and not without reason —that inadequate coordination with the North Vietnamese would lead to serious defeats. However, Hanoi continues to retain exclusive control over VPA troops, although there are some signs that the North Vietnamese military chiefs are ready to make concessions to their comrades in the South. Perhaps the high rate of casualties in several battles in the coastal provinces of Binh Dinh and Quang Ngai forced the Hanoi Communists to change their minds.

The PRP is the political arm of the Liberation Front. Besides the insurgent army, it also controls all semimilitary provincial units and local guerrillas. The functions of party agents are best illustrated by their military and civil organizational work. The district and city committees are —more accurately, were—the most important links in the organizational chain of the South Vietnamese Communists. These committees consist of three to twelve members. Until the end of 1964, these district committees planned and executed almost all military and propaganda operations. At the beginning of 1966, the organizational structure was expanded and the district leaders began establishing subcommittees in the villages and hamlets. Today, these committees compose the infantry of the Communist revolution in Viet-Nam. Five to seven members preside over the village committee; three to twelve Chibos are subordinate to it. A "Chibo" is the smallest organizational group within the PRP, a combat unit that has political as well as military duties and, in the words of NLF leader Nguyen Huu Tho, represents "the connecting link between the party and the masses."

Most members of the Chibos are peasants. They are politically indoctrinated members of the PRP and organize self-defense units and guerrilla groups in their villages—indeed, even in their own families. They collect taxes for the Liberation Front, administer finances, give political as well as military training courses, instruct the peasants in guerrilla strategy, and show them how to produce effective weapons with primitive means.

A PRP official told me that "elections to all committees take place every two years." Actually, elections are rare, and most village chiefs are simply installed without the communities being consulted. The number of people the party can call on to perform political functions is small; besides, elections are held reluctantly because of security problems. A government patrol once entered a village where election meetings were in progress. All the political officials of the community were seized by the soldiers; the self-defense apparatus was crippled by the elections.

I was told that, theoretically, every Vietnamese can join

the PRP. However, "the condition for acceptance is that two party members must endorse the application," the man I was questioning said. "We prefer to look for members in certain social classes: workers, peasants, lower middle-class, students. A wealthy landholder will hardly ever make a good Communist.

"Next, his application is taken up. The two sponsors must look after the candidate's political education. Four to six months later the new man is finally tested for his knowledge. If he meets the requirements he is accepted as a member." He added that members of the NLF must go through the same procedure and that "only about every eighth member of the NLF is also a member of the party." However, by the beginning of 1966, the PRP seemed to have intensified its efforts to win new members.

While the PRP represents the "Marxist-Leninist element" inside the Liberation Front, the leaders of the NLF have the job of covering the entire country with a network of other political, paramilitary, and military organizations. These groups need not be Communist and often are not. The members are students who dream of an independent Viet-Nam, Buddhists who hope to acquire greater power on the Communist side, small landlords who believe present "good deeds" will pay off when the Communists introduce their reforms later, deserters from the government army, or simply people who want to save the country from "the rule of new white masters."

The head of the NLF and, simultaneously, the leader of the rebellion in South Viet-Nam, Nguyen Huu Tho, is a fifty-six-year-old Saigon lawyer who came to the Communist movement relatively late. His name appeared for the first time on a list of left-wing revolutionary leaders in 1950. On March 19, 1950, he led a demonstration in Saigon against the Indochina War; he was arrested and shipped north to prison in Lai Chau. French jails were the real party universities for Vietnamese Communists before World War II; the concentration camps and prisons France built after 1946 for uncontrollable nationalists became the first schools for today's South Vietnamese revolutionaries. Tho was released in 1952 and two years later founded a peace committee in Saigon, serving as its second chairman. He was arrested again and jailed in Phu Yen (central Viet-Nam). He was liberated in 1961—according to the official party version—"with the help of the people from the imperialists' prison." He was elected president of the NLF Presidium at the first congress of the NLF in 1962 and confirmed in his office by the second congress in 1964.

After Tho, Professor Nguyen Van Hieu is the most influential and probably the most prominent personality in the NLF. Hieu, a former journalist, is practically foreign minister of the South Vietnamese rebel movement and also seems to be its chief ideologist.

Huynh Tan Phat, a former Saigon architect, is secretary-general of the NLF. He, too, came late to the rebel movement, his party career beginning in 1955.

Organizationally, the NLF consists of a central committee and committees. It practically constitutes a South Vietnamese shadow government. The committees correspond to ministries and are organized in exactly the same fashion.

Most leaders of the Liberation Front are also members of the People's Revolutionary Party. They have another thing in common. Until quite recently they were almost unknown. Ho Chi Minh, Vo Nguyen Giap, Pham Van Dong, and other North Vietnamese leaders were prominent Communists years before the outbreak of World War II and had become almost legendary characters by the beginning of the Indochina War. But not a single leader of the South Vietnamese revolt has a similar reputation. There are several reasons for this. The North Vietnamese Communists drew all the outstanding Communist officials north in the years after 1941. It was difficult to build a Communist movement in South Viet-Nam because the French colonial rulers had a much firmer grip there. And the North Vietnamese also benefited from China's nearby border. Today Nguyen Huu Tho, Nguyen Van Hieu, Huynh Tan Phat, and Vo Chi Cong remain overshadowed by the men around Ho Chi Minh. This is not by chance. The rebellion in South Viet-Nam was originally a popular uprising against Diem's government. But today it is clear that the South Vietnamese rebel organizations do not have the final word in the Viet-Cong struggle against the U.S. and Saigon. For the Communists, the course of the war is being determined by North Viet-Nam, and for North Viet-Nam by China. The issue in South Viet-Nam is no longer "liberation," but the problems arising from Chinese Communist ideas of world revolution, and it is doubtful that Peking and Hanoi would entrust the future of their brand of Communism to relatively obscure men.

6

The New War

South Viet-Nam is the model for the national liberation movement of our time. If it succeeds in defeating the special war being tested by the American imperialists in South Viet-Nam, this kind of war can be defeated throughout the world.

GENERAL VO NGUYEN GIAP

THIRTY BAFFLED SOLDIERS surrounded the wreck of an American reconnaissance plane lying on the rocky slope of a hill alongside Route 19. Neither the Korean nor South Vietnamese observation posts stationed along the road had seen it crash; no one knew how it had gotten there. From the plane's condition, it was obvious that there were no survivors.

The soldiers wanted to check the plane or, at least, pull out the bodies. Two men tried to bend back the jagged pieces of metal of the smashed cockpit. Somebody suggested turning the plane around to reach the corpses. Ten men began pulling the fuselage, moving it slowly. Suddenly, an explosion blew up the wrecked plane. Eight soldiers were torn to pieces, and almost everybody standing around the wreck was badly wounded. The explosion was so violent that it destroyed the sandbags of a nearby bunker.

At first the explosion was considered an accident. But a

thorough examination showed that it was the result of a clever trap set by the Viet-Cong. Two months earlier the plane had crashed in Binh Dinh Province, about twenty miles from the highway. Viet-Cong guerrillas had taken the wreck apart and, unseen by government sentries, had reassembled it along the road, concealing explosive charges and contact fuses within the fuselage.

"We have learned to use all means to defend ourselves," Bui Van Dieu told me. "Every one of our soldiers must know and be able to do everything."

The ideal Viet-Cong fighter has learned how to turn a tree trunk, a water pitcher, or a bicycle into an effective weapon and to use it ruthlessly. He is a robot of the revolution who must dedicate everything he owns, and is, to the war he serves, a man who has unconditionally subordinated himself to the idea and strategy of guerrilla warfare. It makes no difference where he fights, whether in the jungles, rice fields, or mountains; as a village official, or a member of a terrorist group in the cities. It is not uncommon for a Vietnamese cyclist in Saigon to be suddenly blown up—along with passers-by. The dead rider may have been a Viet-Cong member, a victim of his own act of terrorism.

The Viet-Cong have developed their guerrilla tactics to a fine point. They have drawn on the experiences of the North Vietnamese and the Chinese revolutions, but their combat groups are much more effective and dangerous than their models. The Viet-Cong are constantly learning. They know they cannot expect help and that they must do everything with a specific goal in mind. Their smallest operations are planned in full detail.

Their enemy commands a modern war machine, air

support with helicopters, bombers, artillery cover, and ample supplies. An American soldier wounded in Viet-Nam has every chance of getting to a hospital quickly and an even greater chance of surviving, no matter how badly wounded. At best a Viet-Cong guerrilla may reach the closest jungle base or friendly village, often miles from his area of operation. Many die because they cannot be treated quickly enough. And the possibilities of rescuing trapped Viet-Cong are almost nonexistent.

An American unit can correct its errors much of the time—even if there are casualties—but when the guerrillas blunder, it is almost always fatal. They know they are far inferior to their adversary in arms, equipment, and numbers. They compensate for this through their strategy and precise planning. "The VC sometimes err, but they never make the same mistake twice," a Vietnamese officer said. Others, American as well as South Vietnamese officers, consider Viet-Cong planning with its rehearsals (with mock-ups) a waste of time or propaganda or proof of cowardice, even lack of discipline. "It shows that sometimes this is the only way they can lead their men into battle," a young Marine lieutenant said. A major of the 1st Air Cavalry Division told me: "The pajama boys run when they see us. They're really afraid to fight, so they settle for shooting at us from ambush. They're gangsters, not soldiers."

But the Viet-Cong strategy must be based on ambushes, quick attacks, and brief skirmishes. It is virtually impossible for them to engage in big battles; when they do, they suffer heavy losses. Even in smaller actions the guerrillas face the danger of an annihilating barrage of bombs and napalm. The U.S. Air Force can reach almost any point in South Viet-Nam within thirty minutes. After a guerrilla unit is sighted, within forty-five minutes, at most, the first cluster of bombs may be hurtling toward them. They must call off their attack and withdraw within this brief period. This, too, demands precise planning and knowledge of the objective.

The guerrillas, like the soldiers of the regular NLF Army, follow the strategic concepts of successful revolutionary leaders from Lenin to Mao Tse-tung. Strategy is setting the goal of a war and elaborating on the general methods of attaining that goal. The guerrilla fighter must first of all accurately analyze his enemy's operations and tactics. Communist soldiers and their commanders carefully study the methods of the U.S. forces and the government army. The writings of the NLF, textbooks and documents, contain page after page of analyses of enemy strategy.

In a Viet-Cong village just taken by U.S. troops, I found a hand-drawn poster. It read: "Know the enemy and know yourself, and you will be victorious in a hundred battles." Later I learned that this sentence had not been composed by a Viet-Cong propagandist but by the greatest military theoretician of ancient China, Sun Tzu.

The Viet-Cong employs various methods to collect information about the enemy, but most of it comes from agents. There is probably not one government army unit, camp, public agency, or even ministry without its share of Viet-Cong informants. All of them, together with the regular soldiers and guerrillas, political cadres, and hundreds of thousands of sympathizers work for the goal: to annihilate the enemy. There is probably no bloodier kind of war than guerrilla warfare: Both sides try with all possible means to defeat and kill the enemy. Thus, harshness and horror become the order of the day, for both sides.

The Viet-Cong have perfected the technique of the ambush and trap. "They're the trickiest I've ever seen," General Kinnrad, head of the 1st Air Cavalry Division, said. "They are real military works of art and their men must work for days to plan and prepare."

The Viet-Cong technique extends from the simple ambush, an attack on a highway or in the jungle, to a complicated system of traps in which groups of government or American soldiers run into the guerrillas three or four times. Each time they believe they've escaped the successive traps until, when they feel safe, the last trap snares them with deadly precision. The first ones were decoys with a single purpose: to lure the enemy into the final deadly ambush.

In the delta, in February, 1966, a company of government troops ran into an ambush system of this type and suffered heavy losses. The guerrillas did not lose one man. The company had been ordered to secure a road bordered by bushes, rice fields, and canals that ran through a no-man's-land. Suddenly the men were strafed from a row of bushes. The soldiers dropped to the ground and returned the fire. There was no more sound, and the soldiers believed they had driven off their attackers until they discovered there had not been a single guerrilla there. The guerrillas had set up a self-operating weapon in the bushes that could be triggered from a few hundred yards away. The government troops knew the ways of the enemy, and guessed this was only a diversion, that the real Viet-Cong ambush lay farther up the road. The company split up. The main force marched ahead, and a small force of thirty men was sent out to fall upon the ambushers from the rear. Ten minutes later the second trap snapped shut just as the government commander had anticipated. A hand grenade exploded, bullets whipped from the right side of the road. The men moved to the left and retreated to a field covered with low hedges. They dug in and waited for the thirty-man detail to attack from behind. The shooting from the edge of the road died down. A few black figures were seen hastily retreating, or ducking into the fields to the left.

The soldiers no longer risked returning to the road and advanced through the underbrush. They suddenly came under fire again from the left and had to take to the road. Again they were raked by heavy machine-gun fire from the right. When they tried to take cover behind the hedges on the left, they were fired upon by automatic weapons. Part of the company was already dead or wounded. The rest tried to get back to the road. But after moving forward about thirty yards, they came under mortar fire. They would probably have been wiped out to the last man if the commander had not called for air support in time. When the plane showed up, the guerrillas disappeared. On the march back, the government troops found the thirty-man force that was to have surprised the Viet-Cong from the rear. Not one soldier was alive. They had advanced barely fifty yards before running into a trap. Later it was learned that the company, in eluding the second group of Viet-Cong snipers, had moved very close to the guerrillas' machine-gun positions. But the gunners began to shoot only when the South Vietnamese ran into the third trap—not a minute sooner.

Once I was with a company of the 1st Air Cavalry in

the An Lao Valley in central Viet-Nam when it ran into another kind of trap. The Americans landed on a ridge by helicopter, and descended through a dense jungle into a narrow ravine where, suddenly, they were peppered by enemy fire. On the opposite slope, about 150 yards away, the GI's spotted earthen excavations and a bunker concealed in thick shrubbery; the shots had come from the bunker. Four men set out to take the position. They reached the bunker safely, threw a grenade into it and, after the explosion, entered it, sure that they had killed the snipers. Suddenly we heard shooting from within, and two wounded Americans stumbled out. The shooting inside the bunker stopped. When the Americans finally penetrated the snipers' position, they found the bodies of the other two and an intricate system of fortifications.

What the GI's had thought was the real bunker was not. The real one was on top of it, connected to it by a tunnel. Its entrance could not be seen from outside. As the attackers approached the lower bunker, the defenders climbed to the top, safe from the grenade explosion. Then, the guerrillas fled to safety through an escape tunnel. There had been only two or three guerrillas, but they had held up a whole company for more than an hour and had inflicted casualties as well.

The guerrillas are as careful about camouflage as they are in preparing attack or defense plans. On my trip across the Vietnamese border, I was given two basic lessons. Once I was told to walk in the shade on open trails and paths so that "you won't be seen so easily." I was also told to cover my knapsack with branches: "If something should happen, you can hide behind your pack without being spotted immediately."

The Viet-Cong has turned camouflage into a science. Uniforms often have hooks for fastening branches or other means of concealment. On long marches, branches must be changed and must come from flora in the immediate area of operation. In fields of bushes, the guerrilla can cover his body with a cone-shaped rush mat that has an opening for his head, and someone passing within two or three yards will be unable to see him. For ambushes on highways or roads bordered with little or no shrubbery, the guerrillas prepare artificial bushes, which they plant before an attack. The method of hiding in rice fields, swamps, or canals is simple: Hollow rush stalks are used to breathe under water. A guerrilla can remain below water for hours in this way without being discovered. Weapons can be concealed in big depots in jungle clearings that cannot be seen from the air; such depots are covered with leaves that are replaced almost daily, because the foliage withers so quickly in the intense heat.

Similar methods were used in building the Ho Chi Minh Trail. In December, 1955, observer planes discovered a new stretch of road running from the Sekong, a wide river, to the jungle village of Chavane. The area had been flown over daily, but no one had seen any signs of construction. It was not even known that there were people in this region. The roof of leaves was cleared away when the road was completed, and the pilots suddenly discovered a jungle road more than nine yards wide in some places.

Near Van Hoa, north of Na Thrang, a settlement close to the coast, helicopter pilots noticed two suspicious-looking men in a rice field. They landed, but the men did not stir from the spot, not even when the two helicopter gunners approached with guns at the ready. They said they were peasants from a nearby village and shrugged their shoulders when asked if they had seen any Viet-Cong. The Americans searched them and found no weapons. One of the Americans saw a piece of wood resting against a dike in the rice field. He lifted it up and noticed it was unusually heavy. He was about to throw it into the rice field when the two "peasants" suddenly started running. They were shot at and wounded and put aboard the helicopter. One of the Americans took the piece of wood along. In the helicopter he discovered that the hollowed-out wood contained a rifle.

"At first our lack of weapons represented our greatest problem," I was told by Huynh Thanh Mung, one of the top commanders of the United National Armed Forces and a Viet-Cong colonel. "In the first years of the revolutionary war we had to rely almost exclusively on the arms we got from the depots of the government troops."

One advantage of this was that the guerrillas did not have to worry about getting their equipment to the combat areas. Also, they could use the enemy's ammunition.

"Now we hardly depend on government and American equipment," I was told. Today the Viet-Cong troops are equipped primarily with Chinese, Russian, and Czech weapons. They also have French and East German arms. Some units are outfitted with carbines of the former German Army, Red Army booty sent to South Viet-Nam via China. They continue to use American weapons, especially the machine gun M6o. But the gun they covet most is the new U.S. AR-15 Colt, which, despite its 5.6-mm. caliber, has an extraordinary rate of fire and impact. The Viet-Cong Army is also equipped with 60-mm. and 80-

mm. mortars and even bigger calibers, light and medium artillery, antitank rockets, bazookas, and anti-aircraft guns.

During operations Van Buren and Harrison, the 1st Brigade of the 101st Airborne Division in Tuy Hoa captured seventeen tons of Viet-Cong weapons including Soviet and Chinese weapons, French submachine guns of the latest make, and old German Wehrmacht rocket launchers and shells, date of manufacture, 1939–41. "We've only recovered what these boys swiped from us in the last few years," Colonel Mataxis said as he showed me the captured weapons on display in the officers' mess.

When the guerrillas lack conventional weapons they manufacture their own. They produce a slingshot gun that has a barrel of beaten metal and is loaded with nails, metal scraps, cuts of bamboo, and stones. It is ignited like a flintlock, and the explosive charge can be catapulted up to 100 yards. At a distance of twenty to thirty yards the slingshot gun, while not fatal, can inflict heavy wounds. Some guerrilla groups still fight with arrow slingshot guns, which also have a devastating effect, or they use catapults that can hurl bundles of spears as far as 100 yards; these weapons are not accurate, but when a spear hits home, the wound is often fatal.

In one Viet-Cong village, I saw a homemade "mortar," with a wooden ramrod in its barrel. At the bottom end of the rod there was an explosive charge—a homemade shell. A bottle, attached to the front end, was filled with gasoline or oil, then, gasoline-drenched wadding was stuck into its mouth. The wadding was ignited before the bottle was attached to the ramrod. The weapon was a kind of improved Molotov Cocktail. "We can shoot up to 150 yards with this bottle mortar," its designer, a member of the local guerrilla group, explained.

In March, 1966, guerrillas attacked a camp of the 1st Brigade of the 1st U.S. Infantry Division, located near Xom Bong Trang village, twenty miles from Saigon on the edge of the "iron triangle." The Viet-Cong began its attack at 2:30 A.M. with a round of shells from 18-mm. mortars. The surprised Americans had a hard time defending their position. After a few attempts to storm the camp, the attackers—the independent Viet-Cong Battalion D 800 and a battalion of the 273rd Regiment of the NLF Army —concentrated on the American artillery in the eastern part of the camp. "The Charlies weren't more than a 100 yards away," the artillery commander, Captain Max Tadlock, told me. "We lowered the gun barrels and fired straight at them."

During this attack, for the first time the Americans faced a weapon the Viet-Cong had obviously developed itself, and an effective one. Staff Sergeant Crawford told me what happened: "Suddenly the VC began firing strange objects at us. At first we thought they were only flare bombs because the shells stayed in the air, gave off a dazzling light and sank down slowly. We thought they were forerunners of an assault, but then we saw that they had cooked up something new. The flare shells sank to the ground over our positions—but not completely—because they suddenly exploded three feet from the ground. Shell fragments buzzed all around us and some of our men were badly hit." I later saw one of these new kinds of "floating shrapnel": It was a shell shot from a rocket launcher—or a gun—to a height of 100 yards. Then a small parachute opened as the flare bomb ignited. While the light burned out, the shell descended and detonated right above the ground.

The Viet-Cong attacks became more intense at about 6.00 A.M. Then the GI's saw new movement in the camp's outer fortifications. Women and small children ran through the barrage of shells, into the middle of heavy machine-gun fire, between the explosions of artillery shells, onto the battlefield to carry off the dead and wounded. They were the wives and children of guerrillas recovering their wounded or dead sons, husbands, and fathers. A majority of the attackers came from the villages near the U.S. camp.

The Viet-Cong broke off the fight at 6:30 A.M. The bodies of the guerrillas were piled high in front of the American trenches. In front of one machine-gun emplacement seventeen dead lay on top of each other. Eighty-six scattered corpses were found ten or twenty yards from the trenches and twenty-two dead in front of the artillery positions. Two hours after the attack, I accompanied a patrol searching for wounded guerrillas. The bodies of the attackers lay where they had fallen. It was clear that the guerrillas had run straight into the U.S. fire.

At 10 o'clock, the reconnaissance pilots reported that the people of the surrounding villages—women and children—were leaving their settlements and traveling north to the nearby jungle. They were allowed to proceed. At 11 o'clock, the search of the villages around the camp began; they were abandoned, with not a soul in sight. Bloody bandages were found in one hut; in another the bodies of four guerrillas; in a third a dying man. The guerrillas had attended hastily to their wounded before moving out.

Then we solved the mystery of the flight of the villagers. Hidden inside the huts lay piles of uniforms, the black and gray-green of the NLF regular army, weapons, helmets, sacks of rations. The guerrillas had discarded their uniforms, put on women's clothing and disappeared. There were more than 120 uniforms. Almost an entire company had gotten away without being intercepted. The search for them began, but was futile.

The Americans burned down the villages. The Viet-Cong leaders apparently had blundered in attacking the camp. They had underestimated the defender's ability to resist and had not had enough time to study the exact layout of each objective. The camp had been set up just two days before the attack.

It is possible that the guerrillas had taken on defeat in order to divert the Americans from another operation, such as the transfer of troops, a withdrawal or advance, or because they wanted to disrupt American attack plans; the 1st Infantry Division was there in order to start a big action in the "iron triangle." General Giap says: "Confuse the enemy, keep him in the dark about your real intentions, divert him. Sometimes what seems to be a victory isn't really a victory, and sometimes a defeat isn't really a defeat." There is a good deal of dialectic in this formulation, but the guerrillas measure victory and defeat by different standards.

The extreme conditions under which the South Viet-Nam guerrillas live and fight require suitable and practical equipment. Every guerrilla and every soldier of the regular

Viet-Cong Army is equipped to exist for days or weeks in the jungle without supplies. The guerrillas' equipment is primitive, reduced to the bare necessities, but it serves its purpose: rations—American canned goods included—drugs, a first-aid kit, a knapsack (often just a crude cloth sack tied to the body with a cord), a hammock, and nylon sheets to protect him from the rain and damp. But the guerrilla's most important piece of equipment is his gun.

"Many of our men would rather die than lose their weapons," said Bui Van Dieu. "They know how hard it is to capture weapons, how valuable and irreplaceable every gun is." American statisticians in Saigon have calculated that it takes two months on the average for a carbine to reach the South from North Viet-Nam down the Ho Chi Minh Trail. It requires five men to transport one such gun over this long distance to the battlefields.

In training, a Viet-Cong is repeatedly told that there is no greater shame than losing his gun. A training manual says: "The Liberation Army soldier may lose everything —but not his weapon." After a battle, all weapons and ammunition must be retrieved; it is every soldier's duty, in case a comrade dies, to pick up his gun. And many guerrillas tie their weapons to their arms or bodies with cord or wire so as not to lose them.

American and government troops know how important the gun is to the guerrilla. Often the success of an action is counted by the number of abandoned weapons, not the number of enemy casualties. "When the VC leave heavy weapons behind, we know we've hurt them badly. It doesn't matter if we find ten or two or no bodies on the battlefield. This is true when we capture a large number of automatic weapons, too," said Colonel MacDade of the

1st Air Cavalry Division. The number of weapons taken, as well as the number of killed, wounded, or captured guerrillas, is always contained in the official statistics of the MACV and individual battle reports.

The Viet-Cong no longer depends completely on weapons transported down the Ho Chi Minh Trail or captured in battle. The NLF has a sizable number of factories and workshops hidden deep in the jungles that can produce practically everything needed. These also manufacture army uniforms and the Viet-Cong sandals, which are cut from auto tires and bound to the foot with leather straps. They produce medicines and bandages, canned rice, charts, maps, magazines, food, and above all, weapons. Some jungle printing shops have been discovered as well; their presses had been carried hundreds of miles from the coast. Viet-Cong headquarters are electrically wired and have their own power plants.

Guerrilla arsenals concentrate on producing mines and guns, gun powder, hand grenades, and cartridges. They have developed their own weapons systems, special weapons for a special kind of war. In one Viet-Cong factory in the delta, the South Vietnamese Army captured 12,500 mines and special mortars prepared to be mounted on river boats and sampans.

The Viet-Cong also manufactures its own anti-aircraft guns with simple but accurate sights. They produce mortars, rocket launchers, and armor-piercing weapons. Captured equipment is rebuilt in these factories, too.

Most Viet-Cong factories are located in the "iron triangle" in the provinces along the Cambodian border, and in the highlands. The workshops here are frequently built far underground and can be reached only through complex tunnel systems; they cannot be spotted from the air and are practically impregnable. Even heavy bomb explosions are absorbed by the soft earthen roofs.

All of this and everyone—local guerrillas, cadres, the population—serve one goal: support of the struggle of the NLF Army. This army carries the major burden of the war. Its strength cannot be accurately determined. U.S. officials have estimated it at 180,000 to 200,000 men, sometimes at only 120,000 to 150,000. The president of the NLF Presidium, Nguyen Huu Tho, said in December, 1965, that the army had more than 200,000 men under arms; I was told there were actually more than 250,-000 regular soldiers. The number of troops may have declined somewhat in recent months for two reasons. The large-scale American operations and, above all, the air bombings have seriously damaged the Viet-Cong. And, by its own admission, the NLF is having trouble recruiting young soldiers.

As a result, the South Vietnamese People's Revolutionary Party called upon its members in February, 1966, to put greater pressure on sympathizers and to recruit "new fighters for the liberation of our country." In the January, 1966, issue of its political monthly magazine, *Tien Phong*, the PRP proposed both military and political reorganization because of the heavier U.S. involvement.

Besides the regular troops there are regional units, which can be compared with the South Vietnamese militia, and local guerrilla groups; both organizations together probably number more than 120,000 men. The regional forces have the heaviest casualties, since they are attached to villages and suffer most from bombings; local guerrillas often participate in military actions once or twice and then stop.

The Viet-Cong Army, in the main, is organized along traditional lines. Its smallest combat units are two-man and three-man groups that train, fight, and live together. The section is the basic unit—even today the Viet-Cong still employs this French concept. A section includes 70 to 100 men. Three, sometimes four sections form a battalion; the fourth section is usually a special unit, trained to use automatic weapons, or mortars, rocket launchers, heavy machine guns, and sometimes artillery.

Until spring, 1965, the battalion was the largest unit. In autumn, 1965, plans were made to organize divisions. But the intervention of more American troops, who were soon to strike hard at the Viet-Cong, led the NLF leaders to drop the idea. Units of division strength, that is, concentrations of 6,000 to 10,000 men within a relatively small area, would have provided vulnerable targets for the constant attacks of the powerful U.S. Air Force. The numerical strength of individual Viet-Cong combat groups and individual army units fluctuates greatly; it depends on the situation in the area of operations, on access to supplies and possibilities of retreating. Even if the regular army is built along these traditional lines its table of organization reveals little about the real fighting strength of individual combat groups.

Mao Tse-tung teaches that units no larger than twenty-five men are best suited for swift operations, a piece of advice the Viet-Cong follows. "They operate like a fan. The soldiers are spread out as they advance on the target. Just before they reach it, they unite. The fan closes and becomes a dagger point. After the attack the fan opens again and the soldiers withdraw in small groups," a member of an NLF cell in Saigon explained.

The regional units and the local guerrillas seldom leave their native areas, even more rarely their district or province. The regular army soldiers operate on a supraregional basis and can be ordered to any part of South Viet-Nam. They are separated from their families; the chances of returning to their native provinces or villages are slight. The army equips and supplies them. They are paid, but their pay is barely enough for pocket money. Ordinary soldiers and NCO's receive between 50 and 150 piasters (50 cents to $1.50) a month, officers and commanders a little more, just enough to buy cigarettes or tobacco. To teach soldiers to be frugal, a brochure advises: "Smoke pipes which you have made yourselves. You can enjoy less tobacco longer in a pipe than in a cigarette."

Except for some big battles, the Viet-Cong Army has scarcely changed its method of operation since the war started, and still prefers sudden raids, ambushes, and short attacks to longer battles with heavy casualties. It must be extremely mobile to execute these tactics; this explains why the Viet-Cong rarely uses heavy weapons. The rifle, carbine, and light machine gun are preferred; all others are hard to transport and cumbersome.

Only special units are equipped with heavy weapons, and these are employed only in exceptional actions. All other troop units are under orders to capture light weapons and destroy heavy ones. The arms of Viet-Cong special units are now of high quality. Aside from machine guns and mortars, they have light and heavy artillery and, in the highlands, fairly heavy cannon.

The North Vietnamese units are even better equipped than the Viet-Cong. Laotian and South Vietnamese intelligence services report that the VPA has light armored vehicles and mountain tanks. Heavy antiaircraft rockets have been observed being transported south along the Ho Chi Minh Trail. The Communists began using cargo planes two years ago to fly arms south, although they do not have many.

With the increase in fighting, the Viet-Cong and North Vietnamese troops have been forced to use modern means of communication. The radio equipment they had at the beginning of the war soon became inadequate. Today the Viet-Cong have up-to-date radio stations and network control centers. Much of the equipment is American; some of it has been captured, but more often it has been bought on the black market. Most platoon commanders now have radios. Regiments of the NLF regular army are in constant and direct contact with North Vietnamese command posts. The VPA forces operating in South Viet-Nam are directed by radio from the North.

Many regional troops and local guerrilla units also possess radio equipment. The Viet-Cong has established monitoring posts to disrupt American and South Vietnamese radio communications. In many large settlements, loudspeakers have been set up that resemble those still to be found in Eastern Europe; these blare out NLF broadcasts.

"This is the most confusing war, and the Viet-Cong the weirdest enemy we've ever had to face," a U.S. public information officer said after we had returned to Camp DOG from a village north of Bong Son. There, in a village considered reliable and progovernment, we had seen a Viet-Cong poster with the slogan: "The people are the strongest weapon." Some unknown man had scrawled the slogan in black paint, to help him and his comrades keep faith in the final victory. But the sentence had been thought up, not by a Viet-Cong propagandist, but by Mao Tse-tung.

The Viet-Cong follows Mao's ideas. He is father of the conception of people's war, or national liberation war—total guerrilla warfare. All other theorists of guerrilla war, from Che Guevara to Vo Nguyen Giap, have merely added details from their own experience to Mao's doctrine, but have not altered his ideas in their essentials.

Mao's doctrine starts from the premise that greater fighting powers are stored up in the people—not in the cities but in the countryside population—than in any specialized army. It is the people who must wage war. The new soldier comes from the people, lives with and fights for the people. The people are an ocean in which the guerrilla swims like a fish, while the enemy is fated to drown in it, according to this concept.

"The only correct road to liberation is the employment of revolutionary violence, the revolutionary war. The invention of the atomic bomb is not the only discovery of our time. That gigantic creation of the masses, the highly developed and invincible people's war, is its equal." So wrote Vo Nguyen Giap in July, 1964, in the magazine *Nhan Dan*. "The people's war is the greatest invention of military science in our epoch. . . . No one denies the horrifying destructive power of the atomic weapon. But war is a social phenomenon that follows its own laws of development. Atomic arms have their disadvantages and weaknesses that limit their use. The people's war is absolutely superior to atomic war."

"Today the war in Viet-Nam is the model of a new war for all colored peoples," Chou En-lai stated in March, 1966, "the model for the struggle of the starving, young peoples against the bloated, old [ones]—the oppressed nations against the imperialists."

"The experiences of our compatriots in the South are being watched throughout the world, especially in South America. . . . The struggle of our fellow citizens in the South . . . is a great contribution to the revolution of the peoples of the world," said the North Vietnamese premier, Pham Van Dong.

The inventor of the new form of war, Mao Tse-tung, clearly formulated the goals of his revolution as early as 1936: "The war which the greatest part of China and the greatest part of humanity will wage . . . will be a bridge leading world history into a new epoch."

This is part of the heritage—and the hope—of the Viet-Cong.

7

The American Special War

We can exert enough pressure to make aggression so costly for the enemy, that sooner or later he will understand we are determined to stay until these people are free. This is costly. But what we are now fighting for is worth this price.

PRESIDENT LYNDON B. JOHNSON
May, 1966, to a group of
Illinois Congressmen

FOR FOUR DAYS, the company of *montagnards*, led by a lieutenant and two sergeants of the U.S. Special Forces, made its way through the jungle without sighting the enemy. I joined them in scouting the area between the two Special Forces camps of Duc Co and Plei Me on a search-and-destroy mission against North Vietnamese troops supposed to have infiltrated by way of the Ho Chi Minh Trail. At dawn, on the fifth day, we found something: newly built huts in a fresh clearing. The huts were filled with military equipment: weapons, ammunition, drugs and first-aid kits. We had discovered an enemy supply base. Lieutenant Halloway entered one of the huts and started cursing. In a corner were a pile of ten sacks, each clearly marked, "A gift of the American people."

"The dogs, the dirty dogs," the lieutenant said. "I'll bet that some local chief made himself a couple of thousand Pi." The lieutenant paced back and forth angrily. "Where do you think this stuff comes from?" he asked me as he carried out a sack and dragged it across the ground until it burst open and the rice slowly spilled out.

"American aid, probably," I said.

"You hit the nail on the head," he answered. "Just as soon as we hand over the rice, the Vietnamese sell it to some black-market dealer working for the Charlies! How can you win this God-damned war in this God-damned country—even want to win it—when they keep on pulling tricks like these?"

The lieutenant yelled in tribal dialect to some *montagnard* soldiers. They ran up to the huts and set them on fire. In a few minutes the whole Viet-Cong jungle depot was aflame.

"That's that—now let's get out of here," the American said. We picked up our guns and marched off. Twenty minutes later a terrific detonation blasted the silence. The munitions depot had exploded.

"Now the Charlies for five miles around know we're here," one of the sergeants said.

"Let them," the lieutenant snapped.

Another sergeant, who had a big Winchester rifle with a telescopic sight, said: "Maybe that's how we'll get the bastards in front of our guns."

"Maybe," the lieutenant answered. The fruitless search was beginning to wear him down too.

It was the afternoon of the sixth day and we were pushing through a wide field of brush. The thickets, six feet high, were very dense. We had been marching for four hours, advancing very slowly, when the lieutenant signaled us to take a break. The men were exhausted. It was impossible to walk in an upright position, and each man was carrying about thirty pounds—gun, ammunition, and supplies for several days. I had marched through this brush before, but then my companions had not been *montagnards* in camouflaged uniforms and American soldiers. They had been the men we were now searching for, guerrillas of the Viet-Cong jungle army.

A *montagnard* scouting party returned—two youngsters with old faces. They squatted next to the lieutenant and his interpreter and gave a detailed report: On the hill behind us they had seen several men—they were certain they were guerrillas. "Okay," the lieutenant said. "Let's move. We've got to make sure that they don't catch us here in the field."

The company still had four hours of marching ahead of it. The soldiers moved forward, this time a little faster, more cautiously; they knew the enemy was close. The hunters had spotted the prey, but they were equally the hunted. Then Lieutenant Parker reported by radio. He was in command of a group of about fifty men operating on our left flank. A force of 130 men had left Duc Co under Captain Conway and had quickly run into a VPA company. After a brief battle, they had killed ten men and captured ten weapons. We learned later that the soldiers from Duc Co had captured a far more important piece of booty: On one of the corpses they had found the radio code of the North Vietnamese. Now it was possible to monitor communications between the VPA and its command posts in North Viet-Nam.

Parker had also met up with a group of local guerrillas. After a brief exchange of shots, they had slipped away into the jungle. "What else?" Halloway asked.

"Nothing."

The radio came alive again half an hour later. Parker had seen a group of forty guerrillas moving in our direction toward the field of brush, apparently the same unit our scouts had seen. The lieutenant cursed; if we were ambushed and attacked in the brush, we would be helpless. He ordered us to move on the double. I found myself wondering whether the *montagnards* in our company were reliable. The three Americans and I were at their mercy.

Parker reported again. This time the news was brief and to the point. "The Charlies have set fire to the brush from northeast to southeast." This was the direction from which we had come; the field was burning behind us. "Shall we come over?"

"No. Not yet. That's all."

Lieutenant Halloway called for a spotter plane, and in ten minutes we heard the plane above us. We could not see it above the high and dense thickets. The pilot confirmed Lieutenant Parker's report: The brush was burning.

We had been on the march for hours and had covered less than a mile. It sometimes took minutes to advance a few yards. There was a possibility that the fire would reach us before we got to the edge of the field. We stumbled, practically running, through the thicket. At Plei Me someone had pressed an AR-15 rifle into my hand: "I can't be responsible for letting you go unarmed on this operation," the fort's commander said to me. The gun kept getting caught in the branches, more of a nuisance than a help.

We stopped after another hour's march. "I'm afraid the Charlies are going to lay a trap for us as we come out into the open," the lieutenant said and called for air support.

Two Thunderchiefs were soon circling overhead. We heard them zooming low, then their bombs detonating not 500 yards away. Then the guns on the plane let loose, sounding like the roar of a truck motor starting up. These fighter-bombers are equipped with 20-mm. machine guns that can fire 6,000 rounds a minute, a furious succession of explosions. Lieutenant Halloway talked with the pilots by radio. The conversation went on even as an F-105 thundered a few yards over our heads.

The situation in the field came down to a few fundamentals for our company: hunting and fleeing, dying and having others die. The small radio in the officer's hand was like the key to another world. "Let's go, cut them down," I suddenly heard a sergeant say beside me. He had taken his cigar out of his mouth and was rolling it nervously between his fingers. Every time one of the planes roared over our cover, he groaned softly. "Come on, knock them off, please." The *montagnards* squatted, moving their heads in unison as the planes flashed by.

The planes flew off. We heard their motors fade into silence. In the calm that followed the bomb explosions and the clatter of the planes' machine guns, we thought we heard the crackling of the flames coming uncomfortably close. Lieutenant Halloway talked with the pilot of the reconnaissance plane about the success of the bombardment. His face became serious. He switched off the radio and crept over to us. "Bad news. The brush is burning right where our men dumped their bombs. We have to get out of here as fast as we can." He thought for a moment. "There's only one way out." He pointed toward the brush. "There. If the Charlies are waiting for us there, the war's over for us. Come on." The company swung left, groping forward in single file through the jungle. "Faster, faster," the lieutenant yelled, moving up and down the line. "We have to get out of here."

The men moved dumbly. We could smell the pungent smoke of the nearby fire. Twenty minutes later the company began to fan out. "Stay here," the lieutenant shouted, and disappeared into the shrubbery. I couldn't hear a thing except for branches breaking as the soldiers stepped on them. The minutes dragged by. Then a *montagnard* came out of the brush and motioned us to follow him. After a short hike we reached the end of the thicket. A broad manioc field lay in front of us, beyond it a gentle hill. Dead tired, the men dropped in their tracks to the ground. Ten minutes later the rear guard came staggering out of the field. Two had burns—they had barely escaped the flames. A tiny Jaraï warrior, no older than fifteen, had dropped into a pitfall and a bamboo spike had pierced his shank. He lay on the ground, moaning while a sergeant bandaged him.

Lieutenant Halloway had dispatched two patrols to make sure the surrounding terrain was safe. The men returned half an hour later. Triumphantly, one waved the fragments of a machine gun, a second proudly displayed a wide leather belt with a big Soviet star on the buckle. "The Air Force was okay," the sergeant said and threw a bundle of papers over to the lieutenant. "There are seven corpses over there, the other Charlies scooted off."

"Yeah," Halloway wanted to know, "where to?" The sergeant shrugged his shoulders. "Then I'll tell you where. They're waiting for the next chance to catch us." The lieutenant banged on his gunstock. "Up, let's go. This time we'll hunt *them*."

The men crossed the manioc field, a small river, and a patch of woods. After a two-hour hike they pitched camp. It was 7:00 P.M., and night descended suddenly. "The great black dragon has come," one of the *montagnards* said, pointing to the dark sky. I sat up a long time staring at the bright flames only half a mile away. Not until the next morning did the fire slowly begin to burn out.

At 8:00 A.M. Lieutenant Parker reported that he had come across some guerrillas. After a brief fight, they had retreated in the direction of Plei Lao Chi. A captured guerrilla had said that there were two North Vietnamese companies close to this abandoned settlement near the Chu Drong Mountains. A little later the radio started up again. This time it was Captain Conway from Duc Co. He had discovered a storage dump. The papers they had found showed it was a depot set aside exclusively for North Vietnamese troops. Viet-Cong guerrillas were forbidden to take supplies from it. Besides provisions, they had found some rocket launchers and a few machine guns. "I guess the VPA is marching in your direction," said the captain.

"Thanks, we'll prepare a nice reception for them," Lieutenant Halloway answered.

Ahead of us were rolling hills covered by thin jungles. I stood next to the lieutenant as he scoured the landscape with his telescope. Smoke and dust were spiraling up in the background, signs of combat or of one of the many forest fires. The woods and brush were totally parched, for this was the dry season. One small spark could set several square miles of jungle aflame.

Captain Conway was operating two and a half miles north of us. The jungle lay between his and Lieutenant

Halloway's company, and somewhere in that jungle the North Vietnamese were hidden. Perhaps they had prepared an ambush; perhaps they were trying to escape; perhaps they were getting ready to fight.

The lieutenant came over. "I think you'd better stick close to Sergeant Shelly. We'll soon be in the middle of it. You can fool around with the VPA even less than the VC. Be careful."

Suddenly a crackle of shots burst from a row of bushes alongside a dried-up river bed. The company threw itself to the ground and returned the fire. There was silence on the other side. The men waited about twenty minutes; they saw some figures 500 yards away run across a manioc field and disappear on the other side of a hilltop. "We're right behind them," Sergeant Shelly said.

"Let's go," the lieutenant yelled. A patrol had found a North Vietnamese camp in a thicket. At least 200 men had been there. We saw sleeping quarters, hastily dug trenches, several bloody bandages. A hammock swung between two trees; its owner had been unable to take it along in the retreat.

"They took off about an hour ago," the sergeant said.

"Seems so," the lieutenant answered. The North Vietnamese had marched east, their destination obviously Plei Lao Chi.

The march through the jungle to the abandoned village was an ordeal for Halloway, Parker, Conway, and their men. There were signs of the enemy everywhere, but there was no enemy. It was not the attacking Americans, the hunters, who fixed the time and place for the assault, but the pursued. The terrain was ideal for an ambush.

Skyraiders from Pleiku roared overhead, and we heard

the explosions of their bombs in the distance. The pilots bombed without taking aim; they could not see the enemy below a thick roof of foliage. It was a hopeless chase, as exhausting for the hunter as the hunted. At 4:00 P.M. the company from Duc Co was again skirmishing with the North Vietnamese. An hour later our vanguard sighted some guerrillas, who quickly withdrew.

The American-led forces had penetrated deep into guerrilla territory, they had spent days in this region, their tactics scarcely differed from those of their enemy. Yet, it was an unsuccessful hunt. Where is the enemy, where is he hidden? The problem not only drained the will of American soldiers here, but in all South Vietnamese combat areas. I met GI's who began to hate the guerrillas not because they were ferocious, but because they avoided battle. Neither political problems nor the doubtful nature of many military measures are as capable of sapping the morale of American troops in Viet-Nam as the endless, exhausting search for an enemy who is everywhere and nowhere. When we reached Plei Lao Chi, the enemy had departed long ago. We marched back without seeing a sign of him. He had disappeared somewhere into the depths of the jungles.

Sitting in a Caribou, a cargo transport plane that would take us back to Pleiku, Lieutenant Halloway said to me: "You've seen us in one action of our special war. How are we going to defeat an enemy we can't find? If we keep on fighting like this, we'll need thirty years to flush out and kill the last guerrilla."

I had heard similar opinions in Saigon. An MACV press officer, Colonel Keeler, told me that while the long-term estimate of the military situation was optimistic, pessimists in the U.S. Military Command still thought the Americans would have to fight another five years or more if the Viet-Cong continued with its demoralizing tactics.

I heard more about the "special war" from Captain Moore, a Special Forces officer. Moore is a specialist in psychological warfare and one of 1,000 men actually waging the "special war." I asked Captain Moore how he would define that war. "You might say that in principle we're using the same methods of fighting the Communists do," he answered.

"The Charlies call us counterrevolutionists," said a young lieutenant, who had just returned from a politico-psychological training course in one of the refugee camps near Pleiku.

"That's right, we are," Moore said. He pointed to his bookshelves, which included works by Mao Tse-tung, General Giap, Ho Chi Minh, General Grivas, and others. "For once, why shouldn't we learn from *them*?" I asked whether U.S. counterinsurgency tactics had chalked up any successes yet. "It has, to the degree that any war techniques can be successful," he answered.

I had seen these methods in practice in a highland hamlet. A force of *montagnards*, led by a U.S. sergeant, had been assigned to bring a village near Plei Torr, thirty miles south of Kontum, under control. The village, inhabited by Jaraï, was considered pro-American, and had been watched over for a year by Special Forces men. A Rhadé spy had reported that a Viet-Cong unit had passed through the village some time ago. Four or five tribesmen had been forced to accompany the Viet-Cong, who wanted to dig an underground supply bunker. When these Jaraï returned, there were two other Jaraï with them, members of the Viet-Cong, who obviously had been instructed to win the village back to the Communist side.

It was a poor hamlet, with about fifty people living in its huts. When we entered, the huts seemed abandoned and no one was in sight. Suddenly, I heard shouting from behind a row of bushes. Two *montagnard* soldiers had rounded up the villagers who had been hiding from us, including two men armed with crossbows. A soldier grabbed the weapons and broke them underfoot. The interpreter asked where the other men were. They said that they were at work in the forest or had gone to buy rice at a neighboring village.

The villagers were terrified. Suddenly, an old man began wailing. He stumbled from one soldier to the next, then squatted on the ground and covered his face with trembling hands. "What's wrong?" I asked the sergeant leading the patrol.

"He's the village elder. He's afraid. He thinks we're going to kill him because he let the Charlies into the village."

"Will you?"

"Why should we? If we do, we'll just be helping the Communists," the sergeant replied.

The American began the questioning. Nobody had seen or heard anything. The old man didn't say another word, but sat there sobbing and shaking with fear. There was nothing to be gotten out of the two men either. They, too, were afraid; every time an armed soldier came near they drew back—but said nothing.

"We'll have to question the old man," the sergeant said. Two *montagnards* pulled the village elder to his feet. But he refused to stand up, and the moment they let go, he slumped to the ground again. The American made a sign to two soldiers who grabbed the man and stood him against the wall of a wooden hut. A third released the safety catch on his carbine and pointed the barrel at the old man's chest.

"All right, now talk," the sergeant said. The old man began speaking slowly, while his eyes kept seeking the face of one of the men who had been armed with crossbows. This Jaraï was about thirty, toothless, with long hair tied in a knot. The sergeant noticed that the old man kept looking at this man for help. He ordered that the man be arrested and the village elder freed.

An interpreter climbed up a ladder leading into one of the huts. He called the villagers together and began talking. "The second part of the program—psychological persuasion," the American said, beckoning to a soldier who was dragging a huge knapsack. It was stuffed with leaflets meant to warn the villagers of crimes committed by Viet-Cong guerrillas. They showed how the Communists took away rice and livestock, raped women, stole ornaments and money, seized their menfolk for forced labor. The leaflets were distributed among the villagers.

"Third part—medical care," the sergeant said, and the interpreter on the ladder announced that anybody who was sick should come forward to be helped. Two women and a boy of about ten, his body completely covered by scabs, did so. A medic examined the patients, gave them medicines.

"What happens now?" I asked.

"We tell them we will be coming back tomorrow with rice. As soon as the Viet-Cong show up, they're to send a messenger to Plei Me or Duc Co to inform us. Then we'll get here in a hurry and defend them."

"But it would take a messenger two days," I said, "even if they were to let him go." The American shrugged his shoulders and gave the order to move out. "What about the man you arrested? Do you think he's one of the Viet-Cong?"

"No, I don't. But we're taking him in for security reasons." We left the village two hours later. The villagers stood silently watching us depart.

It was the end of 1961 when American strategists first resorted to "special warfare" with its three elements: unconventional warfare, psychological warfare, and counterinsurgency. Antiguerrilla warfare was then given primacy. Its goal was to counteract the hold of the Communist guerrilla movement on the population through small, well-trained task forces. Each of these groups—like the Communist cadre system—consisted of specialists in unconventional warfare, experts in psychological warfare, sabotage, intelligence, espionage, and political education. In the main, this special war was conducted by Special Forces men. These soldiers were trained to live among the population, to recruit antiguerrilla fighters, to politically "turn around" Communist-infiltrated areas, and to undermine Viet-Cong–controlled zones through sabotage, subversion, and counterterror. In these, the Americans must depend on the native population more than they ever had to elsewhere. "Our work in Europe wasn't half as complicated," Captain Moore said. "Just imagine a six-foot Texan trying to slip unnoticed into a VC-controlled settlement."

In November, 1965, Royal Laotian Army scouts reported the discovery of a huge jungle way station alongside the Ho Chi Minh Trail. The scouts operated out of Savanneketh and had spotted this bunker near the village of Ban Ba Kha in eastern Laos on about the same latitude as the South Vietnamese city of Quang Nghai, some thirty miles from Kontum. They guessed rightly that they had discovered one of the VPA's command posts along the Red Army road through the jungle. The information was sent on to Vientiane and from there to Saigon. The Americans dispatched a native reconnaissance group from Kontum, which quickly confirmed what the Laotians had reported.

At the beginning of January, a Special Forces unit consisting of five American soldiers and ten *montagnards* slipped off to blow up the bunker and to destroy its installations. One of the purposes of the mission was to instill fear in the North Vietnamese and Viet-Cong who felt safe in eastern Laos.

The *montagnards* knew the area. They wore their tribal clothing, because their uniforms would have given them away as members of an antiguerrilla force. The Americans moved by night, protected by the tribal fighters. The task force reached its destination after a ten-day march. They found the North Vietnamese bunker not far from a former French airfield, now overgrown by the jungle. In a jungle garage, they found four Molotova and two Dodge trucks loaded wth weapons and ammunition. The saboteurs laid their mines and left. A few hours later an explosion rocked the jungle. The bunker had been completely destroyed. Some days later reconnaissance planes of the Laotian and American air forces saw the scattered evidence of the successful raid.

The trip back was unusually difficult for the sabotage task force. The Communists knew what had happened and were doing their best to catch the group. But with the help of the natives, the Americans finally reached South Viet-Nam. Not far from Kontum they were attacked by local guerrillas. One American and four *montagnard* soldiers were killed; the others reached the base unharmed.

During this period I interviewed the Laotian Premier, Prince Souvanna Phouma, and a member of the Central Committee of the Neo Lao Haksat (the Laotian Communist organization), Soth Petrasie. Both the premier and the Communist leader denied that there were foreign troops on Laotian soil. Souvanna Phouma said: "It is a slander to say that American troops are operating in Laos." Soth Petrasie said: "It's American atrocity propaganda that has invented the fairy tale about North Vietnamese troops in Laos."

Meanwhile, the hidden war on the Cambodian frontier, in Laos, and in North Viet-Nam goes on. Both American and South Vietnamese antiguerrilla forces operate far behind the lines of the Viet-Cong and are slipped across the 17th Parallel into Ho Chi Minh's republic.

"Yes, we have sabotage detachments in North Viet-Nam. They are small, well-equipped special units. Don't ask me if we've violated permissible limits. The Communist terror groups in South Viet-Nam have never troubled about that either," Premier Nguyen Cao Ky once said to me. He is proud of the fact that he himself had flown such special task forces to North Viet-Nam.

American and South Vietnamese commandos, special action teams, try to carry the war to the enemy's hinterland, where he feels most secure. "They amount to death task forces," a Special Forces major said to me in Na Thrang. "But what surprises us most is that a majority of the boys manage to come back with a whole skin."

Most of the Special Forces teams have limited missions and do not remain behind enemy lines more than a few months. When they have accomplished their missions, they are flown out. The size of a special task force depends on the nature of the assignment. The regular Special Forces teams consist of twelve, in some cases of fourteen or fifteen men and NCO's, led by one or two officers. A major task of these teams, trained at Fort Bragg, is to recruit antiguerrilla fighters from the local population and train them. The Special Forces camps in South Viet-Nam are the centers of these counterinsurgency forces.

Besides military operations, the special fighters carry on a number of activities among the civilian population. But it is a law of war that military actions take priority over civilian interests. The Special Forces teams have pursued their civilian programs in a halfhearted way.

General Maxwell Taylor's original plan called for each American combat unit to train between 1,000 and 1,500 guerrillas. But it seldom happened that any of them won over more than 500 antiguerrillas. For example, Fort Buon Brieng in Darlac, where more than 700 *montagnard* soldiers are stationed, is one of the largest of its kind in South Viet-Nam.

"Can you really trust these men?" I asked Captain Willangby in Plei Me. We were standing on the camp's huge drill ground. The South Vietnamese flag waved in front of us; four companies had marched up under it—*montagnard* soldiers, some Vietnamese NCO's and officers. The camp commander, a captain of the Vietnamese Special Forces, delivered a short speech. His wife stood beside him in a tight-fitting Tiger uniform, two pistols in her belt.

"Here are 350 men," the American said. "Forty are

Viet-Cong or Communist sympathizers. The percentage is higher among the Vietnamese. The rest are completely reliable."

I looked at the small fighters listening impassively to their commander's speech. I remembered the fate of two American Special Forces sergeants who had been killed by their own men in the province of Binh Dinh. They had gone out on patrol with twenty men. By chance most of them were Vietnamese supporters of the Viet-Cong. When the Americans went to the head of the column, they were shot from behind. Wounded, they had enough strength to take cover in the brush—but were killed in the brief fight that followed.

About 1,500 Special Forces soldiers are currently stationed in Viet-Nam. This force has administrative and technical as well as military duties. More than half the Green Berets, as they are called, are tied down by nonmilitary work. In the spring of 1966 not more than 672 were actually engaged in military operations. These special fighters were operating mainly in the strategically important highlands. There are several reasons for this. U.S. strategists considered the sparsely populated mountain provinces particularly suited to the special war plans. At the same time, it was difficult to recruit antiguerrillas among the Vietnamese. The *montagnards,* equally suspicious of the government and the Viet-Cong, were more apt to join the Americans—and besides, the Ho Chi Minh Trail leads into the highlands. There the Special Forces can disrupt the flow of supplies coming from Laos and Cambodia to the Communist guerrillas and observe the infiltration of North Vietnamese troops. They have not been able to stop this infiltration, because they simply do not have the military means. The decision to move Special Forces units into other Vietnamese regions was not made until 1965 and 1966. A new camp was set up in January, 1966, near Bong Son in Binh Dinh Province, near the coast of the South China Sea.

Other groups are in charge of the refugee program. They established the Open Arms policy (*Chieu Hoi*); they advise Vietnamese political officials and try to supervise the distribution of American aid. But their primary mission is to convince the peasants that the government side is better; that it is capable of defending them from the Viet-Cong; and that the government, not the Communists, will win the war.

"There is a critical point in every guerrilla war," wrote David Halberstam, correspondent for *The New York Times*. "That is the moment when the population knows who is winning." The Americans and South Vietnamese have yet to prove they are winners. The Viet-Cong remains the only source of political education the peasant has received till now. The simple Communist arguments make more sense to him than those of the government or Americans; besides, he does not trust the American because he is a member of another race and because he represents a foreign power.

The U.S. Special Forces study the experiences of other guerrilla wars: of the English in Kenya, Cyprus, and Malaya; the French in Indochina and Algeria; and of their own in the Philippines, as well as those of Communist revolutionists. But in spite of a variety of ingenious programs, they are seldom as successful as the Communists.

They draw upon the doctrines of Mao, Lenin, Stalin and Giap, but do not possess that power of persuasion that contributed so decisively to revolutionary Communist victories in other countries. They are outsiders, foreigners, attempting to challenge the Communist-nationalist revolution on its own ground, but they have neither the revolutionist's *élan* nor his ability to sway the population. They are on the defensive from the beginning and find themselves psychologically in a hopelessly inferior position. The revolutionist has always won sympathy because he is "progressive" and seeks to change society; his goal is secondary for his supporters while the struggle is on.

The antiguerrilla, the counterrevolutionist, on the other hand, appears as the tool of the ruling power that must be overthrown. He lacks the aura that surrounds the persecuted rebel at all times. He is devoid of the same appeal since he does not propose to change anything but merely defends the existing order against values that are new or seemingly so.

It is no surprise, then, that the U.S. Special Forces have failed in South Viet-Nam, with the exception, perhaps, of the highlands. There, teams held out for years, steadily harassing the Viet-Cong. The U.S. camps in the highlands became the targets of bloody guerrilla attacks and were furiously denounced by Communist propagandists. The fact that the Viet-Cong and North Vietnamese viewed the Special Forces camps as effective threats may be proof that American antiguerrilla warfare might have been successful had it been launched earlier and given greater emphasis.

Now, the original American concept of special warfare has changed, but the enemy has not. Of course, U.S. commanders must still allow for the distinctive features of the country, but they are operating on a different scale and with a different objective in mind. Today, when a huge action is launched, with 10,000 men or more, to drive the enemy out of his bases, when air strikes hit Viet-Cong zones around the clock in order to wipe out the guerrillas and demoralize the population, there is less room for the more sophisticated methods of counterinsurgency. Moreover, the current internal political disorders prevent a consistent execution of the original program. Viet-Nam is no longer split into two or three camps, but into eight or ten. The growing intervention of strong North Vietnamese units has also made necessary the change in American tactics. The Americans are no longer fighting a special adversary with special means; they are waging a conventional war with conventional means, with special rules almost exclusively imposed by the enemy. The comparison may not be quite accurate but it is not unfair to say that the United States faces a situation in Viet-Nam today similar to that of the French in the last years of the Indochina and Algerian wars.

The people responded to counterrevolutionary ideas without enthusiasm. They were fighting for a national revolution first of all; the Socialist-Communist revolution was subsidiary. The Americans reacted by resorting to the violence which has always accompanied revolution or counterrevolution. There was a single difference: One side terrorized the population in the name of freedom, the other in the name of a new world order.

"We made a big mistake. We thought the South Vietnamese could repulse the Communists by themselves if we gave them everything but our troops," Captain Moore said to me in Pleiku. General Pearson, commander of the 1st Brigade of the 101st Airborne Division in Tuy Hoa, put it more simply: "We overrated the South Vietnamese." The misjudgment turned out to be a disastrous error. The South Vietnamese Army slowly continued losing ground even as it was winning hard-fought battles against the Viet-Cong near Saigon and in the delta at the end of 1965 and the beginning of 1966.

The civil action programs, handed over to the Vietnamese *in toto* by the Americans, with American experts restricted to advisory roles, failed. They foundered on corruption, incompetence, the refusal of the Vietnamese to see the pacification programs through to the end, and internal political turmoil. The Staley Plan, a blueprint for creating strategic hamlets and pacified, prosperous zones, failed as badly as the psychological warfare program. This soon dwindled to random scattering of leaflets and occasional political meetings. But the program never reached the people for whom it was intended: those living in Communist-controlled areas.

A good part of American aid disappeared mysteriously and continues to do so. The goods emerged again on the black market or in Viet-Cong hands. The distribution system, managed by the Vietnamese, functioned badly or not at all until, in some cases, U.S. experts took over.

America's special soldiers realized their indirect form of warfare had achieved little success. The American commitment grew, military escalation began. In February, 1964, there were not more than 14,000 Americans in South Viet-Nam; there were 25,000 by the end of the year. Yet, while this increased number was too small to hold back the flood threatening to inundate the country, it was too large for the United States to withdraw without serious consequences.

The Viet-Cong also started to expand in 1965. Its strength was placed at 200,000 men, consisting of regular units, regional forces, and local guerrillas. According to American figures, 20,000 North Vietnamese soldiers had infiltrated the South between 1961 and 1965. Moreover, 20,000 political cadres were actively engaged in administration, political education of the population, and collecting taxes.

In January, 1965, American intelligence reported that a fully equipped North Vietnamese infantry division, none other than the 325th, had appeared in the highlands near Kontum. The division was armed with medium-heavy weapons and 75-mm. artillery pieces. Colonel Patch, a Special Forces officer, said to me: "The North Vietnamese suddenly came too fast for us to count. It looked as if they wanted to overrun the highlands in one grand offensive."

At about the same time, McGeorge Bundy, White House special adviser, arrived in Saigon. Washington hoped that the new Year of the Snake would bring at least political, if not military success. There are many indications that Bundy had come to probe the possibilities of a peace settlement, an armistice or a neutralization of South Viet-Nam.

But on February 5, 1965, the Viet-Cong "committed the greatest blunder it could have made."[*] It attacked one of the most important components in U.S. strategy of special war, the Pleiku airport, with 18-mm. mortars and heavy machine guns. Nine Americans were killed and 146 wounded. President Johnson reacted immediately by

---

[*] According to U.S. Ambassador Alexis Johnson as quoted by Lothar Rühl, *Vietnam, Brandherd eines Weltkonflicts?* (1966).

ordering "appropriate retaliation" against military targets in North Viet-Nam.*

At this point, the United States took direct charge of the war. Its powerful military machine was set into motion. "We want to and will show them how serious our intentions are," Defense Secretary McNamara said. The United States landed the 3rd Marine Infantry Division at Danang. The Leathernecks were followed by the 1st Infantry Division (the Big Red One), the 1st Air Cavalry Division, the 25th Infantry Division, the 173rd Airmobile Brigade, the 1st Brigade of the 101st Airborne Division, the 2nd Division of the U.S. Air Force and other units. Washington hoped these elite forces would be able to turn the tide of war. There are more than 400,000 American soldiers in Viet-Nam today; a third of them are fighting the Communist troops. Naturally, American casualties have risen. By the end of 1966, there were more than 38,000 U.S. casualties.

The United States now has more armed men in Southeast Asia than it had in Korea. Yet to attain a 6 to 1 superiority, Washington will have to throw another 2 million GI's into the fight; in other words, station practically the entire American Army in Viet-Nam.

Like the Americans, the Communists have also increased their commitment. There are now at least three full North Vietnamese infantry divisions in the South, the 304th, the 308th, and the 325th, and a number of inde-

---

* The first bombings of North Viet-Nam took place on August 5, 1964, however, as a reprisal for a North Vietnamese attack on the U.S. destroyer *Maddox* in Tonkin Gulf three days earlier. Four torpedo boats and a large oil depot were destroyed by bombers of the U.S. 7th Fleet.

pendent regiments and *groupements mobiles,* detached
special combat units. Today the Viet-Cong has about 350,-
000 men, a figure I was given by a member of the NLF.
To these must be added the 50,000 to 60,000 North Vietnamese soldiers. The Communists command a total armed
force of approximately 400,000 men in South Viet-Nam
alone. In numbers, then, the Viet-Cong does not lag far
behind the South Vietnamese Army (reportedly 520,000
to 560,000 men).

The Communist troops fight, but they also continue
their political and propaganda work. Their original strategy has hardly changed. The mission of the new American combat units is clear—to wage war. They have not
been adequately trained to deal with the unique character
of the Viet-Nam War, nor is it their task to follow the
sophisticated methods of the Special Forces: "We are soldiers, our job is to seek out and destroy the enemy. Whatever else happens is none of our business," Colonel Moore
of the 1st Air Cavalry Division said in Bong Son. Soon,
the specific nature of the country and the war will be completely ignored. The guerrillas are looked upon and fought
as soldiers of an enemy army, the population in Viet-Cong–
occupied territory is considered "hostile" and treated ac-
cordingly.

The air force began playing a dominant role too. As
early as 1964 and 1965, American pilots helped save the
South Vietnamese Army from defeat and played a decisive role in many battles. The U.S. Air Force operated
with great accuracy, frequently bombing only fifty yards
in front of its own positions. "Like a knife it cut up enemy
fortifications with a precision I admire," said General Thi,

then commander of the 1st Zone, later discharged by General Ky.

The air force bears much of the brunt of battle today. With U.S. Navy planes it bombs North Viet-Nam and is also involved in the fighting in South Viet-Nam. The U.S. forces have about 1,000 of the most up-to-date helicopters, and some units, like the 1st Air Cavalry Division, are fully equipped with them. "We can throw units of brigade strength into combat as far away as 100 miles within a few hours," said Captain Hitchcock, one of the Division's press officers at An Khe. "There never has been a unit as mobile as ours. They used to figure the movement of large troop units in terms of days; we do it in minutes."

The use of the helicopter as a means of transporting men and weapons is probably the greatest military-technical innovation of the decade. The lightning appearance of American combat units has dealt severe blows to the Viet-Cong, and helicopter crews are among the most hated enemies of the Communists. Helicopter pilots are among the busiest soldiers in Viet-Nam; they land and take off in the midst of enemy territory, evacuate the wounded from the battlefields, and engage in the fighting.

Most of the planes are armed with two heavy machine guns and rockets, attached above the landing gear. A specially developed device allows the copilot to guide the rocket to its target. Many planes also have heavy aircraft cannon mounted on the fuselage.

The destruction of a helicopter is always celebrated by the Viet-Cong as a great victory, and the guerrillas use every possible trick to capture one. In February, 1966, a Caribou, a transport plane, had to make an emergency landing in the delta, in Vinh Binh Province. The pilots brought the plane down undamaged and radioed for a helicopter to ferry them out. A rescue helicopter soon showed up and landed beside the plane. Its two gunners got out and slowly approached. The plane's crew was in the cockpit; all, apparently, had been wounded. Just as the helicopter gunners reached the cockpit, shots whipped at them. The two uniformed figures inside were guerrillas and raked the Americans with submachine-gun fire. One gunner fell dead on the spot; the other was seriously wounded. The pilots in the helicopter heard the shooting and radioed for immediate support. Meanwhile, the two disguised guerrillas blasted away at the helicopter, damaging it badly; then, they made off. Four more helicopters landed ten minutes later. By the time their crews reached the Caribou the second gunner had bled to death. They found the bodies of both Caribou pilots and the plane's mechanic naked and mutilated, in a corner of the storage compartment. The guerrillas had apparently killed the plane's crew, donned their uniforms, and taken their seats in the cockpit in order to capture the rescue helicopter.

It is harder for the Viet-Cong to fight against other types of U.S. planes. The greatest American losses have been due to surprise guerrilla attacks on the big airfields. In January, 1966, I spent a night at Saigon's airport. It was impossible to sleep. Jet fighter-bombers took off and landed at five-minute intervals. At about 3:00 A.M. a squadron of Phantoms moved into line on the strip for take-off. They rose steeply and disappeared into the night. Suddenly, two explosions flared close to one of the planes. The plane could not have been higher than fifty yards and had not yet passed the end of the airfield. The next plane got under way, and again I saw the flashes. The jets were being shelled.

I told an officer on guard duty what I had seen. "We know," he said calmly. "The Charlies have set up an anti-aircraft gun some place out there."

"Right on the edge of the field?"

The American replied: "We've tried to catch them, but no luck. They bang away two or four times, take their guns and disappear."

"Have they ever knocked down a plane?"

"Maybe," was the answer.

By the end of 1965, before the greatly accelerated activity in Viet-Nam, the U.S. Air Force had made 45,000 combat flights, the South Vietnamese Air Force 15,000. During these operations the Americans dropped 56,000 tons of bombs, the Vietnamese more than 25,000 tons. This is more than the French dropped during the first Viet-Nam War over all Indochina. According to official figures, "more than eighty" American planes were shot down in 1965. The Viet-Cong claims it destroyed many more (370 to 657). South Vietnamese losses are unknown, but they are estimated at seventy planes.

Gunners aboard helicopters and planes fired more than 70 million rounds of ammunition in 1965. By June, 1966, an average of one ton of bombs and 1 million rounds had hit every square mile of South Viet-Nam. By the end of 1966, 400,000 tons of bombs in the Second Viet-Nam War had hit the tortured land.

Clearly, the concept of a special, antiguerrilla war has been abandoned. The war has become too big for this kind of strategy. Neither side has changed its original military, political, and ideological goals, but the conditions for breaking the power of the Viet-Cong and Hanoi through effective antiguerrilla warfare and counterinsurgency no longer exist. Neither the vast amount of U.S. aid nor the massive apparatus built up to wage psychological and other warfare* can disguise the fact that the special war has failed. Propaganda and psychology are being employed now as they would be in any conventional war. The special war, the antiguerrilla war, with its concept of a thousand minor fronts remains confined basically to those areas where the Americans began to wage it—in the highlands on the Laotian and Cambodian borders.

* As of mid-1966, 85 million leaflets were dropped over Viet-Nam; 420,000 propaganda pamphlets distributed; 20,000 gifts for children dropped over North Viet-Nam; 4.5 million Vietnamese treated under the U.S. health program; 124,000 tons of food distributed; 100,000 items of clothing distributed; planned U.S. construction reached $1 billion with 2,600 projects under way; and more than 20,000 Vietnamese were working for U.S. agencies, according to MACV reports in Saigon.

8

The Rebellion
in the Mountains

America almost had its first "defectors" at this time. Officers of the Special Forces had to choose between the pledges they had made to the montagnards and discipline.

JEAN LARTEGUY
(In an article on the revolt of the
mountain tribes in the fall of 1965)

T HE COMPANY HAD pitched camp for the night in a small patch of woods in the heart of guerrilla territory, ten miles from the Cambodian border. Lieutenant Halloway of the U.S. Special Forces was supervising the building of a trap to defend us from surprise attacks. A patrol had engaged in a fierce skirmish with Viet-Cong partisans in the late afternoon. "The Charlies are just waiting for the chance to grab us," said the lieutenant, his bearded face covered by scratches from the day-long march through the brush.

At the bottom of a sandy hill we had found the entrance to a deserted underground guerrilla bunker. Used radio batteries "made in the U.S.A." lay in a corner. For a moment we stood atop the hill. The misty twilight blotted out the field in front of us. The trees on the opposite hilltop looked like a group of uniformed soldiers standing guard. "You'd better go down," the lieutenant said, "the VC's have first-rate sharpshooters."

I returned to camp. Sergeant Shelly had given me some plastic explosive—a white substance that burns quickly with a hot flame and is excellent for heating food. I took out my canned rations and began preparing my meal. Sergeant Broune squatted next to me; his long Winchester, which he always carried to knock snipers out of jungle trees, lay beside him on a nylon cloth. He was out of sorts. It had not been a good day for him. He had lost one of his men on a morning patrol. A little later he had almost run afoul of a Viet-Cong ambush himself. A native scout had warned him just in time.

Three *montagnards* were whispering near us. They were squatting on their heels, smoking small, curved pipes. Two of them—Ban Nie, native commander of the unit, and Ilhuc, the interpreter—belonged to the Rhadé tribe. The third was a Jaraï. Most of the *montagnards* are even smaller than the slightly built Vietnamese, but this Jaraï was almost six feet tall and towered two heads over his tribal brothers. I never learned his real name; his comrades called him *Beaucoup Kilo*. He was a sergeant and considered a brave, reliable soldier. He had won some medals that he did not think much of—his great joy was drinking. He was shot in a mountain ambush at the end of February.

I sat down beside the three men. Ban Nie and Ilhuc spoke excellent French. Ban Nie had attended a missionary school in Kontum; Ilhuc had studied for several years at the *lycée* at Ban Me Thuot. The interpreter had light eyes and brown hair, proving that the old white colonial masters had known how to combine pleasure with duty. I hoped that here in the highlands I would get an answer to a question that had long baffled me.

"What is FULRO" I asked.

I had already raised the question with Captain Schwikar, intelligence officer of the Special Forces in Pleiku. Instead of answering, the captain had invited me to have a whisky, and said I had better forget all about FULRO; no one would be able to supply me with information about it. Sergeant Christina, a tall Negro soldier and psychological warfare expert in Pleiku, said: "Better not talk about it. They don't like questions about FULRO here." Colonel Patch, commander of the Special Forces in Pleiku, had explained to me that he would first have to get permission before he could discuss FULRO.

Finally, the Vietnamese province chief, Major General Vinh Lac, said that FULRO was a movement started and financed by the French for the purpose of re-establishing French colonial rule over Viet-Nam; in addition, FULRO was controlled by Sihanouk in Cambodia, the Pathet Lao, and the Viet-Cong. It was a criminal organization, and the best thing was not to waste time talking about it. But still no real information.

And now, suddenly, here in the middle of no-man's-land stood two *montagnard* soldiers, part of an American-led company, who were both members of FULRO (United Front for the Liberation of the Oppressed Race). Ban Nie, a slender young man, reversed the lapel of his too tight uniform jacket, and touched a narrow badge pinned inside. "This is FULRO," he said. I saw a small flag with three stripes whose colors I could not make out in the darkness. There were three bright stars on the center stripe. "This is the symbol of our liberation movement." he said. "If there will be peace, FULRO will have been victorious too."

"He is an officer of the fighting front troops," Ilhuc said, pointing to Ban Nie. "He has already been sentenced to death twice. The Americans saved him both times."

"Who condemned him?"

"Once the province chief and then some Vietnamese officer in Ban Me Thuot," Ilhuc said, grinning. "He's a dangerous enemy of the state."

"Then why is he fighting on the Vietnamese side?"

"He's not fighting for the Vietnamese, but for the Americans. He is fighting for the liberation of the national minorities in Viet-Nam."

"But he's fighting against the Viet-Cong."

"Yes, and for the same reason. The Communists threaten the freedom of minorities as much as the Saigon government. Never forget one thing: The Viet-Cong are Vietnamese first and then Communists—and that won't change so quickly."

I recalled a conversation with an NLF official, who said the mountain tribes had spontaneously joined the Liberation Front to fight with the Communists against Ngo Dinh Diem's government. "In fact, the mountain tribes were the first to revolt against Diem," Ilhuc said. "But they had nothing in common with the Communists. Later, the Viet-Cong used the successes of the *montagnards* in their propaganda."

Ban Nie said that the tyrannical way the Vietnamese treated them had driven the national minorities to create a fighting front, which all the highland tribes supported.

It opposed both the Communists and the Saigon government.

South Viet-Nam has a population of about 15 million—of these, 12 million are Vietnamese, the rest belong to different ethnic groups. A large Cambodian minority, the Khmer Krom, lives in the western provinces of the delta; it ruled the Mekong Delta before the Viets. About 500,-000 Chinese live in Saigon and the coastal cities—a Chinese minority, the Nungs, has also joined the fighting front of the mountain tribes; there are Nung soldiers in all Special Forces camps.

Approximately 1.5 million *montagnards* (the French term for mountaineers) live in the central highlands, members of mountain tribes that ruled the region in earlier times and claim to be the original inhabitants of Viet-Nam. They are Malay-Polynesian in origin. In part, the tribes are direct descendants of the Champas, who had established a highly civilized kingdom around A.D. 200 in central Viet-Nam, southern Laos, and eastern Cambodia. The kingdom of Champa was first conquered by the Mongol emperor Kublai Khan, then by the Viets, who destroyed it. The Champas lapsed into primitive poverty.

The Vietnamese rulers oppressed the mountain tribes brutally, and today still call them *Moi*—"savages"—and treat them as such. Viet-Nam's thirty-two mountain tribes, which in many cases differ greatly in language and culture, repeatedly tried to throw off the Vietnamese yoke—but all revolts by the "savages" were bloodily suppressed.

"French colonial policy is to blame for the new uprisings of the *montagnards* against the government," an official of the Vietnamese Ministry of Information said. "We had completely pacified the highlands—the savages would have never again dared revolt had not the French aided them. They supported the savages against the government—it's unfortunate and really best not to discuss it."

"Do you want a look at the savages?" a young American lieutenant asked me in Pleiku. We drove, escorted by ten heavily armed *montagnard* soldiers, to a Rhadé village. "If you were staying longer, I could show you other, nicer settlements," my guide said apologetically as we reached the village.

I am no stranger to the misery and poverty of Southeast Asia, but what I saw here shocked me. A few ramshackle huts built on short stilts surrounded the center of the hamlet where the shabbily dressed villagers had gathered for our arrival. The people were grimy with dirt and appeared starved and sick. A toothless old man with filthy, matted hair welcomed us. His pierced ear lobes may once have glittered with ornaments; now they hung like strips of dry skin down to his shoulders. His wrinkled face had faint traces of tattoos; his clawlike hands were crippled by arthritis.

"These people came here from Kontum. I don't know how often they've had to flee: First the government persecuted them, then the VC burned down their huts. They have been living here for a few months. Later on they will move into a newly built hamlet near Pleiku," the lieutenant explained.

A young boy, who showed black tooth stumps when he laughed, brought a huge earthen jar containing a liquid.

"Numpai," the American grinned, "rice wine. They forget their troubles with Numpai, and they have a lot to forget." A few men sat down with us and we began drinking through thin bamboo straws. The villagers stood around, the men in front, wearing loin cloths and smoking curved pipes; behind them, the curious but fearful women and children.

"All these people are sick," the American said, "80 per cent or more have malaria, 60 per cent tuberculosis, 50 per cent dysentery, half of them have incurable festering sores. Leprosy reaches 10 per cent in some tribes. This is the highest rate of the disease in the world. Instead of isolating the lepers, they keep them in the villages and spread more infection. They die like flies. Their average life span is twenty-five years. Of the babies born, 60 per cent die within a few weeks. Those who escape disease, and are not killed by government troops or Communists, face every prospect of slowing starving to death."

The chieftain was talking away in a monotonous, sing-song voice. "He's furious at the government soldiers—and besides, he hates the Viet-Cong. He hates everybody in fact, except us, because at least we give his people food," the American officer said. He had acquired a fair knowledge of the tribal dialects during his year of service in the highlands.

A few boys guided me around the village, made up of primitive huts mounted on stilts. The huts are entered by ladders hacked out of tree trunks. The homes seldom contain more than several rice-straw mats and some cooking utensils. One of the boys proudly showed me a mosquito net full of holes. It belonged to his mother and was their only possession.

The village elder called me over and made another long speech. Then he offered me a jar of rice wine. They had an ingenious way of finding out how much a guest had drunk. Two bamboo rods stuck up out of the jar, and the more you drank the higher they rose above the rim. "Drink a lot," the lieutenant said. "The more you drink, the more they'll respect you."

When I finished, the old man inspected the position of the rods. He was obviously satisfied because he nodded approvingly. A young warrior grabbed my right arm and pushed my hand toward the chief, who slipped a narrow brass band on my wrist. "You are now an honorary member of this Rhadé village," said the lieutenant. He wore several clinking brass bands on his right wrist. "They usually present these bracelets only during a big buffalo feast. But they no longer have any buffaloes to slaughter, and the war has disrupted all their customs." We left the village after a noisy farewell ceremony.

"For centuries, the mountain tribes were almost helpless in the face of Vietnamese oppression," Ban Nie later told me. The condition of the mountaineers began to change when the French realized how strategically important the highlands were. They moved fast to get a foothold there and skillfully succeeded in winning over the oppressed mountain tribes. Since then the *montagnards* have been pro-white.

Later, during the Indochina War, the mountain tribes were the most reliable troops in the fight against the Communist Viet-Minh. After the Geneva Treaty, the French evacuated the country, and the *montagnards* were again subject to Vietnamese rule: Ho Chi Minh's in the North, Diem's in the South. Both used almost the same methods to pacify the rebellious highlands. At first, Ho Chi Minh created a few autonomous zones for the mountain tribes in the North. Since he wanted to secure the mountainous border territory between South Viet-Nam and Laos, he soon began a major resettlement program: Unreliable tribes were driven to the lowlands, and Vietnamese peasants from Tonkin were moved to the highlands.

In the South, Diem's first step was to send troops to subdue the highland tribes. These expeditions began expropriating the mountaineers' property and turning it over to Vietnamese landowners. When tribes resisted, Diem's agents demanded that they produce deeds proving they owned their lands legally.

Under French rule, the *montagnards* had lived in an autonomous zone. Many tribesmen rose to relatively high positions in the colonial administration and army, and only 30,000 Vietnamese had succeeded in settling on the high plateau. This changed very quickly after 1954. Today, more than 350,000 Vietnamese civilians live in the mountain provinces, and it is almost impossible for a *montagnard* to attain a high post in the civil administration or the army.

Like Ho Chi Minh in the North, Diem started a large-scale resettlement campaign. Rebellious delta peasants were forced to settle in the highlands; mountaineers were to be settled on the coast. Diem hoped to bring the highlands under control and create a buffer zone between North and South Viet-Nam that, he believed, he could keep free of Communist infiltration. Diem's scheme could hardly be called a success. A large number of Viet-Minh veterans and other government opponents accompanied the people moving from the delta to the highlands. What Diem had done was to open the gates to Communist agitation.

About 5,000 Viet-Minh soldiers were in the highlands

when the first Viet-Nam War ended. Some had infiltrated the mountain tribes to win them over to the Communist cause. Now they turned out to be invaluable in bringing the rebellion to birth. Many cadres had lived for years among the mountain people, had adopted their customs, and often had become tribal members. They began inciting the *montagnards,* telling them of the army's atrocities and the oppression of other tribes by province chiefs. It was easy to arouse the already angry tribesmen. Of course, the *montagnards* distrusted the Communists too, since they were also Vietnamese, but the Communist officials, unlike the Saigon government, succeeded in winning over some tribes through promises and a skillful policy.

Saigon was alarmed by the growing Communist infiltration and resorted to terror. Punitive expeditions swept the highlands; tribal villages were plundered, their men pressed into army service after they had been forced to surrender all their weapons, including bows and arrows and crossbows.

Many villages were on the verge of revolt in Darlac. In Ban Me Thuot, I met a *montagnard* sergeant, a Bahnar, who had served with the French and had been in the French Army when it entered Germany in 1945. He told me that some tribal leaders had planned an uprising, but they had dropped the plan because the rebellion—inadequately prepared—would have been drowned in blood. Instead, a manifesto was drawn up protesting the "extermination policy" of Diem's government. The manifesto was presented to the U.N., where it was forgotten.

Diem did not forget. First, he accused the French of fomenting rebellion; then, he ordered all signers of the protest arrested. Some were executed, others sentenced to long prison terms; a few were lucky enough to flee in time. Among those who fled was a former official in the French colonial administration, a Rhadé by the name of Y-Bhame, who would later cause the government a good deal of trouble.

The simmering revolution in the highlands could no longer be suppressed. The Kor, led by its chief, Pho Moc Ghia, was the first tribe to rise up. This tribe, which lives on the border between the provinces of Kontum and Quang Ngai, attacked a Vietnamese garrison in the village of Teo Reo in January, 1959. Sixty soldiers were killed. A little later the Sedang and Hré tribes also rebelled.

Today, these uprisings are considered the first successes of the nascent liberation movement, but this is only partly true. The Kor and Sedang revolted spontaneously; only the Hré were led by the Viet-Cong. The leader of the Communist underground movement in Binh Dinh Province was a Viet-Minh veteran named Nguyen Van Hao. He had already succeeded in building several tightly organized resistance committees among the Hré in 1956 and 1957.

Other tribes, such as the Sedang and Bahnar, joined the Viet-Cong. The government persecuted the rebels without mercy. Two regiments of the 26th Infantry Division marched against them, but their expedition was a failure. The tribesmen had left their villages and withdrawn into the jungle where they built strong defenses. The government soldiers did not dare pursue them. Afterward, the Kor joined the Viet-Cong.

"At first our organization in the mountains was not very big, but the support we received from the tribes made up for that," an NLF member in Phnom Penh had said. He claimed that as early as 1959 there was at least one cadre in almost every village. The NLF functionaries in the larger settlements kept in constant contact with each other by radio. The tribesmen were instructed to fortify their villages, and they were also forced to build bunkers and retreat positions in the highlands for the Viet-Cong Army. They were taught how to use guns and how to produce their own weapons.

The highlands were important for the guerrillas. It was even harder to suppress them there than in the thickly settled delta provinces. And guerrilla soldiers trained in North Viet-Nam could now be infiltrated into the South; they brought equipment and weapons down the Ho Chi Minh Trail into the highlands for transfer to other centers. At that time, many Viet-Cong cadres were already receiving radio orders directly from North Viet-Nam.

The Communists set out to build ideological as well as military bases. They started a huge propaganda campaign. Radio Hanoi broadcast programs in the different tribal dialects and thundered against "the racist policy of the Diem government and American imperialists."

Attacks by Communist guerrillas multiplied; without exception, all these forces consisted of *montagnards* led by Viet-Cong officials. In Binh Dinh a Viet-Cong functionary named Phy Nie led the Hré against Diem's 42nd Regiment, which was supposed to subdue the tribe, in a bloody battle. Other tribes joined the rebellion in Kontum, Quang Ngai, and Darlac.

After the Viet-Cong succeeded in getting a foothold in the mountains, the Communists began a large-scale purge to force the tribes to support the NLF. Their main targets were the men who had fought under the French against the Viet-Minh—more than 10,000. These former colonial soldiers were executed, murdered, tortured, and kidnaped; anti-Communist tribal chiefs were replaced by pro-Communist or neutral ones. The purge claimed several thousand victims, including French missionaries and teachers who had lived for years in the mountain provinces. By 1960, the Viet-Cong had a sizable armed force in the highlands and undertook some major operations.* The goal was to drive the government troops out of Pleiku, Kontum, and Darlac provinces. The insurgents were well equipped. They had 81-mm. mortars—still a rarity for the guerrillas—and recoilless 57-mm. cannon. The first uniformed Viet-Cong troops appeared in Kontum at that time. Their uniforms had been sewn by women in the mountain villages.

Several tribes began to break with the Viet-Cong, even though the purge was under way. Since the NLF guerrillas were Vietnamese nationalists first and Communists second, they soon turned their guns on these *Mois*. "Some insurgent leaders behaved no differently toward the mountain tribes than government officials," Ban Nie told me.

Despite these difficulties, Communist policy was more successful than the government's. The minorities had their own committee; agitprop officials preached racial equality and promised the tribes autonomy after the Saigon "puppet regime" was destroyed. They toned down talk about Vietnamese national freedom; it was not an idea you could sell easily to the *montagnards*.

Soon after the NLF was founded, the national minori-

* Saigon charged at the time that the 325th North Vietnamese Infantry Division was in the highlands. Probably the first North Vietnamese units were already in the mountains, but there was no proof of an entire division being present.

ties got their own commission. The South Vietnamese Government did not establish a minorities commission until February, 1966. A *montagnard* from the Rhadé tribe, Ybih Aleo, is vice-president of the NLF. For the first time in their history, the minorities have a representative in a Vietnamese organization, though it is only a shadow government. Tran Nam Trung, one of the NLF's military heads, was able to boast: "Ninety per cent of Darlac Province is controlled by the people." The Viet-Cong leader of the province, Tran Dinh Minh, declared that more than 80 per cent of the population "adhered to the just cause."*

The government had few bases in the highlands, and these were exposed to constant guerrilla attack. Darlac's capital, Ban Me Thuot, was an island in a Red sea. The insurgents collected custom duties on roads leading from the south and the coast to the mountain provinces; the situation has not changed much since. The surest way of being captured by the guerrillas is to take a bus to Darlac or other highland provinces. The Viet-Cong stop them all. The passengers pay a "road tax" and in most cases continue on their journey unharmed. But a white man can expect to be taken prisoner, and Americans run the risk of immediate execution by a guerrilla firing squad.

The NLF has not blocked all roads, for this would hurt them more than the enemy. But in Saigon, no one questions the fact that the guerrillas could totally paralyze traffic at will on these provincial routes.

---

* Darlac Province has a population of 176,130, of which 59 per cent belong to national minority groups; Pleiku has 153,880 people, and 71 per cent belong to minorities; Kontum has a population of 105,120, with 72 per cent belonging to minority groups; and Binh Dinh has 855,860 inhabitants, with only 6 per cent members of national minorities.

To a degree, the situation in the highlands improved in 1962. U.S. Special Forces units were sent to hold this strategically important area. In the struggle against the Communist guerrillas, the Darlac Plateau, northwest of Ban Me Thuot, assumed a significance similar to that held by the bitterly contested Plain of Jarres in central Laos. The Special Forces were supposed to pacify the region. They tried winning the tribes back to the government, but no sooner had they established contact with the *monta-gnards* than the government would undo their work by senseless and arbitrary repressions of the *Moi*.

At the beginning of 1962, the government had resettled members of the Rhadé and Jaraï in a strategic hamlet near My Tach in Pleiku Province; the mountaineers first re-fused to abandon their villages, but finally agreed to reset-tlement. They were promised clean huts, decent provi-sions, and, most important, adequate defense from the Viet-Cong. But the camp was barely fortified, the living quarters consisted of dirty, hastily built barracks, and the Vietnamese camp chief and his soldiers took half the food rations supplied by the Americans. Fourteen days after the forced resettlement, the Viet-Cong attacked the "strategic hamlet." The barracks were burned down as the members of the defense unit fled. Those who did not run fast enough were shot. The province chief ordered the *mon-tagnards* to rebuild the hamlet, arguing that the *Moi* themselves were to blame for the attack on the village: if *they* had not been living there, the guerrillas would not have attacked. The huts were rebuilt—only to be overrun and destroyed again a few days later. The government dis-patched an infantry battalion to the hamlet. A spokesman for the tribesmen told the commander that his people wanted to return to their old villages, because they were safer there than under government protection. The people were promised they could leave, but first they had to rebuild the huts. However, when the huts were rebuilt, the camp commander reneged on his promise. The "savages" protested, whereupon the Vietnamese ordered sixty *montagnards* seized and shot. Women and children were among those killed.

Y-Bhame, one of the few surviving *montagnard* leaders, was living in Cambodia under Sihanouk's protection, who readily supported the mountain tribes against the Saigon government he hated. "Y-Bhame could still not return to Viet-Nam," Ban Nie told me. "The government troops would have shot him, and the Viet-Cong would have hanged him if they had captured him."

Y-Bhame was fifty-four. He dreamed of restoring the legendary kingdom of Champa, and assumed the title of first President of the Provisional Government of Champa. His hopes rested on the American Special Forces, who began training *montagnard* soldiers in their own camps and soon had a private army, made up of reliable, first-class fighting men, under their command.

A Special Forces officer in Kontum told me that "I prefer one *montagnard* to ten Vietnamese. I know that I can trust him. Five out of ten Vietnamese are open or secret supporters of the Viet-Cong, two are completely unreliable, and the other three run away as soon as they hear the first shots." This judgment is harsh, but in the highlands I rarely heard the Americans say anything friendly about their Vietnamese allies. Of course, they attempted to maintain an appearance of friendly cooperation.

The Americans began organizing the tribal soldiers into commando units to keep tabs on the Ho Chi Minh Trail and the Laotian border. They trained an antiguerrilla force that infiltrated Viet-Cong–occupied areas. "The small sabotage groups of *montagnards* often cause the Charlies more trouble than an entire Vietnamese regiment," I was told. The mountaineers proved to be born fighters and even better scouts. Several times, while on patrol missions in the jungle, I believed we were hopelessly lost, but the *montagnards* always brought us back to the right trail.

I was talking to an intelligence officer in Pleiku when a Jaraï entered, wearing short black pants and a dirty white shirt. He stood, grinning broadly, in the doorway. The American called the unarmed Jaraï over and said to me: "Now you'll see what these guys can do." The tribesman was a scout who had been sent to watch a road controlled by the Viet-Cong. He could neither read nor write, but he could draw. He sketched everything he had seen on a piece of paper: a Viet-Cong rice depot, a small underground bunker, two footpaths which, he thought, led to a guerrilla camp in the brush, and, most important, the points where the Viet-Cong had mined the road. I learned later that the *montagnard's* observations had been astonishingly precise.

"I don't believe the Americans would be so well informed about everything that goes on in the highlands behind their lines and on the Ho Chi Minh Trail if they didn't have the mountain tribes on their side," a French officer said to me in Vientiane.

Despite the adroit American policy toward the minorities, *montagnard* resistance against the government began to stiffen. The FULRO movement was established, and Y-Bhame demanded autonomy for his mountain tribes. The *montagnard* fighting front had an army of roughly

5,000 men. Many of them served in the Special Forces camps and had been fully trained and equipped by the Americans. On September 20, 1964, the first dangerous revolt occurred.

Tribal soldiers in the American camps were the first to rebel; under the eyes of their American advisers, they disarmed the Vietnamese officers commanding them. The rebels shot eighty-four Vietnamese in four days—including two district chiefs. Soon FULRO controlled a total of seven Special Forces camps, and the blue-red-green flag of its liberation movement waved over these camps.

The Americans tried desperately to settle the conflict, but the Vietnamese refused to negotiate with the *Moi*. About 1,000 *montagnard* soldiers marched on Ban Me Thuot, a vitally important city in the highlands that Diem's government had selected as its temporary capital in case Saigon should fall to the Communists.

The rebels occupied parts of Ban Me Thuot and took over a radio station. A broadcast called on all mountain tribes to revolt. Y-Bhame stated his demands:

1. National minorities were henceforth to be represented in the government.

2. American aid to *montagnards* was to be given directly instead of being distributed by Vietnamese administrative agencies.

3. *Montagnard* soldiers were to be commanded only by their own officers, not Vietnamese.

4. Saigon was to draw up a treaty guaranteeing the mountaineers full autonomy and independence.

"Colonial domination is finished," Y-Bhame announced, confident of victory.

The government delivered an ultimatum to the rebels: Either submit or the revolt will be drowned in blood. Air Marshal Nguyen Cao Ky announced he would destroy all rebel villages with his fighter-bombers.

Again the Americans tried to mediate, but they were caught in a difficult situation. They had gradually won the trust of the mountain people after years of hard work, but they had to obey orders from their superiors in Saigon and Washington. And their superiors had no intention of risking a conflict with the government because of a few rebellious mountain tribes.

The *montagnards* had to surrender unconditionally; they were forbidden to fly their own flag and would continue to be commanded by Vietnamese. Their proposal to receive American aid directly was not considered, and a substantial share of this aid flowed into the pockets of Vietnamese officers. The government could not afford to antagonize its officer corps by cutting off this secondary source of income.

After this defeat, Y-Bhame left Viet-Nam. With him went 3,000 well-armed tribal fighters. The camps on the border began emptying. The highlands were again open to the Communists, who quickly began exploiting the new opportunity.

"It was unbearable," I was told in Pleiku. "We had to watch while one village after another deserted us and was infiltrated by the Communists. It didn't happen all at once, but after several weeks, we noticed that the people had become unfriendlier. In a few months we were being fired upon from hamlets that we thought were friendly."

Y-Bhame went to Phnom Penh. Meanwhile, the NLF proclaimed a great victory in the highlands, stating that

FULRO had joined the common struggle against the "imperialists and puppet government." This was not true, but some tribal chiefs, believing the Americans had betrayed them, considered joining the Communist rebellion.

In Phnom Penh, a former French officer—who had good relations with the Viet-Cong and FULRO—told me that Y-Bhame had taken a position after comparing the proposals of NLF agents and U.S. representatives. The Americans showed diplomatic skill again in winning Y-Bhame over to their side. Y-Bhame declared he was ready to send his men back to Viet-Nam. He had to be given a guarantee, however, that U.S. troops would protect the *montagnards* in future conflicts. He also insisted on a promise that the mountain tribes be given full autonomy after the war.

One of the strangest operations in a war filled with strange events now began: American helicopters landed in northern Cambodia. Six hundred heavily armed tribal fighters boarded them and were flown back to the highlands. They were soon followed by 1,500 more men. The Special Forces camps slowly began filling again. The angry *montagnards* sometimes attacked their Vietnamese officers, but the Americans let the *Moi* have their way—they were happy to have reliable native-born troops under their command again.

The *montagnards* quickly resumed the bitter struggle with the Communist guerrillas. Fort Buon Brieng was now a major FULRO base. It held 700 *montagnard* soldiers, and over it flew FULRO's three-starred flag, not Vietnam's. The Americans regained lost terrain. Tribes that resisted the entry of U.S. Special Forces men into their villages a few months before now sent representatives requesting protection from the Viet-Cong.

However, General Ky was now acting up. In September, 1965, he ordered a thorough investigation of all activities in the highlands; he regarded the Special Forces camps as hotbeds of rebellion against the government and wanted to bring them under Saigon's control again. Ky threatened to have the camps bombed if his troops were denied access to them. Then he announced he was sending troops to the highlands to "pacify" the *montagnards*.

The Americans refused to supply Ky with transportation to carry his forces to the highlands. In spite of this, Ky dispatched his troops after forcing cancellation of a planned meeting between government representatives and FULRO.

The Vietnamese Marine infantry occupied Buon Brieng. This camp, the scene of the first *montagnard* rebellion in 1965, was described by Ky as the center of the uprising. I was told in Ban Me Thuot and Pleiku that Vietnamese officers and Americans had almost come to blows. The Americans were fond of the *montgnards*, whom they had promised to protect, but their orders were clear. After all, the United States was fighting in Viet-Nam as an ally of the government. The men of the Special Forces had to look on helplessly as the mountaineers were disarmed and arrested.

The tribal fighters did not resist. They still believed their American friends would defend them. They did not realize until too late that the hands of the Americans were tied, that they could not move against the Vietnamese. "There were mass arrests in the cities and camps," an American sergeant said. "Every suspect was seized. The Vietnamese knew that most educated *montagnards* had joined the FULRO movement, and those who could read and write were the first to be arrested. We were soon stripped of interpreters, and the troops lacked noncoms. Hell broke loose for a few days in Pleiku and other towns."

I later discovered what he meant. Alleged and real members of the rebel movement were herded together and publicly shot. Government execution squads swept through the highlands and took revenge on the "savages." In Plei Me, Sergeant Duke said to me, "If the Vietnamese had fought as passionately against the Communists, there would be nothing more for us to do here now." Ban Nie, the FULRO officer, who was still fighting beside the Americans against the Viet-Cong, estimated that more than 400 members of the Rhadé, Jaraï, Bahnar, and other tribes were killed at the time. Most FULRO troops left Viet-Nam once more.

The job of organizing the natives against the Communists would have to be started again practically from scratch. The U.S. position was not as bad as it had been the year before, but it was still bad enough. The men in the green berets were furious at the Vietnamese Government for undoing all their work.

What happened in December, 1965, and January, 1966, was exactly what the Special Forces had tried to prevent from the beginning by all possible means. Several fully armed FULRO companies went over to the Viet-Cong. They were welcomed with open arms; not because the Communists in the highlands needed military support, but because by changing sides, these FULRO men were living proof that the government's policy in the mountain region was bankrupt.

9

Victories Without Victory

Find, fix, fight.

General William C. Westmoreland

In the fall of 1965 and the beginning of 1966, the U.S. armed forces in South Viet-Nam concentrated on a new tactic to isolate the foe. They succeeded in establishing strongholds in the highlands and along the coast, where rebel influence had always been weaker than in the countryside. A broad strip of territory was freed between Ban Me Thuot and Pleiku; in addition, the Americans were able to open Route 19—strategically very important because it links the highlands to the coast—from An Khe to Binh Dinh. The next major operational objective was to win control of the coastal roads and railroads. The French had pursued a similar tactic during the Indochina War, when they named coastal Route 1 *la rue sans joie* ("the street without joy"). The American fight for Route 1 was no more joyful. U.S. troops were to clear the coast step by step and try to drive the Viet-Cong westward into the interior. Simultaneously, American influence was to spread from U.S. bases.

The U.S. military plans envisioned pushing the Viet-

199

Cong into a few western provinces and isolating it. Then, the guerrilla army could be crushed with a few concentrated attacks. More than anywhere else, the rebels would be exposed to annihilating air strikes in the thinly settled, mountainous western provinces. The war would no longer hold the entire country and people in its grip.

American troops began their operations on the coast in 1965 and continued on a larger scale in 1966. The brunt of the fighting was borne by the 3rd U.S. Marine Infantry Division, the 1st Air Cavalry Division, a brigade of the 101st Airborne Division, along with units of the 25th Infantry Division. They were supported by one Korean division and some South Vietnamese units.

The Viet-Cong had consolidated its positions on the coast and in the valleys running parallel to the coast. Many villages were fortified, the roads and railroad lines destroyed or mined. The NLF had stationed elite units there, and seasoned local guerrilla troops were available. Strong units of the North Vietnamese Army also operated in the area.

On January 25, 1966, the 1st Air Cavalry Division mounted Operation Masher; it was the start of a series of massive sweeps in the coastal region. The air cavalry men advanced north and west from Bong Son. A few days later the Marine infantry joined in, moving out of Quang Ngai. The 101st Airborne Division operated in the south, with Tuy Hoa as its base.

I arrived in Bong Son and went on to the air cavalry camp DOG. A few hours later a helicopter was ferrying me to the area of operations. It was January 28, 1966. Company C of the 2nd Battalion of the Cavalry's 7th Regiment had come to a halt; the GI's lay behind low thorn bushes along a 200-yard-wide row of palms at the edge of a narrow rice paddy. The Viet-Cong held a tree line on the other side of the field.

It was 10:00 A.M. The men were tired and drenched. They had spent a rainy night in a field camp right in the middle of guerrilla territory. Sleep was out of the question. There had been firing back and forth hour after hour; Viet-Cong snipers had not withdrawn until 4:00 A.M. The company struck camp at 7:00 A.M. to pursue the enemy. "I hope this is going to be a nice, easy, and peaceful job," Sergeant Wright of the 2nd Battalion said when I reported to him. His answer came in the sound of distant machine-gun and rifle fire.

The company pushed through a palm grove and across a manioc field to a bare hill. The machine-gun fire came closer. Company A, operating on the left flank, had made contact with the guerrillas. We learned from the radio that the Viet-Cong's main force estimated at battalion strength—had probably dug in near the village of Luon Thon. The company was to advance to the village before the guerrillas disappeared.

It was a gray, rainy morning, and a mist was rising. "Just the weather we don't need," Wright said. The reconnaissance planes could not spot the enemy positions to direct artillery fire. The helicopters and bombers were also out of action.

A stretch of Route 1 between Bong Son and Quang Ngai was the operational target. The coastal highway from Bong Son to Hué was to be opened up. The land extending from the South China Sea was made up of several large, natural tiers. The coast, level and covered by hard sand, formed the first section. One hundred yards behind it began the dunes, 4 to 18 yards high and hard to climb, with fishing villages scattered throughout. Next came a thickly settled zone, with small temples, gravestones, and pagodas. Beyond lay Highway 1; then a series of hamlets, often only 200 or 300 yards apart. Each village is a labyrinth of sorts, ringed by palm trees and small fences, bushes, hedges, and bamboo shrubs.

The Communists have controlled these villages for years. The Viet-Minh ruled them during the Indochina War, and today they are subject to the Viet-Cong. The villagers have worked for years to fortify the settlements with an interlocking system of trenches, tunnels, underground weapon depots, and field-dressing stations; sometimes entire settlements are linked with each other by tunnels or trenches.

Luon Thon, one of these villages, was our objective. We had to cross two wide rice fields to reach it. The company slowly approached the first one. It was January, and the peasants had just finished with the planting. Narrow embankments divided the surface into larger and smaller rectangular fields. The colors dissolved in the fine-spun curtain of rain that stretched across the landscape. I felt as though I were moving through a Chinese watercolor.

A burst of fire whipped across the paddy. The GI's answered with their automatic weapons. Nothing moved in the palm grove on the other side. I crawled out of the hedge into which I had dived. A tall Negro soldier standing behind me called over a couple of soldiers; he wanted to surprise the enemy from the rear. Wide bandoliers hung across his chest; his belt bristled with hand grenades; the gun he held in his black-gloved hands seemed small and delicate, and he the prototype of the soldier of our century. (A few hours later I would see him again in a trench—dead.)

His patrol began crossing the rice paddy. They groped forward slowly along the narrow embankments. They reached the other side without a shot being fired. The rest of the men could now follow.

When we crossed the first paddy, we reached a palm grove where we found two abandoned huts and some hens. Then, the shooting near us became fiercer. A platoon covering the company's left flank had run into resistance.

The Americans crept forward, crossed the rows of palm trees, and prepared to go through the bushes separating us from the second paddy. I remained behind in the tree line. Henri Huet, a French Associated Press photographer who had been a reporter during the Indochina War, was next to me. The rifle fire had stopped. I asked Huet whether the Viet Cong had withdrawn. "Maybe," he said.

The GI's started crawling along the row of bushes. At the end of the bushes they found the beginning of a low bamboo fence. Two gates stood open—the rice paddy lay beyond. The men crept as far as the gates, rose slowly and —since not a shot had been fired—beckoned to the others to follow them. Ten soldiers crawled to the gate. The first American stood up to enter the rice paddy, when hell broke loose.

The Viet-Cong had dug in on the tree line on the other side of the field. I hit the ground, but without real cover. Henri Huet lay on his back beside me. He was trying to clean the lens of a camera that had been smeared. The guerrillas were about fifty yards away, and their bullets whistled uncomfortably close. "This kind of thing is usually over in a few minutes," Huet said as he tried to turn over to take some pictures. At that moment a shot landed right next to us. "Merde," Henri said.

In about an hour the guerrillas began moving out, and the company resumed its advance. Two platoons crossed the rice field. Several snipers forced them to crawl through the mud, but they crossed without any losses.

When I crept up to the bushes I could see how heavy the guerrillas' fire had been. Eight Americans were wounded. Two medics bandaged them hastily and tried to arrange ponchos to carry them. Ten soldiers and Huet and I remained with the wounded.

"When the Charlies see they can no longer hold the tree line they break off. They leave four or five men behind who wait until we bring our wounded across the paddy, then they start shooting. When you're carrying wounded men, you're slow and immobile," a young lieutenant had told me in Saigon.

After we placed the first wounded man on a poncho, four men tried to carry him across the rice field. But the guerrillas opened fire. The group was about five yards into the field. It had no cover and could not move forward or backward. The bullets kicked up sprays near the soldiers, who lay a few yards in front of us in the slimy water. "Advance, advance," a sergeant yelled from somewhere. Had the men remained lying there, sooner or later they would have been shot one by one. The four slowly rose, their faces distorted. They dragged their burden through the water, while the bullets from the invisible snipers fell around them. The GI's finally reached the other side unharmed. It had taken them half an hour to cover fifty yards.

It was our turn now. We prepared to move out of the bushes into the open paddy. Huet stuffed his cameras into a water-proof bag, exhaled loudly and gave me a friendly punch in the ribs. We picked up the ends of a poncho containing a groaning, wounded American and started out. Two steps and we were down in the mud, the snipers' bullets spraying the water all around us; from the small fountains they kicked up I could tell the shots were moving steadily closer. An automatic gun let loose briefly. Then, Huet signaled me. We leaped up, plunged a few steps further, then dived back into the water, and continued this way—plunging, stumbling, sinking into the mud—until we finally crept, gasping, to the other side.

The wounded soldier had fainted. Behind us the next group was hurrying across the paddy, falling and stumbling forward as we had, until it reached us.

The guerrillas were entrenched in a village facing us; a strip of sand separated us. Evening fell, and the Americans had not made any progress. Neither helicopters nor other planes could get at the guerrillas. Bombings and napalm would have been as ineffective as hours of artillery barrages in driving them off.

The men knew the Communists would surround them during the night. A Viet-Cong elite battalion and units of the 330th North Vietnamese Infantry Division confronted them. The U.S. company had suffered heavy casualties on the first day of fighting: fifty-six wounded and five dead lay on the sandy ground of the trench.

Small foxholes had been dug around the trench containing the main force of the American unit. Young Americans, scarcely in their twenties, crouched waiting for the darkness. The artillery boomed away most of the night, yet the guerrillas repeatedly tried to breach the American positions with surprise attacks. All were thrown back by thick defensive fire. It was an eerie business, groping and waiting on a rainy night. Every sound could be a guerrilla crawling toward us; a soft snap in the nearby bush could be a carbine being loaded. Rising above every other sound was the howling of artillery shells exploding in the enemy positions—just 100 yards away.

Gradually, dawn began to break. The American losses had increased during the night to seventy-two wounded and nine dead. Almost half the men were out of action. It had stopped raining, and I went toward one of the huts to light a fire and dry my uniform. I jumped back when I reached the door. The small room was crammed full of ten Vietnamese soldiers squatting around a fire. They had marched with the company as reinforcements. A lieutenant stood up and welcomed me. "Come close to the fire. After all, you spent the whole night outside in the rain," he said. I asked where he had been. "Oh, we were here. It's dry and warm," the lieutenant answered. His men laughed.

"War is horrible," a young soldier said in good English. He handed me a coconut shell with some rice in it. I took it gladly. It was my first warm meal in forty-eight hours.

The Vietnamese whispered and laughed among themselves. They seemed oblivious to the fighting going on just a few yards away. "We came in here at 9:00 P.M. last night," the lieutenant explained to me. The forty-eight-hour-a-week war! I wanted to look around the hut but the Vietnamese held me back gently. "Careful, stay here." He pointed to the next room. "Everything is mined in there."

I crept back to the trench. They kept bringing in more

wounded. I moved further on to look at the civilians. Some women, children, and men had been flushed out of hiding and brought into the trench. Many were wounded, all were paralyzed with fear and terror.

At noon the Americans resumed bombing the Viet-Cong positions. A wall of flame flared up from the village; yet, every time a U.S. patrol tried to advance, it was immediately greeted by furious machine-gun fire.

Skyraiders sped over. Black napalm canisters tumbled to the ground, then a sea of flames heaved upward. When the flames ebbed, the palm trees were cracked and charred; ruins burned beyond them.

The bombardments had not broken the Viet-Cong. They began swarming out, trying in individual attacks to reach the American trench. Once, the bullets from an automatic weapon sped directly into the wounded groups. One Viet-Cong even succeeded in getting within ten yards of the trench. He seemed astonished when he found himself in front of the American positions and tried to leap forward; but as he leapt, a burst of machine-gun fire ripped his skull apart.

The guerrillas slowly withdrew at 4:00 P.M. The planes came in with another napalm strike; the flames again blazed up; another patrol sought to reach the village and was thrown back by machine-gun fire. Finally, one commando unit succeeded in cleaning out the guerrilla nest. The GI's found one badly wounded guerrilla who still kept his finger on his trigger. His gun finally had to be torn from him; he could not walk and was carried into the trench, where he died an hour later.

The village had been taken. Up to this point the Americans had eighty-six wounded and fifteen dead. There were still other sniper nests around us. Their mortar fire caught us as we tried to bring some wounded across a rice field to the trench; I was wounded by a shell fragment.

A helicopter ferried me back to Camp DOG. Just before my flight to the hospital of the 1st Air Cavalry Division in An Khe I had discussed the casualties of the battle with Colonel Moore. The colonel described his own losses as light. One of his press officers figured the casualties of the Viet-Cong at more than 100 killed; 57 had supposedly been found in the village. "How did you establish this figure?" I asked. "I was out here the whole time. We didn't find more than fifteen dead VC."

He answered briskly, "We made a recount."

A short time later several U.S. newspapers published articles critical of the official figures on enemy casualties. The stories were hotly discussed in Saigon. I spoke later with Patrick Nieburg, a U.S. information officer, about the casualty figures. Nieburg said, "You correspondents always make the same mistake. You see the individual actions, not the whole picture of an operation."

"But if a company has fought the Viet-Cong and lost more than two-thirds of its strength, and the enemy has probably had no higher casualties, it's difficult to claim we had light losses while the Viet-Cong's were heavy," I objected.

"As far as I know two battalions were engaged in the Luon Thon operations," Nieburg said. "Our losses came to no more than 10 per cent of all troops involved—therefore, they are light."

"But the battalions had no contact with the enemy during the whole battle," I replied.

"That doesn't count. The total results are important."

The Americans are fighting a war on many fronts in Viet-Nam. Perhaps their most difficult struggle is the one to win favorable public opinion around the world. U.S. public information officers in Saigon seem obsessed by the idea that, no matter what else it loses, the United States must retain its image as the most powerful and successful military nation on earth. They tabulate and juggle and present figures on enemy losses as proof that the war in Viet-Nam is being waged successfully. Vietnamese press officers do the same. Every correspondent arriving in Viet-Nam is impressed by these tallies at first. It takes some time to learn how to assess the real value of figures released after each victory of the government troops. Once, I met a young American major after a South Vietnamese press conference. He had left in anger, saying to his fellow officers: "Today we've wiped out a Viet-Cong battalion. Tomorrow, we'll wipe out the same battalion. The day after, the same thing, until the time comes when we'll be crushed ourselves. The awful thing is that the army command believes in its own figures." The major had been in Viet-Nam for several years and served as an adviser to a South Vietnamese Ranger battalion.

The official casualty ratio is 1:3. That is, for every allied soldier killed or wounded in battle, three guerrillas are put out of action. Yet, it is almost impossible to determine the exact number of Viet-Cong casualties. The rebels seldom leave their dead and wounded on the field; in most instances, it is they who decide when to break off the fight, disengage, and withdraw. The Americans, like the South Vietnamese, must depend on estimates. They support their claims by presenting the number of weapons captured. But the quantity of captured weapons hardly serves as an ab-

solute basis for determining casualties. It is even more difficult to establish guerrilla losses after bombing strikes and
artillery barrages than after a field battle; no one can state
with any degree of accuracy after several villages have
been bombed that "80 or 100 or 150 Viet-Cong were
killed." The pilots I have talked to concede that it is seldom possible to fix the number of guerrillas killed.

During these attacks many civilians, not just rebel soldiers, are hit. I have heard private but authoritative estimates that more than 30 per cent of those officially reported to be Viet-Cong dead are really noncombatants, old
men, women, and children. Officials in Saigon told me
that a 30 per cent margin of error must be considered
when figuring the number of casualties. The ratio of losses
—wounded and dead—is probably closer to 1:2, if one
grants the allies the benefit of the doubt.

I stayed in An Khe four days and then returned to
DOG. Meanwhile the 1st Air Cavalry mopped up an area
stretching thirteen miles north from Bong Son. In the
north, the Marine Corps began Operation Double Eagle
on the coast. I flew back to the combat zone with five
heavily armed GI's. Our helicopter squadron flew high at
first, about 300 feet, but when we neared the target, the
planes descended to a few yards above the tree tops. The
advantage of this tactic is clear: The Viet-Cong hear
the copters, yet they cannot see them until they are just
overhead.

We flew over rice fields filled with black-clad peasants
wearing cone-shaped hats. They did not acknowledge our
presence but just stood there.

Before, the guerrillas had urged the peasants to flee as
soon as a plane or helicopter appeared. The peasants had

run, and the air gunners, believing they were fleeing guerrillas, shot at them. Hundreds had been killed in the first
years of the war, especially in the delta, because of such
misunderstanding. But the Viet-Cong had learned from
these incidents and told the peasants what to do. They
now stand still when a plane approaches; their best defense is no defense.

We flew in a wide arc over the paddies. Suddenly a machine gun in one of the helicopters near us began to ham-
mer away. Our gunners immediately opened fire too. Then
I saw two men below trying to reach the protecting embankments dividing the fields. We were about ten yards
above them. They sank to their knees in the slime and
could scarcely move; desperately they paddled the water
with their hands trying to advance faster. They took a few
more steps and fell; one tried to get up, collapsed, and
sank into the mud.

The two dark specks lay below us in the gray water.
Peasants who had made a thoughtless motion? Guerrillas
who had tried recklessly to stop the approaching armada
in its flight? Local partisans who had lost their nerve? I
did not know. Two nameless dead. The peasants in the
fields had continued working undisturbed. The war had
worn them down to the point where they no longer
showed fear or concern.

It was a routine landing. Escort planes and helicopters
of the lead group launched rockets, then the other helicopters let loose with heavy machine-gun fire. Dry bushes
began to burn; smoke bombs were dropped to screen off
the terrain; the helicopters carrying troops dropped, behind these fireworks.

We had landed on the flat top of a hill. The troops went

down through tall elephant grass to An Lao Valley. Presumably, the guerrillas driven from the coast had taken shelter here. The mission of these troops was to comb the valley and "pacify" it; the guerrillas were to be driven farther west.

We soon reached a dense jungle, about 100 yards down the hill. We ran into a sniper, who was dragged out of a small foxhole by a GI. The sniper tried to escape, but was caught in a blast of fire and fell among the thick lianas. We went over to him; he was bleeding to death.

Then we came upon a Viet-Cong system of fortifications that began about halfway up the slope. The woods were laced with communication trenches. Holes had been dug beneath trees, roots, and rocks to the right and left of a narrow path—small bunkers for one or two men. A wide trench ran along the slope, roofed by thick tree trunks, concealed and camouflaged by palms, bushes, and rocks. Both the valley and the rising slopes could be strafed from this trench. Farther below we found traps and fields of punji stakes—steel-hard, bamboo spikes—which we carefully skirted.

"The Charlies could have held us up here for days with one company," Major Henry said later. "We would have had to wait until their ammunition ran out or our bombs flattened the jungle." The unit reached the bottom of the valley without trouble. It had taken fourteen hours just to descend about 900 feet and penetrate the jungle.

The next morning the U.S. troops reached the first village. It was abandoned. The GI's knocked on the floors of the huts looking for hidden tunnels and trenches, but there was nothing. Then I saw smoke rising from one of the huts. I thought some peasants were there, but inside were two young American soldiers. They had started the fire, then they moved to the next hut and burned it down too; in half an hour, the village was burning. I asked one of the soldiers why he had started the fire. He laughed and said, "The Charlies will know we've been here."

A few days later this incident became the subject of controversy at a press conference in Camp DOG. A Swedish colleague, who had also seen the houses put to the torch, asked whether there was an explicit order to burn peasant huts. "No, there is no such order," came the answer. "But we didn't know the houses were burned down." I said that I had personally seen the village set on fire. The colonel in charge of the press conference said he believed me, but he doubted that the village was harmless. "Perhaps the soldiers found weapons or a Viet-Cong flag; perhaps the Americans had been shot at from the huts," he said.

"No, they weren't," the Swedish correspondent answered. "The houses were empty, and there were no weapons or flags or anything else in them to show that guerrillas had been there." However, a few American correspondents made the point that the burned huts weren't important; after all, this was war, and such incidents always happened.

The colonel still doubted that we had the facts straight. After the Swede offered to develop the photos he took to show what had happened, the colonel finally admitted, "Yes, it can happen." I was confused by the officer's attitude, but was more disturbed by that of the American correspondents, who apparently viewed our questions as a betrayal of America's just cause. We were unable to make them understand that to burn down one hut arbitrarily could nullify years of political and psychological work and an investment of tens of thousands of dollars.

At another village in the An Lao Valley, a small, gray-haired man, driving a herd of emaciated cows, suddenly showed up. He was seized and questioned. Had he heard anything about the Viet-Cong? Oh, yes, but he didn't bother with politics. Had the guerrillas ever been in this village? Yes, several times. When? Oh, perhaps many days ago, perhaps just a few days ago; he didn't know exactly. Besides, he was old, and the Viet-Cong always appeared suddenly and then disappeared. Had he seen many guerrillas in the valley? Perhaps 100, perhaps 1,000, perhaps even 5,000. Where had the guerrillas gone? That way, and that way, and that way. The old man took in all four points on the compass, and it seemed as if he wanted to turn the interrogation into a farce. He was tied up and turned over to the Vietnamese soldiers accompanying the American troops.

The next village had already been hit badly. More than half the huts were burned down and the rice fields were pock-marked with bomb craters. The villagers assembled as the Americans marched in. They sat silently in front of their ruined huts. Women held crying children in their arms. When a young American tried to comfort a child, it began screaming while the mother stared in terror at the foreign white giant.

Two young peasants came from behind the huts, followed by their families. They were all dragging sacks and boxes, apparently everything they owned. One man waved a small colored leaflet, a safe-conduct pass dropped by allied planes over guerrilla areas. The young Vietnamese told the interpreter that he and his friend, together with their families, wanted to go with the Americans: They feared the Viet-Cong and had to flee.

After some discussion helicopters were called in. They flew both families and a few other peasants, who had been arrested, out of the valley. I saw the families later in the main camp. Both men were behind barbed wire in a prisoner camp for Viet-Cong insurgents. The women and children squatted apathetically in a small grass-covered area also ringed by barbed wire. American military police stood guard.

"Why are these people under arrest?" I asked one of the guards.

"They are VC suspects."

"What will happen to them?"

"They will be questioned and then turned over to the Vietnamese authorities. They know what to do with Communists."

The operation in An Lao Valley continued. According to Saigon, 40 per cent of the structures in this valley of 8,000 people had been destroyed in the months preceding the attack. The Viet-Cong avoided the Americans except for brief skirmishes that always ended the same way. The guerrillas would break off contact after ten or twenty minutes or half an hour at the most. The Marine infantry, operating to the north, did not have much luck either. NLF leaders had obviously ordered their troops to leave the valley without putting up a fight. There was no other explanation for the lack of resistance.

The search for the wounded after the first days of combat was equally unsuccessful. U.S. intelligence believed the Viet-Cong had two large field hospitals in the valley. About 1,000 guerrillas wounded in the fierce clashes at the beginning of the operation must have headed for them —1,000 wounded men cannot disappear without a trace— and yet, it was difficult to find them.

Operation Masher was renamed White Wing. By February 5, 1966, 518 enemy had been killed, 120 captured, and 582 suspects seized. The Marines, conducting Operation Double Eagle north of the 1st Air Cavalry, had killed 116 Viet-Cong and arrested 216 suspects by the same date. The air cavalry troops soon uncovered new and larger fortifications in An Lao Valley. Almost every village was ringed by trenches and reinforced by bunkers. Some of the larger settlements contained the symbols of Viet-Cong control: speakers' stands, large posters, meeting halls decorated with NLF flags, memorial statues of Liberation Front heroes, obelisks—some reaching an impressive height of thirty feet—with red stars glittering at the top.

In most cases, the villagers were unfriendly toward the American troops. Sometimes the hostility was hidden by fear. They passively submitted to arrest, questioning, and search.

The guerrillas ventured into brief combat almost every day. These encounters could not affect the course of the American operation, nor were they intended to be defensive battles. Their obvious purpose was to demonstrate the guerrillas' presence.

Three weeks passed and the air cavalry men finally discovered the field hospitals, extensive installations in the jungle where hundreds of wounded had been cared for. They also found arms and rice depots. The wounded had already been transported elsewhere; however, the few defenders of the bunkers put up a hard and bloody fight.

The Viet-Cong finally struck on February 20, not in An

Lao Valley, but in An Khe, the air cavalry's divisional headquarters. The guerrillas began bombarding the American camp with mortars at about midnight. The attacking unit seemed to be of company size. It first concentrated its fire on the camp of the 2nd Brigade and then shifted to the helicopter landing field. Within a few minutes the guerrillas had fired sixty mortar shells into the camp, then penetrated it and strafed the Americans with automatic guns. Seven GI's were killed, more than thirty wounded.

The attackers withdrew at 2:00 A.M., after shooting off more than eighty shells and losing only six men. Several helicopters were badly damaged. This surprise guerrilla assault had not been particularly successful, but it was important, because for the first time since the beginning of the war, the guerrillas had attacked an American division camp with mortars—a tactic they would repeat later.

Meanwhile, the cavalry had reached the southern end of An Lao Valley and cleared Route 1 from Bong Son to Quang Ngai. When I returned to Camp DOG, Colonel Moore held a brief press conference and said that the Viet-Cong had been driven from the area surrounding the camp and the road to Bong Son, and that these were now controlled by American troops. The operation had been unusually successful: The guerrillas had withdrawn all along the line and refrained from fighting. It seemed as if they had decided to abandon the entire province without striking a blow.

That evening I was sitting with four other correspondents in front of the press tent in DOG. We discussed the operations of the last few days. All of us agreed the sweep had really been successful. It was a warm night. We had left the tent open, and the light from our acetylene lamps showed outside. About 9:00 P.M. one machine gun started hammering away near us, then a second.

"One of our boys is a little loaded," one of the U.S. correspondents said. We laughed. Two minutes later our good humor turned to fear. A guerrilla had crawled to about fifty yards of our tent and was firing at us. Four or five shots whistled over our heads. The guard sounded the alarm. Guerrillas had sneaked into other parts of the camp as well. The shooting was wild, and only a miracle saved the Americans from wounding each other as they rallied to fight back. By then, the guerrillas had vanished without a trace.

The next day I wanted to go alone to Bong Son, about two and a half miles from the camp. I was advised not to travel alone, because the road was unsafe.

Two days later guerrillas attacked the artillery emplacements in the southern part of the camp. The assault was quickly beaten back, and the guerrillas vanished into a nearby wood. The Americans tried to pursue them but had no luck. Then, they shelled the woods in which a few still undamaged structures stood; in a few minutes, fifteen huts were aflame. But the guerrillas had vanished long before a commando unit began combing the area.

A few days later I spoke to Colonel Moore again about the progress of the operation. "It's a success," he said. "We've driven the enemy out of a large territory they called their own until now."

"What will happen to the civilian population?" I asked.

"The government will look after them."

"You mopped up An Lao Valley and expelled the Viet-Cong. Have you any idea of how the reconquered area is going to be held? Will American troops remain in the valley as an occupation force?" I asked.

"No. I don't know what will happen next. It's not my business. I'm a soldier, and my job is to beat the enemy."

"Isn't it possible the Viet-Cong will reinfiltrate its old settlements after the U.S. troops leave?"

"It's possible," the colonel answered, "if the government doesn't really succeed in taking over the valley."

Later I learned that Viet-Cong units had appeared again in the center of the valley. Villages liberated a few days earlier by U.S. forces were again controlled by the guerrillas. Until now, the government has failed to get a solid foothold in the valley and is unlikely to do so in the foreseeable future; it is beset by too many other domestic political problems.

Operation White Wing ended on March 4, 1966. Approximately 10,000 allied troops had been deployed during the entire operation, 4,500 of them Americans. The U.S. troops killed 1,280 guerrillas and captured 331. As in many other Viet-Nam battles, the disproportion between dead and captured enemies is striking. More than 1,500 suspects were seized.

In the south, fanning out from Tuy Hoa, the 101st Airborne Division ended Operation Van Buren on February 22 and began Operation Harrison. During Operation Van Buren, the airborne troops—supported by Korean marines —killed 670 enemy soldiers and took only 45 prisoners; they arrested 725 suspects and seized more than 30,000 tons of rice in a guerrilla supply depot.

Before Operation Harrison started, I flew over the new combat area in a reconnaissance plane. The fighting zone stretched north from Tuy Hoa to the coastal town of Tuy An and westward to Van Hoa. The mountainous area consisted of villages on steep slopes, thick brush, and jungle. The whole region was strongly fortified. It was easy to spot Viet-Cong bunkers and trenches from the air. Rails had been ripped from nearby tracks and laid across the highways as roadblocks. Strong enemy units held the zone of operations: the 95th North Vietnamese Infantry Regiment, five battalions of local guerrillas, and three battalions of regular Viet-Cong troops.

"There are about 4,500 Communist soldiers on the coast," Colonel Mataxis told me. "We know this because we used our own observation teams. If we relied on the Vietnamese intelligence service we'd be lost." The airborne troops landed small reconnaissance groups by helicopter in enemy territory before night fell. Three or four days later they would be evacuated. "We have to do this," Colonel Mataxis said, "because all information supplied by the Vietnamese Army and local police units is wrong or inaccurate."

The airborne troops were flown into the combat area by helicopter. In addition, the 101st Airborne Division follows another tactic: Its troops parachute into combat directly over the Viet-Cong. The Americans have mounted several successful actions by taking the guerrillas completely by surprise.

I soon had my chance to go along on one of these operations. Three airborne companies had taken off from Tuy Hoa and come down in the Van Hoa region, about ten miles west of the coast. The Americans landed without opposition. Then came word that a strong Viet-Cong force

had withdrawn to a village two and a half miles north of
the landing zone.

"These operations are lousy," an American major told
me. "You learn the Viet-Cong are in a village; you get
near it and see only women and children. You can't attack because you'll kill them. But you can be sure that as
soon as you enter it you'll lose a couple of men."

The Americans fortified their landing zone in a surprisingly short time. Fifteen minutes after the landing, helicopters were unloading small ground vehicles, heavy
mortars, ammunition, and rations. Twenty minutes later
the radio equipment had been set up, the command staff
tent raised, and foxholes dug. The fortifications were complete in less than thirty minutes.

The colonel in charge called a staff meeting at 2:00
P.M. Should the village be attacked today? A young captain volunteered for the action. A helicopter squadron
landed in camp at 3:30 P.M. It would ferry us to the village. This was to be the most dangerous operation I had
yet been in.

"We're flying without life insurance," the company
commander said, offering me a gun. "Take it. You'll need
it." I refused. The men buckled their helmets and climbed
into the helicopters. I was in the first plane. The pilot ges-
tured "thumbs up," and the helicopter rose slowly from
the ground.

"We haven't called for bombers because we want to
surprise the Charlies. We'll drop straight from heaven on
their heads," the colonel said. We sighted the target after
flying for ten minutes. Two observation planes flew above
us. Three or four helicopters circled the objective at a

great height. The line of helicopters came closer. Just before reaching the village, they suddenly veered off. Machine guns were strafing us from the ground. Five "gun ships" dropped out of formation and flew at the village. Their rockets shot downward as the machine guns roared.

The attacking group flew a wide loop and returned to the village. Puffs began appearing near the helicopters; I later learned that they were small antihelicopter rockets the guerrillas had developed themselves and that were now being used for the first time.

The helicopters circled the village for half an hour. The guerrilla defense was too strong to risk a landing. The company commander, crouching near the exit hatch, became restless. He ordered: "Down!" The helicopters descended gradually to a height of about 150 feet. Suddenly, the pilots let the planes drop straight down, as if into a bottomless pit. I grasped the straps; my first thought was that we had been hit. Twelve feet from the ground, the pilot leveled off. The huts were in front of us—and inside them, the guerrillas.

Now, everything happened fast. I leaped to the ground and raced between the flaming huts. The company commander had jumped before me. He ran, firing an AR-15 rifle, toward one of the huts, stumbled and fell, motionless. For a moment I thought of dropping to the ground and staying put. But then I ran toward one of the huts and threw myself against its wall. I saw a foxhole and jumped into it.

By now, the entire company had landed. The bodies of five GI's lay in front of the huts. Six feet in front of me a young American was desperately trying to crawl to cover. He had hurt his foot in jumping from the plane; a machine-gun blast killed him.

The main force of Americans plunged straight into the houses without seeking cover. I heard the carbine shots whipping by, the roar of machine guns, and the crackling of burning huts. The guerrillas tried to flee; some succeeded. The others lay sprawled in the huts or trenches. There were no prisoners.

The American airborne troops drove back the enemy almost everywhere in the combat zone. They won every battle. Yet, the same thing happened here as at Bong Son. The Viet Cong infiltrated their old positions again. It was a victory without victory.

At Tuy Hoa and Bong Son the Viet-Cong avoided throwing large units, matching the enemy's, into battle. But elsewhere the U.S. Marines succeeded in forcing a North Vietnamese unit into untypical large-scale combat. The second phase of Operation Double Eagle ended on March 2, 1966; 125 guerrillas had been killed, 15 captured. Operation Utah began in the Quang Ngai area. The Marine Corps was operating five miles from coastal Route 1, near the villages of Khanh My and Son Chau. Nothing indicated the presence of large enemy units. Two dead North Vietnamese were found on February 17, soldiers of the 21st VPA Infantry Regiment. Four days later, a U.S. convoy ran into an ambush, but the Communist mines exploded prematurely, and the attack failed. From February 22 until March 1, the U.S. Marines had repeated light run-ins with guerrilla groups, and probably with North Vietnamese as well. But the enemy kept trying to avoid these clashes.

The Marines, in turn, set a trap for a North Vietnamese unit on the night of March 2 and took two prisoners. One belonged to an engineer unit, whose mission had been to mine the coastal highway and the railroad embankments. Another North Vietnamese soldier, captured on March 3, disclosed that the entire 21st North Vietnamese Infantry Regiment was near the coast, with the regimental command quartered in Son Chau village. That day the Marines seized a VPA radio station, and at 6:00 P.M. a Viet-Cong deserter surrendered. The monitored radio and the deserter's statements confirmed the presence of the enemy regimental headquarters in Son Chau.

A Vietnamese airborne battalion, the 2nd Battalion of the 7th Marine Infantry Regiment, and a Vietnamese Ranger battalion were ordered to Son Chau. The Vietnamese paratroopers, jumping a bare 800 yards from Son Chau, immediately came under savage enemy fire, and suffered heavy losses; they could not advance and dug in in front of the village. On March 4, three Marine battalions converged on Son Chau from the east, north, and south. They were followed by the 37th Vietnamese Ranger Battalion. The 2nd Battalion of the 4th Marine Infantry Regiment had landed a mile south of Son Chau by helicopters. It encountered large enemy units.

"The Marines are brainwashed," I was told by a fellow correspondent who witnessed this operation. "They fixed their bayonets, buckled their bullet-proof vests tight, and ran straight into the enemy fire." So heavy were Marine casualties that a hospital ship lying off the coast had to be prepared for them.

Up to this point only two enemy battalions—a maximum of 1,000 men—were engaged in the fighting; North Vietnamese losses stood at about 250 dead, those of the Americans and government troops at 200 men.

Two artillery batteries were brought to clear the way for the attack on Son Chau. On March 5, the North Vietnamese were practically surrounded. A steady artillery barrage beat upon them, but the defenders showed no sign of weakening. That afternoon a company of Marines was ambushed and more than thirty men killed. New troops were to be flown into the combat zone the next day, but the defensive fire was so intense that the Americans could not throw them into battle. Colonel Johnson, commander of the Marine Corps helicopter group, reported that he had never yet met such tremendous ground fire in Viet-Nam. Of the 125 helicopters in operation, 14 had been shot down and more than 35 damaged.

The 1st Marine Aircraft Wing flew sortie after sortie; the North Vietnamese positions were smothered with bombs and napalm. But the Marine fliers felt the defensive counterblows as well. One plane was brought down, 4 had to make emergency landings in the combat area and were destroyed, 12 were badly damaged.

The allies, with artillery and bomber support, renewed their attack on the Communist positions on March 6. They finally took Son Chau after unusually bloody fighting. The bunkers and tunnels around the village were full of bodies. Just one trench, 20 yards long, held 40 dead Vietnamese; a tunnel contained 46 bodies, a hut that had served as an emergency hospital was filled with 52 dead and dying. A total of 533 North Vietnamese had fallen, and over 200 local guerrillas had been killed.

The wounded regimental commander was captured. He stated that he had defended Son Chau with more than 2,500 men; 1,000 of these had been wounded.

Bitter disappointment awaited the allies despite this momentary success. They found nothing in Son Chau except the dead and wounded. The regiment's survivors had moved out unnoticed. How they had done it was a mystery to the allied commanders.

"Somehow they slipped through our ring," Colonel Pietross of the Marine Infantry Regiment said. "We don't know when or how they managed to do it." The fleeing men were spotted days after the battle, fighting their way westward in groups of 50 to 100. It was impossible to block their escape.

Colonel Johnson's helicopters had flown 2,754 sorties in three days. The allies had used up a total of 137 tons of matériel and medicines. Marine fliers had made 191 sorties in three days, dropped 154 tons of bombs and napalm, launched 254 rockets, and fired 15,625 rounds from the guns of their planes. The bombardment had completely destroyed 136 out of 162 buildings.

The Son Chau command headquarters of the North Vietnamese forces stationed in Quang Ngai had been smashed, but the chance to annihilate an entire VPA regiment had been lost. The enormous expenditure of matériel, all the sacrifices, had not been enough to win decisive victory.

IO

No-Man's-Land

To liberate the South, let us all advance together.

Opening of the hymn of the NLF

WESTERN CIVILIZATION ARRIVED in An Khe with the American troops. And with civilization came money. A few months earlier this highland town had been exactly like hundreds of other forsaken small towns in Southeast Asia. Now, on its main street, stood shops and flourishing businesses. A "Hollywood" laundry, a "San Francisco" barbershop, a "Broadway" tailor, a "George Washington" watch repair shop.

The headquarters of the 1st U.S. Air Cavalry Division is located in An Khe. The first small shops appeared a few weeks before the Americans arrived—and the first bars: wooden frames encased in corrugated tin, with a couple of wobbly stools inside, a few bottles of beer, cola, whisky, a jukebox, and some girls.

The first time I visited An Khe I counted ten bars; two weeks later more than thirty. The girls came in crowds from the coastal towns and from Saigon to the highlands; often with their husbands and children, all young, pretty, tired, cynical female sutlers of the atom age. Daughters of mothers who had performed the same services in another war—but for less money, of course.

"Why have you come to the highlands?" I asked a Saigonese who had worked as a taxi girl in the capital.

"There's less competition; you make more because there are fewer girls. Only a very few dare come up here because it's too dangerous," she said. She had earned about $500 a month in Saigon. Her income had tripled working "at the front."

Her boss is a thirty-five-year-old Vietnamese, who previously had run a restaurant in An Khe. He had located his first "bar" in the living room of the hut he lived in. He divided the room by a curtain. His children romped on one side where his family lived, and on the other side of the curtain, four girls collected American dollars for whisky, cola, beer, and entertainment.

Today, this Vietnamese owns four tailor shops, two bars, and two laundries. An industrious little man, he wears a watch on each wrist as a token of his wealth. A government flag waves in front of his house—a new wooden hut. Just a few months ago he had been paying taxes to the Viet-Cong. Now he wants nothing to do with the "damned Communists," but silently continues paying 12,000 piasters monthly to the guerrillas' tax collector. "I can't tell this to the Americans," he admitted to me and broke into a smile of complicity. "But you, as a Frenchman, understand me."

The Viet-Cong is everywhere despite the presence of American troops and the fact that the area is considered "liberated." "Twenty per cent of all government officials are Communist fellow travelers, another 30 per cent are disloyal, and the rest untrustworthy," an American information officer once told me bitterly before he left Viet-Nam. His judgment was harsh, but it exposed the vicious circle in which the Americans in Viet-Nam are caught.

"We want to stay alive," a clever An Khe bar owner said to me. "To do so, we have to accept all sides. Politics no longer interests me. Why should I risk my head?" In Nha Trang the Viet-Cong had raised no objections when a bar owner hung a picture of President Johnson at his entrance and an American flag behind the bar. But when he refused to pay off the Communists because he felt protected by the U.S. troops, his bar girls left him overnight. Two days later his place was blown up. One day in Gui Nhon a restaurant owner was taken away by two policemen. They told him he had to settle some minor official matter. He was found fourteen days later in a rice field—headless.

An Khe is a town on the edge of the war. Its few brick houses are surrounded by barbed-wire fences; its main street lined with earthen bunkers and trenches. Government soldiers stand guard in heavily protected positions: It is a settlement with a doubtful future, and nobody knows whether it is rising or falling. Green rolling hills stretch into the distance, and binoculars are focused on the guerrillas. Not much effort was needed to fortify the town. Some of its fortifications are a heritage of the old Indochina War. The French stationed a garrison in An Khe to keep Route 19 open to Pleiku and the coast. During the battle of Dien Bien Phu, the Viet-Minh encircled and took An Khe. Fighting continued near the town for a month after the cease-fire agreement. The French lost more than 1,000 men there in a few days.

When Viet-Nam was divided, the Communists had to

leave An Khe. Soldiers of the new government replaced the Viet-Minh. When the Second Viet-Nam War began, Viet-Cong troops controlled An Khe for a time. Then, the guerrillas were succeeded by government forces, which, in turn, were replaced by the Americans. Five different occupations in twelve years. Even now the area around An Khe is only "conditionally safe."

I rode through the no-man's-land from An Khe to the coast with an American convoy. The column was stopped for the first time for a road check ten miles beyond town. Two Korean soldiers inspected a bus crowded with Vietnamese peasants. The bus was allowed to proceed ten minutes later. Groaning, it rolled onward into territory ruled simultaneously by four masters: Americans, Vietnamese, Koreans, and the guerrillas.

A young peasant woman approached the convoy as it slowly began moving through the roadblock. She ran alongside a truck carrying a basket with four bottles of lemonade, which she wanted to sell to the GI's. It was all she had. Several cans of rations were thrown from one of the heavy trucks to the road. The woman stopped in her tracks, then walked over to the cans, picked them up, hid them in her basket, and disappeared.

The convoy left Route 19 before reaching the coast and swung north on Route 1. The villages along the highway bore the scars of recent fighting. In some places the countryside was completely depopulated. Barbed-wire entanglements protected still-inhabited villages from guerrilla attacks. Temporary bridges led across rivers; the guerrillas had blown up all bridges as they retreated. The railroads were impassable, the rails torn up, the embankments mined.

The villages and towns were full of heavily armed soldiers of the South Vietnamese Government. They did not act like "citizens in uniform" in their own country, but like members of an occupation power in hostile territory.

The convoy stopped in a small town. I walked down the street and came upon two tailor shops where a dozen boys behind old sewing machines were busily producing green uniforms. Two months earlier they might have been sitting there manufacturing gray or black uniforms for the rebel army. I lingered in front of one of the shops. An old woman, her lips red from chewing betel, offered to sell me a comic pennant: Donald Duck in a helicopter with an inscription reading, "Welcome to Viet-Nam." I thanked her politely; she spat past me into the street.

On my way back to the car I was surrounded by about thirty yelling children. I do not believe any American soldier who has ever served in Viet-Nam will ever forget such children. Their entire English vocabulary—"Okay," "Hello," and "Number one"—may have been acquired in a few days, but it will suffice for the months to come.

The children tirelessly yelled at every passing truck and soldier; they ran after each vehicle for a while and then played the same game with the next one. It was a triumphal procession, with the children providing the crowds. The U.S. convoy passed through about forty villages on its fifty-mile trip northward along Route 1. In each one the children yelled and waved, but not once did I see a man or woman greet the foreign soldiers or even give them a friendly glance. Instead, they just plodded through the dust raised by the vehicles.

"It's always like this," said a GI sitting up front beside the driver. His left hand gripped a carbine at the ready;

with his right hand he waved tiredly at a pack of children who were yelling "Number one" at us: "The kids shout, and the grown-ups keep silent."

The young Vietnamese signaled me to follow. We were at the door of an old one-story house in Saigon-Cholon. Across the street, a girl behind a lemonade cart was grinding up ice cubes. A Chinese leaned in the doorway of a bookstore opposite, staring at us. A bicycle rickshaw was parked at the crub. Its driver had put down the top to shade him from the noonday sun and was curled up asleep on the seat. Two jeeps, horns honking, moved through a side street.

We entered the house where I was to be introduced to a NLF official. I wanted to visit a village in a Viet-Cong–controlled zone. Once I had the right contact, I would have to leave the Saigon area and wait until a guerrilla patrol picked me up. But I knew that there was a fair chance that I would never get to see Saigon again.

In November, 1965, a Swiss journalist who had tried to visit a Viet-Cong district in the delta on his own had been captured by guerrillas, tortured, and killed. Americans later found his mutilated body. In February, 1966, two French TV reporters were seized by the guerrillas and imprisoned. Their cameras were destroyed. Ten hours later they succeeded in escaping. Twenty-four hours later, they were compelled to leave Saigon. They were suspected of having voluntarily surrendered to the guerrillas and were subject to government action. A correspondent seeking to contact the rebels faces, at the minimum, the threat of expulsion. He cannot rely on American help in any case: The guerrillas are *the enemy;* a reporter who tries to meet the other side is considered *a priori* a traitor or, at least, highly suspect.

There are, of course, American journalists who have Viet-Cong connections. They must keep their contacts a secret. If it were known that they "contact" the NLF to keep informed, they would probably be expelled from the country, a risk few want to take.

In the course of my efforts to see the guerrillas at first-hand, I was introduced to a Vietnamese in his early forties. From behind steel-rimmed glasses he carefully studied me. "I don't understand where you got the idea I could take you into the liberated zones," he said in a soft voice. "You are obviously the victim of a misunderstanding."

He had the same deliberate tone and reserve I had met so often in Viet-Nam. "We have learned not to be ourselves any longer," a friendly physician in Saigon once said. He had been jailed by the Ky regime for six weeks because he had signed a peace petition. Two of his friends had been executed. He expected to be arrested again any day. "They'll take me into custody because I'm not active any more. I'm really suspect because I'm keeping quiet." Why didn't he try to flee, I asked him. "Where to?" was his answer. "I'm not a Communst. But perhaps going over to them is the one thing that might bring me temporary peace. I really don't have much of a choice left."

Now the man sitting opposite me remained silent for a long while, then said: "It's a misunderstanding that I regret." He waited for me to rise.

"I'm sorry too," I answered and said good-bye. But four days later, somehow, I was trudging over a muddy path alongside a rice paddy in the company of this man and a younger one.

Our destination was a village in the Viet-Cong–controlled border region of Bien Hoa and Long Khanh provinces, east of Saigon. There were straw-covered huts to our right and left. A small arch stood in the middle of our path; woven in its center was a five-pointed star made of straw. My escort stopped and pointed to it.

"The symbol of the Front," he said.

"An Arc de Triomphe," I said jokingly.

"Yes, it is an arch of triumph," he answered seriously. "It was put up after a victory of the Liberation Army over government troops."

We passed under the arch and entered a small clearing full of women and children who looked at us distrustfully. My escort explained lengthily who I was and seemed to calm the villagers somewhat. However, I again became an object of suspicion when I entered the huts and was shown the trenches and defense installations. The villagers did not like the interest I showed in their affairs.

I was introduced to the village chief. Nguyen Hoi was mayor of the community and leader of the local guerrilla unit. He was about thirty-five and, outwardly, scarcely different from the other peasants I had seen in Viet-Nam. But he was self-confident, his answers clear, his orders precise. When he spoke of the Americans—and he did often—his eyes darkened and his voice rose a pitch higher. Here he could afford to show his hatred.

He had been imprisoned by the government several times and told me that once—under Diem's regime—he had been tortured because he had insulted government soldiers. I asked what he had said. "I called them thieves when they tried to steal pigs after inspecting the village," he answered.

He proudly showed me the village fortifications. They were not particularly impressive, but I knew from experience how long a group of guerrillas could defend themselves in such trenches and foxholes. Barbed wire had been stretched in front of some of the trenches. "It's hard to get hold of barbed wire now," he said, and added cynically: "The black market in Saigon is always sold out. The Americans aren't keeping up the supplies." He told me that the village had been bombed recently and pointed to a trench that had caved in. It was covered by the splintered trunks of two coconut trees. "Nobody was hurt."

My escort rummaged through his brief case and came up with a piece of paper. It enumerated the damage done by bombings in 1965: 200,000 structures, it said, had been destroyed by bombs on South Vietnamese territory.

I was taken into a house—"our meeting hall, our school, our village administration, everything in one." I entered a room with some rough-hewn benches as its only furniture. The blue-red flag of the NLF hung from the wall. Beneath it was a hand-drawn poster listing all the victories of the rebel army. I read the names of Bien Hoa, Binh Gia, An Lao, Ap Bac, Binh Dinh, Pleiku. A chart hung beside it outlining the organizational structure of the village administration.

"Unfortunately, we don't have much educational material," my Saigon escort explained. "Cadres visit the village once or twice a month to hold classes." The teaching staff consists of five or six people, and usually includes one or two women. The education officials come with a set program to the village and stay several days, seldom more than a week. They have a variety of tasks, ranging from classes for the village children to holding political meetings.

I saw several children's school notebooks with the French word *Cahier* on the covers, printed in Saigon. Neat corrections had been made with red ink. "Since we can't buy ink for the pupils, we produce it ourselves," Nguyen Hoi explained. The class schedule of the village school was listed on the back of the notebook: writing, arithmetic, agricultural instruction, geography, history, and history of the South Vietnamese National Liberation Front—agitprop for elementary school pupils.

Usually, the education cadres bring the textbooks when they visit the villages. This village had some of its own schoolbooks: several volumes of poetry, readers, old French textbooks. I was astonished to find a biography of Napoleon among the books.

On a bench was a folder of song lyrics. "We sing these songs on meeting nights," he said. The folder included some old Vietnamese folk songs, but most were new Viet-Cong battle songs with such titles as "Brothers in Arms," "On the Way with Our Heroic Soldiers," "Defend Yourselves, Brothers." One song, "Brave Uniform Makers," began:

> Our fighters stand outside in sun and rain and bitter cold.
> We are making uniforms from our clothes so that our
> fighters will be courageous and kill the foe.
> You, warrior, fight at the front, and we promise we will give
> our best for you.
> Work faster, brothers and sisters, work faster.

Today, your uniforms are still in our busy hands. Tomorrow
they will be outside on the front.
Work faster, brothers and sisters, work faster.

Another song, "Youth in the Free Villages," is a summons
to rise up and "liberate our beloved homeland from the
terrible enemy."

The NLF cadres hold classes for adults as well. The
villagers are given agricultural advice, political indoctrination, and some military training. "Every village in the liberated zones fights along with the Front troops," my escort
said. "This village volunteered to produce baskets for
transporting rice." I was shown a hut piled with fifty baskets. They were made of split woven bamboo, and each
contained six to eight pounds of cooked rice. The baskets
are smeared with resin and have small lids. This preserves
the rice for a long time.

"A neighboring village produced 150 straw mats in two
months, a great record," Nguyen Hoi said proudly. I
asked what the mats were used for. "They are taken to the
cities and sold. We buy medicines for our wounded soldiers with the earnings," the guerrilla leader answered.
"Many Americans buy our mats and send them home as
souvenirs."

"Do the peasants retain part of the money?"

"No, their labor is voluntary."

Nguyen Hoi led me into another hut. A young woman
shooed her two small children away from the front steps
and disappeared with them behind a nearby shed. Several
homemade weapons lay in a recess of the room. One was
a slingshot gun, and the guerrilla leader showed me how it
worked. He stretched the rubber bands and aimed at a
palm tree about ninety feet away. The rubber thong

snapped forward, and the short iron arrow hit the tree trunk with a dull bang. I tried, but could not pull it out. "This arrow pierces a man's body," the guerrilla said as he pulled it out of the wood with a jerk.

A pistol-shaped piece of wood protruded from Nguyen Hoi's belt. He explained that it was used for training "as long as we didn't have real weapons." He reached for a piece of wood carved like a carbine. "This is also a practice weapon. We train the women with it and once they get hold of a real gun they know exactly what to do."

He took me into his house. Behind a woven wall were thin bamboo spikes, three to six feet long, with knife-sharp pointed ends. "We stick these bamboo spikes in the rice fields when our village is in danger. They are almost as effective as gun bullets. They are cut by the old people and the children."

Nguyen Hoi pulled a small, worn notebook out of his shirt. The yellowed, graph-lined pages were crowded with sketches of traps, pitfalls, and the like, with instructions for waging guerrilla warfare in neat writing. A girl from one of the education teams had prepared it for the villagers. I leafed through the notebook and found information on ambushes, sketches of weapons, instructions on making mines from old tin cans, drawings of tunnels and trenches, data on how to protect fortifications with bamboo spikes and traps, on how to manufacture foot traps, and the best ways of concealing them on paths and in rice paddies.

The Americans call the Viet-Cong bamboo spikes punji stakes. The spikes vary in size and are used for different purposes. Bamboo rods up to nine feet long are rammed into level ground where a helicopter might land. Helicopters trying to land on punji-stake fields have been greatly damaged by the iron-hard points. And I have seen men with frightful wounds, their thighs or lower bodies run through by the spikes.

Nguyen Hoi left to prepare a surprise he had promised me. He wanted to demonstrate the military discipline of his villagers.

I stayed behind with the Saigon official. "You can't imagine how these villagers are suffering," he said. "For years it has been practically impossible for them to work in the rice fields because they may be shot down, their crops confiscated, their houses burned." The Vietnamese had suddenly dropped the reserved attitude of the functionary: "It's not hard to understand why the people here hate the war and all those who force them to keep on fighting. But . . ." again he resumed his official tone, "but we will win."

The village was suddenly empty as if in response to some signal from the jungle. The children romping in front of the huts, the wives sitting on the mud steps, had all vanished. The silent village seemed gripped by the threat of danger which might fall from the sky or rise from the gray rice paddies. It was impalpable yet near.

A withered sheaf of rice stalks dangled beneath the low roof of Nguyen Hoi's hut. Discarded implements lay next to the well nearby. It was the only well in the settlement and the pride and joy of the villagers. A Soviet star, symbol of the Viet-Cong rebels, and the date "1964" had been chiseled into its gray concrete base. A guerrilla labor unit had helped the villagers build it during the period when the provincial cadre had adopted the slogan: "Better water for the villages."

Nguyen Hoi entered his hut. Its cracked walls were covered with black writing. He translated the inscriptions for me. They were the kind of propaganda slogans often found in the huts of Viet-Cong–controlled villages: "Youth leads the way," "We, the soldiers of the Liberation Front, are very brave"; a third motto read "Liberty and equality," only the word "fraternity" was missing.

The hut was filled with the smell of cold smoke. The single room contained a tall, elaborately carved wardrobe of the type sometimes found in expensive European homes. Here it served as a sort of shrine, the only visible reminder to the villagers of the period when the French still ruled Indochina. Perhaps some plantation owner had made a gift of it to the peasants; perhaps they had taken it when the French had to leave the country; perhaps its former owner had fallen in battle against the Viet-Minh.

Nguyen Hoi went out a back door into the glaring sunlight and turned to a narrow palm grove that surrounded the village. He moved cautiously along a hedge, eyes fixed to the ground like someone fearful of falling into a trap. He approached the trenches close to the tree line encircling the village. The peasants had labored for years at these trenches and the bunkers in front of their houses. They had originally been intended as a defense against the French, then against the Japanese, then plundering bands, and finally, when the villagers began to rebel against the government, their own countrymen. Now they served as defensive installations against the U.S. military machine.

These fortifications had been ruined repeatedly because bombs or mortar shells had hit them, because the peasants had been forced to destroy them, or simply because the soft earth had given way. Now a sixteen-year-old boy, Le Duy Can, squatted in one of the trenches. He had run to his post at the first alert, and there he sat, barefoot, clad only in short black pants and torn shirt, waiting.

Le Duy Can was a soldier and had been one, really, as far back as he could remember. There is no distinct time of which he can say: "That was before the war." His childhood flowed without transition into the harsh life of a guerrilla; he could recall just one break in his existence. A year ago he had been taken into the forest and, together with many youngsters his age, had lived for two months in a concealed camp where he received military training.

He had already fought for the guerrillas before that, as a spy, a guard, or a courier. Several times he had been ordered to carry rice to secret hideouts in the nearby forest. When his military training ended he returned to the village as a soldier of the NLF. He had brought back one other thing with him: the weapon that now rested on his bare knees. It was an old Mauser rifle. The rust-scarred bolt was stamped with the German imperial eagle and a small swastika beneath with the date 1939/41. The wooden gun stock had turned gray.

Nguyen Hoi leaped into the trench after testing the thick bamboo stalks that covered it at many points. The boy got up and moved to the side of the guerrilla chief. Neither said a word as they leaned against the trench wall. The boy placed his rifle on a parapet and both gazed out into the rice paddies.

The water was a shimmering gray; tiny rice shoots flickered above the surface. A palm tree grove rose some 200 yards away. Beyond it was the dark green line of the jungle. There, smoke clouds were rising. Above them circled a helicopter. It was too far away to hear the rattle of its rotor blades.

The village chief squinted and stared at the helicopter. Then he looked at the boy. Le Duy Can understood the glance, picked up his gun, pointed it toward the fields and aimed. It was a useless gesture. Even if the helicopter had come closer to the village, the chances of hitting it were slight. Le Duy Can knew this and so did Nguyen Hoi, but both were faithfully obeying the defense orders issued by the district cadre: "Weapons against planes."

Nguyen Hoi continued his tour of the trench around the village. Whenever danger threatened, the leader of the local guerrilla unit inspected the defense positions. Next, he reviewed his "self-defense unit" (the villages use the same term as the government hamlets). This consisted of six men. Then, he went to see about the women and children.

They had disappeared into the bunkers and tunnels at the first warning. These villagers had not been able to create an extensive system of tunnels to protect the peasants for hours from napalm bombs and artillery barrages. However, Nguyen Hoi had accomplished one thing in his four years as commander of the self-defense units: Almost every family had its own bunker, most of them right next to the dwellings. Some of these shelters were already connected by narrow tunnels. In a few years, this village, too, would have a full network of tunnels. "One time, government troops wanted to destroy the bunkers, but we said we needed them to preserve our rice and fruits," Nguyen

Hoi recalled. "They accepted our reasons after we gave them some small gifts, and they didn't touch the bunkers."

All the villagers had fled underground except for two old women, who had refused to leave their huts and squatted in the dark in front of their extinguished hearths. Those ordered to take cover were well hidden. "I've told the people to cover the bunkers with tools, implements, fruit, and even garbage. It's harder to camouflage huts in a village than it is out in the jungle," the chief said.

Nguyen Hoi pushed aside a basket used to dry meat and vegetables. Beneath was a dark, narrow hole. Nguyen Hoi crawled into it, and quickly disappeared also. I forced my way after him, my feet touching soft earth. A hand groped for me. A narrow, slanted shaft stretched about six feet underground, wide enough for two people, but impossible to stand in because of its steep angle. The entrance to the defense shelter was located at the center of the shaft. It, too, could be camouflaged by a bamboo-plaited cover. The unknowing observer would mistake the shaft for a garbage pit and never recognize it as the entrance to a bunker. The villagers would probably remain undetected even if the hamlet were temporarily occupied.

I crept through the opening into the cave. It was completely dark. Nguyen Hoi said something and was answered by a woman. There were two families, or at least two women and seven children, in the shelter. Their husbands and fathers were serving in Saigon's army.

"These woman are very poor," Nguyen Hoi said. "Their husbands deserted them. They left to make more money."

"You mean they weren't forced into the government army?" I asked.

"No, they volunteered."

"What will happen to them when they leave the army and want to return?"

"We will have to re-educate them," the guerrilla leader answered gently.

I had seen only seven men in this 200-family settlement and asked where the rest were.

"They are working," Nguyen Hoi answered. "Perhaps here—perhaps far away."

"What kind of work?"

"The same as ours," he said. "We no longer know how many men we have in the village. Perhaps ten, perhaps thirty, perhaps just seven," he continued in the darkness.

A child began crying, and a woman sought to calm it. I had been in the heat of the cave about twenty minutes, people breathing heavily around me. The sweat was streaming down my body; when I squeezed my way back into the open air, I was very tired.

Nguyen Hoi came up after me and carefully covered the shaft hole again. The bamboo basket he used, with its rotting vegetables and meat, resembled a gravestone. When I returned with him to the trench I saw an old peasant armed with a primitive gun that had obviously been produced in some jungle workshop. He stared out at the rice paddies over its barrel. Nguyen Hoi slowly, wearily, entered the trench.

What baffled me was the determination of these people to fight no matter how great the odds. I knew how little remained of such villages after being pounded for hours with high explosives and napalm. The people of this village knew that as well as I did, yet still they kept their resolve.

What gives these guerrillas their strength and their courage? I kept looking for the answer as long as I was in Viet-Nam; but there is no easy answer. I do not believe political arguments alone instill these simple peasants with their determination. It is not due to the NLF commissar, from whom many of them hear the word "Communism" for the first time. He is too clever to burden his countrymen with the confusing notions of Communist ideology. Nor are the peasants driven by terror alone to fight against their rulers and a more powerful enemy.

Unquestionably the Viet-Cong functionaries exert pressure on the peasantry, which fears its own leaders as much as it does the enemy. Yet this, too, is not the only reason for the peasants' determination. The political cadres of the Viet-Cong had to *convince* the people it was necessary to fight. Had they relied on force alone the revolt would probably have been crushed at the outset.

The peasants felt they were fighting for their own cause and interests. They knew (or at least believed they knew) they were struggling for themselves, not for the wishes of distant, feudal war lords, as they had been made to do in the past.

Desperate, landless peasants need nothing more than the belief that it is possible for them to defeat an enemy who hitherto seemed invincible. They have already gotten rid of their landlords, revolted against arrogant province chiefs and government troops. Cannot they also ultimately defeat the white, foreign enemy? The NLF cadres seem to have given them this conviction.

These poorly armed village guerrillas—who cannot even count on the support of regular Viet-Cong units—are not guided by profound political ideas. More likely, I believe, they have a feeling, an intuition, of the common strength latent in masses of people. Faith in the power of the common cause and hatred of the mighty are the motives driving the village guerrillas to fight. Certainly, a few defect, but those who have taken their stand have only the choice between different kinds of death. They are doomed and desperate and therefore have the nerve to leap at their enemy no matter how superior his strength. I recalled what the Chinese military writer, Sun Tzu, taught in 400 B.C.: "Leave an escape route open for the encircled enemy, else despair will make him fearless."

Nguyen Hoi and his guerrillas are not completely cut off by enemy soldiers, but they are caught in the deadly escalation of the Viet-Nam conflict. They have made up their minds—and they have no way out. It is the system under which they live that is more to blame for their situation than the Allied troops. However, they do not ask about the causes, they merely see the effects.

Nguyen Hoi picked up his weapon and leaned against the trench wall. His eyes searched the sky; then, he looked toward me and said: "Well, let the planes come if they want to." But now he appeared to relax. Le Duy Can turned around, laid down his gun, and stood beside Nguyen Hoi. The guerrilla chief lowered his weapon too and looked at me wearily.

"Over?" I asked.

"Over," he replied and climbed out of the trench. We returned to his hut.

The village came to life. The bunker covers opened and women and children crawled into the open air. They were all serious, silent, dirty. Not one of the children, who had spent more than an hour underground, spoke loudly.

"We have these air-raid drills once a week. It's necessary. Each must know exactly what he has to do—including the children," Nguyen Hoi said.

"Would you actually shoot if planes or helicopters flew over the village?" I asked.

"No. We have orders to shoot only under certain conditions," he said. "We can fire at reconnaissance planes or helicopters on scouting flights outside the village. If we attacked them from the village more planes would return. But, naturally, we defend ourselves when we are the target of an attack. Two years ago a fighter bomber was knocked down by guerrillas near Bien Hoa. So you see, we can fight back." A victory could still inspire him with faith two years afterward.

The war had obviously shaped his life. True, he worked in the fields, but infrequently. Besides running his village smoothly, he had the extra job of checking the trails to several neighboring villages. "The moment we see something unusual—more helicopters, more planes—we immediately report it to the higher cadres responsible for a number of villages," he explained. He had participated in several operations by large guerrilla groups but spoke of them reluctantly. "They were routine actions on the province border."

Sentinels patrolled the village outskirts day and night. "They are lookouts, and the women serve too, to warn us of planes and surprise attacks. Of course, the enemy has not dared to strike yet. But some nearby villages were attacked, quite suddenly, by small raiding parties. These groups operate exactly like our own. Sometimes they are dangerous," Nguyen Hoi commented.

I learned that commando groups had kidnaped guerrillas from two neighboring villages by night and shot them in front of the settlements about a year ago. In the following months the village chief had slept in a different place every night. "But the commando teams have discontinued their activity; we haven't heard any news about them for a long time," Hoi added.

My escort indicated it was time to leave. Nguyen Hoi and a young boy accompanied us to the road. Four guerrillas, looking like any other peasants, were waiting for us there. Again I had to admire the improvised but effective way the Viet-Cong organization operated.

I had felt relatively safe in the village. But here, in the open, in no-man's-land, where government troops or American planes might suddenly appear, I felt defenseless. Had a government patrol checked us, as a white man, I would not have had any chance of escape.

The men around me, who silently guided me down narrow trails, across canals and rice paddies, restored my confidence. I could see they were accustomed to long marches. I tried talking to them, but my escort had become very quiet. A couple of jets flew over us. Dull explosions sounded in the distance.

We reached the outskirts of Bien Hoa. I don't know how our guides succeeded in getting us there unnoticed. My escort took swift leave of me. He told me to visit him again in Saigon.

Four hours later I sat in a small bar on Hai Ba Trung street, drinking my fourth glass of lemonade. I was exhausted and tired. Two waifs came into the bar and shined the shoes of a young American. A waiter asked me if I wanted to order. His face was the face of a Vietnamese peasant.

Outside two armored personnel carriers rattled by, their sides covered with the mud of the rice paddies they had crossed in pursuit of "Charlies." A tall GI climbed off his stool, put his arm around a girl who barely came to his hips, and disappeared with her behind a curtain at the back of the bar. I paid and left.

Searchlights glowed on the Saigon River shore road. The pale fingers of light groped across the river and glided to the other bank. The Viet-Cong ruled there now that it was dark. Flares trembled on the horizon, then there were the flashes of more distant bombs. Flames sprang up from the east, from the direction of the village from which I had just returned.

II

The Struggle for the People

Everyone knows material resources in themselves are not the decisive factor in war. Whether one can fight on and conquer in this prolonged struggle depends on the aims and character of the war, on political, military, and geographical factors, and especially on the strength and inner attitude of the people.

Excerpt from a statement on the fifth anniversary of the NLF

NORTH VIET-NAM's General Giap has called the Viet-Nam conflict "the model of the people's total war." The country has become the testing ground for the clash between Peking's revolutionary Communism and the West's liberal-democratic philosophy. The people, not soldiers and armies, are the decisive factor in this war; and both revolution and counterrevolution are wooing them. The side that wins the people over—convinces and controls them—will be victorious.

Saigon seemed to have practically lost the war by 1961. At that point General Maxwell Taylor began to develop the idea of a special war against the Communist rebels. He still opposed direct intervention by American troops; the Korean War had convinced him that the United States should not again allow itself to be drawn into a conflict on the Asian mainland, and he cast about for other ways of reversing the struggle against the Communists.

251

The United States simply could not afford to let the Communists take over the country without a fight, so it decided to provide the Saigon government with everything it needed for victory over the Viet-Cong—except American troops. From 1955 to 1961 Washington had pumped over $2 billion into South Viet-Nam, but the money had disappeared in a morass of corruption and incompetence. Now, it was hoped, things would change: The conduct of the war was to be tightened and American control of financial aid made more effective.

The struggle on the civilian front was also to be intensified. An American economist, Dr. Eugene Staley, drew up a plan. After several visits to South Viet-Nam, he recognized that the first order of business was to free the peasants from Communist influence. They had to be given protection, and the revolutionary drive of the landless had to be satisfied by a program of social reform.

The Taylor-Staley Plan envisaged close cooperation between military and civil authorities and coordination of South Vietnamese and American activities. The war against the Communist rebels was to move into a new phase—political struggle.

Staley planned the creation of wide strips of unsettled areas, primarily along the Cambodian and Laotian borders. The guerrillas were to be driven into these pockets and then destroyed in massive military operations. Simultaneously, government "prosperity zones" were to be established with American aid in which the civilian population would be able to live safely under the protection of government troops. This scheme was meant to isolate the population from the influence of Communist agitprop teams.

Staley divided South Viet-Nam into three regions:

1. Yellow zones: Areas already under government control. These would be the first to receive large amounts of American aid.

2. Blue zones: Areas not directly influenced by the government. This was the no-man's-land in which both Saigon and Viet-Cong troops operated. The NLF had not yet consolidated its position in these districts to the point where the peasants could not be won back to the government.

3. Red zones: Areas controlled by the Viet-Cong. The first step in these territories would be to establish "yellow islands," from which the government's influence could gradually spread. Military actions would have priority over civil programs.

The Diem family originally opposed Taylor's plans, but on January 4, 1962, the Staley Plan became official policy. In all three zones—yellow, blue, and red—fortified centers, strategic hamlets, were to be built and the peasants resettled. The hamlets would be strongly defended: The villagers would receive military training, and regional troops—together with army units—would protect the countryside population. (The idea of fortified villages was not new; during the Indochina War and in Algeria, the French believed they were the key to military and political success. The French *agrovilles* and *camps de regroupement* resembled concentration camps more than they did peaceful settlements, however, and they were not at all successful.)

President Diem had already tried building strategic hamlets as strongholds against the guerrillas. He first called his strategic hamlets Camps of the Just Cause or "political reorientation centers." Between 2,000 and 6,000 people, preferably inhabitants of former Viet-Minh zones, were packed in each of these villages. In 1957, Diem built *agrovilles* (*Dinh Dien*). Up until 1961, 147 such villages were built, each for 500 to 1,000 persons. In 1959, the Saigon government—with American help—concentrated on establishing the first "prosperity zones" (*Khu tru mat*). This operation did not affect more than 100,000 people. Before the Staley Plan was set in motion, Diem sought to continue his policy of strategic hamlets (*Ap chien luoc*) but failed. Communist propaganda began comparing these villages to Auschwitz and Buchenwald before the United States had entered the picture and taken over their organization. The Communists insisted that Diem's pacification actions had caused the death of more than 300,000 people by 1961. The figure seems grossly exaggerated.

The United States thought it could do better. Within eighteen months, 116 "prosperity zones" with 15,000 strategic hamlets were to be established. Each village would contain 500 to 900 people. While existing villages in the thickly populated delta and coastal areas could be expanded and fortified, the inhabitants of the thinly settled provinces had to be concentrated—in other words, they had to leave their old homes and be resettled.

The Staley Plan may not have been bad as a blueprint. Its basic premise was that the peasants wanted to resist Communist infiltration but were powerless to do so. Unquestionably, many peasants wanted security from the Viet-Cong because they knew that the moment they fell into their hands or submitted, the government would strike back. Moreover, they hoped to gain economic benefits—

especially from the Americans—that the Viet-Cong could never offer.

But the Americans were caught in a dilemma. They could not satisfactorily explain to the peasants the reasons for the resettlement program, not even to those who were progovernment. And without the agreement of the villagers, the operation was doomed. The peasants did not want to abandon their villages or to endure the hardships of relocation.

More than 80 per cent of the South Vietnamese cultivate the land. The peasants are bound by a thousand ties to their soil, even though, in many cases, they do not own it. Both the NLF and the Saigon government know how strong these bonds are. One of the Viet-Cong's greatest problems is to organize units that will operate in several provinces. Most guerrillas refuse to leave their villages and families when asked to join such groups. The NLF leadership frankly admitted that it had problems with soldiers assigned far from their native regions, and it had to engage in a propaganda campaign to make "service for the homeland" in "distant provinces" palatable.

I once discussed this with an NLF official. "Why do you think our troops so rarely leave their dead and wounded behind?" he asked.

"To hide the number of casualties from the enemy," I answered. He said that was true, but also gave a second reason.

"Before our soldiers begin a battle, we must often promise that we will not leave them on the field if they are killed. We must agree to take their bodies with us and bury them as near to their villages as possible."

American psychological warfare experts have told me

that the increasing number of dead left on battlefields by the Viet-Cong in the last few months is not so much proof that the U.S. troops are waging war successfully, but a sign of some disorganization within the NLF due to the massive use of troops.

One of the peculiarities of this war is the way government soldiers take their wives and children along with them. Even today families often live in military camps or right near the men. An important reason for the U.S. Special Forces' success in organizing the *montagnards* into hard-fighting troops was because they permitted the tribal warriors to bring their families into the camps. At the battle of Plei Me, in addition to the fifteen-man team of the U.S. Special Forces and 400 *montagnards,* over 200 women and children lived in the camp's bunkers—and often the trenches—and many are still living there.

The Vietnamese peasant is bound to his village, and when he dies he wants to be buried in his field or in front of his hut or village, in his soil. Vietnamese often are ancestor worshipers, and in many regions, fields and groves are crowded with the small pyramids built over graves.

However, the success of the Staley Plan demanded that the peasants abandon their villages. The depopulated settlements were burned down, and the crops destroyed to deprive the guerrillas of hiding places and food. Frequently the peasants had nothing but their personal belongings when they moved into the strategic hamlets.

When peasants resisted resettlement—this happened often—they were driven out of their villages by force. The Vietnamese Army did not always use humane methods. The ambitious American program was a disaster before it really got started. Other unfortunate measures, too, damaged the reputations of the Saigon government and the United States. In some cases, villages were burned down when their inhabitants put up determined resistance to resettlement. Peasants or village elders who opposed resettlement were often executed by government troops to serve as examples. Both unoccupied and occupied areas were poisoned. Rice fields, plantations, and jungles were sprayed with chemicals to destroy plant life—a measure that has done the United States tremendous harm throughout the nonwhite world. The chemicals were not injurious to man and beast in most cases—but this is hard to explain to a peasant who sees his meager crop wither after it has been poisoned.

Nonlethal gases—such as tear gas—were also used. I have seen unconscious women and children dragged out of tunnels and bunkers into which tear-gas bombs had been thrown. The effect on the peasants was frightful. Several times peasants who had been brought under control this way tried to flee, screaming. They believed that the troops wanted to gas them to death.

Communist agitprop teams had an easy job convincing them that the Americans intended "to exterminate the entire Vietnamese people in a horrible way with gas." NLF propaganda alleges that 320,000 hectares of arable land were devastated by chemicals in 1963, 500,000 hectares in 1964, and 700,000 hectares in 1965. It also says that 50 per cent of the cattle were destroyed and "several hundred thousand people" killed or their health seriously damaged. Thousands still believe this. Prince Sihanouk's minister of information in Cambodia told me he was convinced the Americans wanted to gas the South Vietnamese people to death in enormous concentration camps.

Laotian General Ma knew "for a fact" that the Americans in Viet-Nam had already gassed close to a million peasants. None of this is true, but when relatively educated Asians believe such rumors, how difficult it is to explain to a peasant the difference between chemical spray, tear gas, and lethal gas! Defoliating the jungle with chemical sprays to deny the guerrillas protection, or destroying crops to deprive them of food may have seemed worthwhile to the U.S. military, but no aid program, whatever its size, can easily restore the reputation the United States has thus lost in Viet-Nam. The use of such weapons may have been militarily justified, but given the political aspects of the war—and its effects on the nonwhite world—their use can only have been counterproductive.

I once asked a U.S. Operations Mission official in Saigon why Americans believed they could win over the peasant at the same time they were ravaging his crops and razing his village. His reply was: "The United States pays compensation for all damages—down to the last dollar and beyond." I believe the idea that payment of money can solve political and social problems reveals a profound misunderstanding of the issues that today agitate the nonwhite world.

The Vietnamese peasants were promised protection, security, and economic aid in the strategic hamlets. What actually happened was that the U.S. supplied tools, clothing, food, medicines, and money. The peasants were compensated for the damages they had suffered during resettlement, but individual sums rarely came to more than 1,500 piasters. They received a daily cash allowance for themselves and their families as long as they did not work, and they could expect a degree of medical care.

In 1962, a Vietnamese peasant earned about 1,000 piasters a month, the price of about 100 kilograms of rice.
From this, he had to pay between 200 and 400 piasters
in defense taxes, 4 piasters for the government flag everyone in a strategic hamlet had to own, 50 piasters for a uniform, 30 piasters for the hamlet administration, and so on.
He had to undergo premilitary training and was assigned
to semiregular units. He had to wear a uniform: adult
men—blue jacket and white pants; youth—white jackets
and white pants; women—white jackets and black pants;
old women—black jackets and white pants. To the resettled people these measures were a form of tyranny and
persecution.

Government representatives started a program of political purges. Those whose families lived in guerrilla areas
were officially ordered to join relatives in strategic hamlets within three months. If they did not comply, the people in the hamlets were punished. The hamlets were
combed for Communists; anyone suspected of having collaborated or maintained contact with the Viet-Cong was
arrested, jailed, and often executed.

Life in the hamlets was strictly controlled. The people
were provided with identity papers. Some were required
for moving about inside the hamlet, others for moving
about outside. A guard was kept on entrance and exit
gates. They were open from 6:00 A.M. to 7:00 P.M. No
one was allowed to leave or enter the village during the
night.

The Americans had turned over implementation of the
Staley Plan to Vietnamese authorities. In line with the
motto, "We can do for Viet-Nam only what the Saigon
government wants to do," U.S. experts served as advisers.

This was another basic defect, which caused the plan to misfire.

Many officials simply did not grasp the strategy of the resettlement project and the strategic hamlets. They were given a task that called for a knowledge of psychological problems, a great deal of sympathy and self-sacrifice. But the Vietnamese officials considered their status a privilege; they were not servants of the people, but representatives of an authoritarian state. Americans who called for a quick change in this attitude were ridiculed. They had to look on helplessly while one mistake followed another.

Their hamlet jobs offered most Vietnamese officials a chance to make easy money too. The Americans paid big bonuses to province and district chiefs for every hamlet erected; in addition, they bore the costs of resettlement, provided the means of transportation, handed over millions of dollars—with little control over the way the money was spent. It was a field day for corruption.

Peasant housing was either shoddy or not built at all. The promised compensation money was not paid out; unjustified deductions and taxes were imposed. Food supplies and other aid were partly or totally kept back. "A few people were driven together, a roll of barbed wire was thrown over their heads and the strategic hamlet was finished," a *New York Times* article said in 1963, accurately describing what was wrong with the program.

U.S. experts intervened without much avail when they saw the Staley Plan foundering. Revolts occurred in many hamlets—and the Viet-Cong were not always behind them. The people tried to break out; they held demonstrations; in some cases they set fire to their own hamlets. The result was always the same: harsher punishment and penalties.

At first, the Viet-Cong had been disturbed by Dr. Staley's sweeping plan. But they soon realized that the strategic hamlets did not represent a danger. Instead, they offered new possibilities for undermining the prestige of the government and its supporters. The villages became favorite targets of attacks; the guerrillas forcefully demonstrated to the peasants that Saigon was incapable of defending them. One village was destroyed or attacked thirty-six times in one year. In the same province, 105 of the 117 strategic hamlets were attacked in a seven-month period ending November, 1962. The guerrillas destroyed 547 villages in the delta. According to NLF figures, over 2,000 fortified hamlets were attacked more than once throughout South Viet-Nam in 1962. More than 625 miles of barbed wire and palisade entanglements surrounding the hamlets were destroyed. In June, 1962, guerrillas in the central highlands ravaged 139 strategic hamlets, 75 of them more than twice.

The guerrillas followed one consistent tactic in all these assaults: The peasant's life was spared whenever possible; government soldiers and officials alone were the victims. "The peasants must not be killed," a guerrilla order said. "The fortifications, above all the barbed-wire entanglements, must be destroyed."

The Viet-Cong method reaped a double harvest. Many Vietnamese officers refused to serve in the threatened hamlets, and the villages' defense units deteriorated. Also, the village garrisons believed the peasants were betraying them to the Communists—which was sometimes true. New repressions and reprisals resulted, since Saigon authorities were convinced that peasants spared during a Viet-Cong assault must be working hand in glove with the guerrillas.

The peasants became bitter. They had expected the government to protect and help them, but they were having a harder time defending themselves from the guerrillas in many of the poorly fortified hamlets than they had in their native settlements. In addition, they were exposed anew —and even more oppressively—to all the abuses of a corrupt government they had never trusted but to whose side they could conceivably have been won. "Anyone unlucky enough to end up in a badly managed strategic hamlet, who was not yet a Viet-Cong supporter, inevitably turned into one there," a French owner of a plantation east of Saigon told me.

The plan had been to erect 15,000 strategic villages in all South Viet-Nam within eighteen months. "Outposts of freedom in the heart of Communist-ruled territory," President Diem's brother, Nhu, had phrased it. In April, 1963, fourteen months after the program had been launched, Radio Saigon reported that 5,917 hamlets had been completed—a figure not accepted by even the most optimistic Americans. Probably no more than 2,500 fortified villages existed in South Viet-Nam that resembled Staley's model.

Staley's plan was dropped around the time of Diem's overthrow. The first and—until now—last real attempt to rally the population in a massive and effective program for all Viet-Nam had failed.

In the meantime, the course of events had outstripped both the Staley Plan and General Taylor's thesis of a special antiguerrilla war. The general, who had opposed the involvement of American ground troops in Asia, is today a strong proponent of escalation. The guerrillas are to be forced to their knees by the relentless blows of concentrated military power.

The expansion of the U.S. military presence in South

Viet-Nam was accompanied by new, large aid programs for the civil population. They are truly impressive—but their influence on the war's outcome is probably slight. The economy is in such a catastrophic state after seven years of war that all the aid programs can do is prevent total economic collapse.

A screaming woman tried to break through a heavy police cordon but was pushed back. Her cries, and those of her children, were almost drowned out by the crowd. In an area cleared by the police, a blindfolded man stood bound to a post. An execution squad marched into position before him as cameras flashed. Again the woman tried to break through the police lines. Two policemen held her firmly by the arms so she could not avoid seeing her husband die.

A special South Vietnamese court had condemned him to death a few days before, on March 7, 1966. Now, in the center of Saigon he was being publicly executed, as an example. He was the first and practically the only victim of the campaign started by Premier Ky to wipe out corruption.

The executed man had been a Chinese millionaire. Ta Vinh had carried on a thriving textile business in Saigon-Cholon. Fast deals and speculation had made him rich in a short time. During his trial, he was accused of trying to bribe government officials. Actually, Ta Vinh had offered two policemen, who had come to arrest him, $1,500 if they would let him escape. His main crime was that he had tried to transfer $20,000 to secret bank accounts in Hong Kong and Tokyo. By his own confession, Ta Vinh had made a profit of more than $300,000 in textile speculations between November, 1965, and March, 1966. Ta Vinh's offense was no different than that of thousands of other Vietnamese war profiteers, but he had a fatal stroke of bad luck—the government chose to make an example of him. The reason, obviously, was that he did not have the right connections. Besides, he was Chinese, and nobody in Saigon likes the Chinese very much.

Corruption is one of the many outgrowths of the economic, social, and military crises that are convulsing South Viet-Nam. Beneath the surface prosperity, South Viet-Nam is suffering from the steady rise in prices of consumer goods and the constant depreciation of its currency. (Food prices rose by 49.5 per cent between December 1, 1964, and December 1, 1965, according to the Saigon Office for Statistics.) The peasants suffer most from this, and many are now totally impoverished. Salaries of the military and high government officials are regularly raised to match new price levels, while peasant incomes continue to sink.

The number of people who are doing really well is small. The peasantry, the tiny middle class, and the workers in the cities are hardly benefiting from the sudden boom. The consequences, of course, are discontent and injustice. The beneficiaries, of course, are the Communists.

South Viet-Nam exported rice up until a few years ago, 250,000 tons in 1960, 100,000 tons in 1964. Today it must import this staple—more than 200,000 tons in 1966. Harvests have rapidly declined because of the war, and not even price increases have been able to compensate the peasants for their losses. Prices are set by the merchants in the city; the peasants have no voice in the matter.

U.S. economic experts have expressed satisfaction because they believe they have succeeded in fixing and controlling the prices of some consumer goods. This may be true in theory. The official price for a can of condensed milk was 16 piasters in February, 1966. Theoretically, every family could buy one can daily with its ration card. But, when I checked the situation in Ba Lieu, a provincial capital in the delta about 125 miles south of Saigon, the police chief responsible for price control said that a can of condensed milk cost 19, not 16, piasters. In fact, no store sold it for less than 30 piasters. The profiteers are the merchants, a small layer of people who are raking in millions in the wake of the Southeast Asian crisis.

Corruption is one of the most effective weapons the Communists have against the Saigon government. It strikes the United States as well. Official U.S. agencies calculate that more than 20 per cent of the goods landed in Saigon's port is stolen. It is even worse in Danang. A U.S. Marine Corps general said in the spring of 1966 that in this central Vietnamese port city as much as 50 per cent of all cargoes, except for food and ammunition, disappeared. A large part of the stolen goods is resold to the Communists, who use it themselves or re-export it back to South Viet-Nam through other Asian countries at a high profit.

A British businessman reported to the heads of the U.S. aid program in Saigon that Communist agents in Hong Kong had offered Louisiana rice for sale. The sacks were stamped with clasped hands, the symbol of American economic aid. The rice had been smuggled out of South Viet-Nam and resold in Hong Kong to Cambodian customers.

A South Vietnamese Army unit received a large quantity of cement for building bunkers. The sacks bore two markings: one was the American aid symbol of clasped hands, covered over by a stenciled inscription—"Made in North Viet-Nam." The cement had been stolen from American aid supplies, sent to Cambodia, and resold there to South Viet-Nam. It had been paid for a second time with American aid funds.

The flourishing Vietnamese trade in cinnamon is totally corrupt. Cinnamon grows mainly in Viet-Cong–controlled areas, yet is exported on an increasing scale from South Viet-Nam; it hardly appears in the official balance of trade. An investigation revealed that Vietnamese officials were buying the cinnamon from the Viet-Cong. They certified that the cinnamon came from government-controlled regions and received export licenses. The officials collected one dollar for every kilogram of cinnamon, but the Communists profited most; they were paid for it with American aid money.

It has been estimated that about 60 per cent of American economic aid—which comes to more than $800,000 a day—is embezzled through transactions of this type; more than 50 per cent of all the money sent by the free world to South Viet-Nam flows back to private bank accounts in the West. The Ky government has done little to stop this corruption except publicize anticorruption programs and laws and promise radical changes. It cannot afford to upset the war lords and province chiefs, officers, and high officials.

At the end of November, 1965, the Ky government announced it had fired lieutenant colonels Pham Ding Chi and Nguyen Ngoc Diep, chiefs, respectively, of Binh Tuy and Ba Xuyen provinces. The real reasons for their sudden dismissals leaked out slowly.

Two U.S. aid officials in Binh Tuy resigned. They said, in an interview, they could no longer stand by and watch American aid being abused. As province chief, Lieutenant Colonel Chi represented both military and civil authority; he also supervised the entire relief program for refugees from the guerrilla areas. Refugee relief for Binh Tuy Province amounted to more than $600,000 up to October, 1965. It was charged that the province chief had pocketed more than 50 per cent of the aid money—at least $300,000.

It was a delicate situation for the U.S. mission in Saigon. Its officials usually close their eyes in such cases. But the Colonel Chi affair had become a public scandal. However, Chi enjoyed excellent relations with top government officials and could call the premier his friend. Ky came to the defense of the provincial boss and declared that the Western press had slandered him.

U.S. officials investigated the charges against Chi and discovered that he had actually embezzled $300,000 and more. They threatened to cut off all relief for Binh Tuy Province if Chi was not immediately disciplined. Saigon bowed; Chi was ousted, recalled to the capital, and promoted to full Colonel.

Lieutenant Colonel Diep was guilty of the same offenses. He, too, was dismissed from office, shifted to Saigon, and promoted "for his outstanding service in the struggle against Communism."

"What can we do?" a USOM official said. "If we crack down on all the cases of embezzlement and corruption, we'd have to fire the whole Vietnamese officer corps and half the government officials. Who would be left to carry on the war?" Obviously, he could barely stomach the extent of the corruption. "Theoretically, the Reds can buy everything from us or our Vietnamese friends. They can equip their entire army on the black market. Go find out for yourself."

I did. A brand-new Colt AR-15 rifle cost between $60 and $90 "retail"; a box of 25 rifles cost between $1,000 and $1,300. Machine guns sold at $200 each. An 81-mm. mortar, used, did not cost more than $120; a complete American combat uniform, with steel helmet and jump boots, cost $20 to $30; a carton of American Army rations cost $15.

Rising prices and inflation are one of the major problems of the South Vietnamese civil authorities. Finance Minister Tran Van Kiem told me that he saw no possibility of stopping them. "The piaster will continue to depreciate as long as American dollars flow into the country uncontrolled and as long as we fail to stabilize the economy. I know that 80 per cent of the population is suffering from the depreciation, but I can't do anything about it."

It was estimated that 300,000 Americans in South Viet-Nam would spend about $200 a month per capita in 1966. This comes to $60 million a month—$720 million annually. A large part of this is spent on entertainment. Hotels, shopkeepers, restaurant and bar owners expect to make more than ever. Consumer goods will become more expensive, and social differences will widen.

The owner of a second-class Saigon hotel told me that he makes more than $10,000 a month; I think he was greatly understating his earnings. His guests were American officers and soldiers, and he could "ask any price I want to" for his rooms. He had previously been a post office official earning $700 annually, a good income for a Vietnamese civil servant.

I spoke to a strikingly beautiful Vietnamese girl of 19, a native of Saigon, who had been a hostess in a bar for a year. She said she had been a student before that. The girl's job was to talk with customers and get them to buy "whisteas"—slang for whisky and tea. A glass of this "come on" drink cost 165 piasters and the girl received a 50 per cent share of her total sales. She earned over 2,000 piasters a day, 50,000 piasters a month, which at the official rate of exchange comes to about $5,000. "Madame Nhu banned prostitution in Viet-Nam," she said laughing. "She didn't have to. Most of the girls here make so much as hostesses that they would be crazy to go to bed with the men too."

GI dollars circulate uncontrolled and benefit a small part of the population, but free-world aid is designed to help the country as a whole. Twenty-seven countries have made commitments to give South Viet-Nam economic support. West Germany, England, Japan, and Canada, along with the United States, are the major contributors of development aid. Western aid is affecting every sphere of life; schools and hospitals are being built, agricultural programs developed, and modest industrial plans initiated. More than 200,000 Vietnamese workers are employed on gigantic American construction projects.

An attempt is being made to rebuild destroyed villages; there is an army of refugees to be cared for. More than 1 million people have fled the guerrilla regions since the start of the war, and the stream of refugees has swollen again in recent months. Yet, all these measures are not much help to the people in coping with the real hardships of the war, rising prices and inflation.

"Who controls whom in South Viet-Nam?"

The American spread several maps in front of him.

"Here's Charlie," he said in his soft voice. He pointed to the big red patches that covered the map of South Viet-Nam. "Here we are," he said, indicating yellow areas that extended mainly around Saigon and along the coast. "And here are the both of us." His finger moved over several green, crosshatched points that seemed to divide the red and yellow regions. Suddenly he pushed the maps aside. He bowed his head and stared at me: "Everything you've seen here is wrong. It simply doesn't make sense . . . we can go where we want and so can Charlie. Everybody controls everybody else. Yet nobody can control anybody or anything."

The man giving me this unusual explanation was Douglas Pike, one of the most intelligent and experienced Americans in South Viet-Nam, an expert on all questions pertaining to the Viet-Cong. "When none of us even knew where Viet-Nam was located, he was already interested in the VC, the way others are interested in Indians or chameleons," a friend of his once told me.

The data Douglas Pike has collected on the Viet-Cong fill an enormous file cabinet. "Things are tough for us because the guerrillas are everywhere and can move everywhere. True, some things have changed now—but we have to start over with the civic program from the very beginning."

The Viet-Cong controls about 60 per cent of South Viet-Nam. Around 7 million South Vietnamese are more or less subject to its direct influence. Its armed units and cadres are everywhere. If the NLF leadership wanted to, it could cut off the supply of electricity to Saigon and other large cities, blow up the water mains, and cripple transportation —with the exception of air traffic. Any time they want the guerrillas could block all traffic on Saigon River, and even the American Embassy in Saigon lies within range of their mortars.

But while the insurgents control about half of South Viet-Nam's population, the NLF's membership is comparatively small; it probably does not exceed 700,000. The membership of the People's Revolutionary Party is even smaller, perhaps 100,000. Three million Vietnamese live in a no-man's-land, between fronts that really do not exist, in areas neither government troops nor the Viet-Cong occupy.

The government controls around 5 million South Vietnamese, and real want does not exist in the areas where these people live: the coastal regions, many parts of the delta, and the cities. American aid, for obvious reasons, flows primarily into the territories where the government seems to have established its authority. Those who suffer most from the war are the peasants in the no-man's-land and the guerrilla territories.

In a refugee camp near Chu Lai, I talked to an old peasant who had fled from a guerrilla region. His only explanation for flight was: "We simply didn't have anything more to eat." Another man, in his thirties, said he had run away because they wanted to evacuate him from his village; the Viet-Cong leaders expected an American attack and decided to concentrate the peasants in several poorly fortified villages and let them defend themselves there. It was the Staley Plan in reverse.

The ability to move about freely in their own regions— plus the support of the population, which provides them with lodging and food—were among the sources of guerrilla strength in the first years of the war. But this advan-

tage was lost as the war expanded. The peasants living in
no-man's-land often refused to take in and feed large guerrilla units because they feared reprisals and bombing attacks. Although American bombings in South Viet-Nam
are not as effective as many believe—about three-quarters
of all bombs crash somewhere in the jungle without even
sending up a smoke cloud—such attacks are powerful psychologically.

The civil population suffers far more from the bombs
than the guerrillas do, for the Viet-Cong is trained and accustomed to living a spartan and dangerous existence. The
Viet-Cong can retreat to hideouts in the dense rain forests,
but the peasants cannot escape the planes; their villages
are easy targets and many American pilots prefer to unload
their bombs on visible objectives than drop them somewhere in the jungle.

By mid-1966, more than 100,000 houses or huts had
been destroyed from the air; by the end of 1966, the number will probably have reached 200,000. In other words,
about one-fifth of all South Vietnamese housing will have
been razed. Seventy per cent of the destruction is in the
"liberated zones" of the NLF.

"I don't know the extent of civilian losses in the liberated zones," an NLF official in Phnom Penh said to me.
"But I know they are very great." American statisticians
are not any more precise. It is estimated that since the beginning of the war, 600,000 people have died, more than
half of them civilians. The number of wounded civilians
is certainly even higher.

There are no more than 200 native-born physicians in
all of Viet-Nam. The American medical programs are
truly generous, but they are inadequate. They cannot

take care of the hundreds of thousands injured by the war. The situation of the peasants in guerrilla areas is particularly serious. Medical services are practically nonexistent there, and thousands of people who need not die do, under the most wretched conditions.

The war has afflicted the fields and soil just as much as it has the hamlets and villages, because the Americans are using sprays on a wider scale now to defoliate the jungle and destroy the food sources of the guerrillas. In many areas crops have declined by 50 to 70 per cent. At the same time, the Viet-Cong keeps demanding greater tributes in produce and money from the peasants.

The guerrillas have expanded their army too. Their combat units are larger than ever, and food and supplies have become real problems for them. Previously they could live off the villages; today, the "rice taxes" are inadequate because of the poor and destroyed crops. Besides, the Americans have captured tens of thousands of tons of rice in Viet-Cong supply caches, most of them underground bunkers. This has been a serious blow to the Liberation Army.

A refugee from the village of Xa Nham reported an incident that explains the problem. A group of NLF cadres entered the village. They were accompanied by a young woman who had been appointed administrator of the district rice depot. The group leader ordered the villagers to assemble. He stood under the blue-red flag of the NLF, and a banner fluttered behind him. "You are all good patriots," his speech began. "You all want the victory of the people." His companions voiced their agreement. The peasants said nothing.

"Until now you have worked and lived under the protection of the Liberation Army. You have paid your taxes and received land in return, land which you previously had to cultivate for the landlords. The Liberation Front Army is now beginning the final struggle for victory. All forces must be united. Every man, woman, and child fights on our side."

The peasants were still quiet; they had heard these speeches often. The leader continued: "The People's Army needs weapons to crush the enemy, and it needs strength in order to fight. That is why we must ask you to increase your efforts, to double them, to contribute even more to the people's victory." At the end of his speech, the official announced that the rice tax would have to be raised from 40 per cent to 60 per cent. His escorts searched the village for secret rice caches. They departed with four sacks, which the peasants themselves had to carry to the depot.

The refugee's story resembled those of thousands of other peasants who had streamed into the camps from guerrilla regions after the large-scale refugee operation, the Open Arms program had started. They had not fled because they had suddenly been converted to the cause of the government or the United States, but because they wanted deliverance from bitter poverty.

"We'll smoke Charlie out and then starve him to death. There's no other way of getting at the little yellow devils," an American Air Force colonel said to me. Until now, it is not "Charlie" whom the U.S. troops have smoked out and starved, but mainly the peasants in the guerrilla zones.

12

The Ho Chi Minh Trail

The Communist transports no longer roll south on a narrow trail but on a boulevard through the jungle.

GENERAL WILLIAM C. WESTMORELAND
March, 1966

T HE CLOUDS from the explosion billowed up between the trees, as the fighter plane twisted into the sky. The pilot flew a wide loop, turned the plane downward, and plunged to within a few yards of the treetops. Two more 500-pound bombs exploded with a muffled thud. A second plane dived, then a third. The bombs clicked out from under their wings and burst.

The fighter planes skimmed over the ground away from the target, following the curve of a narrow valley, then returned to the bombed area. A small section of road was visible between white scraps of smoke and dark evergreen trees. The red earth was clearly distinguishable from the brush and foliage. Flames flickered from the dry forest, and the brush began to burn. But the road for which the bombs had been intended remained undamaged.

Squadron 765, commanded by Lieutenant Chanh, had not completed its mission. Its bombs had failed to hit the road, a source of trouble for South Vietnamese and American military and political officials, the legendary trail through the Indochinese rain forests, the Communist military highway to the battlefields of South Viet-Nam—the Ho Chi Minh Trail.

I flew on this bombing strike against the jungle trail in December, 1965, when Washington and Saigon were still denying ever having bombed the Communist military highway in Laos and Cambodia. Since then the American Military Command in South Viet-Nam, Lieutenant General Nguyen Van Thieu, and Air Marshal Nguyen Cao Ky have admitted that for years American, Vietnamese, and Laotian bombers have been attacking the Viet-Cong supply trails.

As the fighting in South Viet-Nam grows more intense, the trail has become a major military issue, perhaps a key one in determining the war's outcome. The flow of troops, weapons, and ammunition from the North to the South, through Laos, swells from month to month and invests the struggle of U.S. troops against the guerrillas and the North Vietnamese Army with what Defense Secretary Robert McNamara has described as a "quasi-conventional" character.

The first transports from the North started as long ago as 1959. Once Hanoi had decided to support and strengthen the guerrilla war in South Viet-Nam, the first Communist combat units—Viet-Minh veterans, who had fled the South to North Viet-Nam after 1954—started returning. These groups, which soon became the core of the Viet-Cong Army, crossed the 17th Parallel by two main routes: down the South China Sea in fishing boats, junks, and freighters, or through the mountainous jungles of eastern Laos on foot, elephant, and bicycle. They used old paths through the mountains, former colonial routes, and trails through the jungle that had been constructed during the Indochina War. They followed the route that the French had first called the Ho Chi Minh Trail. During the first Viet-Nam War, the trail had served merely as a line of communication for Communist couriers and small combat units. However, the men around General Vo Nguyen Giap were aware of its strategic importance and began making fuller use of it. The Ho Chi Minh Trail runs through territory that in popular fancy once seemed to be a dreamlike tropical landscape of dense forests, rice paddies, palm groves, straw-covered huts, and golden pagodas. In fact, more than 70 per cent of the country is covered by thick jungle, and in the central highlands of Viet-Nam and in Laos there are mountains rising to more than 6,000 feet. The landscape is often savage and sparsely settled, occupied by mountain tribes, many of them still living in the stone age. The jungles are almost impenetrable primeval forests; the mountains, steep and rocky. The trackless, barely explored country begins at the Chinese border and extends 750 miles to Viet-Nam's southern provinces—a natural area for effective guerrilla warfare.

The French colonial rulers could not control this region. Saigon's troops and the Laotian Army have not done any better. The U.S. camps in the highlands are nothing more than small islands in an enormous sea that has still not been accurately charted.

The trail played a lesser role in the Indochina War because the major fighting took place in North Viet-Nam. It made military history for the first time in the fall of 1953 and the spring of 1954. Before the battle of Dien Bien Phu, Viet-Minh troops pushed down the trail into South

Viet-Nam and dealt crushing blows to elite French units. Even while the decisive battle of the "small district town on the border"—the Vietnamese name for Dien Bien Phu —raged in May, 1954, Giap succeeded in tying up French troops in South Viet-Nam's central highlands. Without exception the Viet-Minh soldiers reached the South via the jungle trails. After the Indochina War, the region through which the trail runs remained a no-man's-land.

The Pathet Lao guerrillas then occupied eastern Laos. The Laotian Communists picked up where their comrades from North Viet-Nam had left off. They began improving the trail. The occupants of villages along the way were obliged to maintain the route, widen it, and construct new sections. Work gangs began building road extensions through the rain forests in 1958.

The Communists controlled the trail from the little town of Tchepone in eastern Laos, just twenty miles away from the 17th Parallel. Tchepone became the first large way station for cadres and guerrilla fighters trained in North Viet-Nam, who were already infiltrating the South. Until 1963, Soviet and North Vietnamese planes dropped supplies for the troops of the "Red prince," Souphanouvong, and the security units of the Viet-Cong and North Vietnamese Army stationed along the trail.

But the airdrops soon had to be called off. Several airfields still exist along the trail and are occasionally used. But flights to the Ho Chi Minh Trail are too risky since American, South Vietnamese, and Laotian fighter planes started their regular patrols and began to bomb the jungle trails.

I had trouble when I first tried to get permission to go along on a bombing mission along the trail. General Thao

Ma looked at me suspiciously. The thirty-three-year-old head of the Laotian Air Force leaned back in a wicker chair and noisily sipped a soft drink. A few young pilots leaned against a bunk, one of them lightly plucking a guitar. In the next room, a portable radio played American jazz; on the veranda of the small barracks—the command center of the Laotian Air Force in Savannaketh—a couple of lieutenants were enjoying themselves killing a giant centipede.

"Excuse me—we don't have glasses," the general said as he finished his soda and threw the bottle to the ground. He wiped his hands and studied my press card again. My comment that Austria was not Australia, but a small neutral country in the heart of Europe, had aroused the general's suspicion. I had a hard time convincing him Austria did not lie behind the Iron Curtain, that I was neither a Russian nor an American agent. Not even a reference to the Kennedy-Khrushchev summit meeting in Vienna, at which the fate of Laos had been discussed, seemed to satisfy the general.

I changed my tactics. "There are people in Europe who simply refuse to believe the trail exists." A fist crashed on the table; the general jumped up and stood squarely before me. "We'll prove to you that the trail exists," he snarled. The man with the guitar kept playing. One of his comrades gave me a friendly nod. The radio was now playing Gershwin's "Summertime." The lieutenants outside had finished off the centipede and were nailing it to the door of General Ma's office.

Twelve hours later I was sitting in a T-28 rolling down the sandy runway of the Savannaketh airport. Savannaketh, on the banks of the Mekong, is the second largest city in Laos, and the headquarters of the Laotian Air Force. Aircraft attacking the Ho Chi Minh Trail take off from there. The combat order for our three-plane squadron was to bomb a jungle road near Ban Bac, a small village on the trail, and to attack a large assembly area on the road near the village of Chavane in southern Laos.

Lieutenant Chanh, the pilot, opened the throttle, and soon the broad ribbon of the Mekong disappeared behind us. The squadron reached Tchepone in half an hour. The planes veered south toward the district town of Muong Phine. There, for the first time, I saw the jungle route; a great number of closely intertwined lines running south-ward; narrow paths, trails, small stretches of road—a red artery with an elaborate system of branches, daily pumping new Communist strength into South Viet-Nam.

We passed Muong Nuong, a small settlement of *mon-tagnards,* who build their houses in a circle to protect themselves from evil spirits. Here it was easy to distinguish the main trail from the many auxiliary paths; the road is six to nine feet wide at many points. Soon we came to a large clearing the size of a soccer field. The earth was furrowed with the tracks of vehicles and pocked with bomb craters. This was Pu Yon, an airfield where North Vietnamese pilots formerly landed cargo planes and one of the big crossroads in the southern section of the highway. A maze of paths and trails leads from it past the mountain villages of Kraman and Pahe into the South Vietnamese provinces of Quang Nam and Thua Thien. The main route continues southward past the village of Ban Bac to Chavane, the last big assembly point on Laotian territory.

The squadron followed the main route. I spotted several burned-out villages near the road. The clearings where huts once stood were filled with bomb craters.

Lieutenant Chanh said: "Look below, to the left." I saw the burned wrecks of two trucks in a small open area. "Did you destroy them?" I asked the pilot.

"No, Americans," he said.

Ban Bac is one of the villages along the trail that exists now only on maps. Where the village had been, I saw a new part of the trail. U.S. reconnaissance fliers first discovered this section in October, 1965; another new stretch of road in this area was found a few weeks later. The work had been done under the cover of a roof of leaves. The length and width of this section alarmed U.S. officials; the heaviest transport, including trucks and tanks, could travel along this road.

"When they discovered this road and saw whole columns of trucks rolling south, the Americans were as astonished as the Romans must have been when Hannibal crossed the Alps and suddenly appeared in northern Italy," a French press attaché in Vientiane later told me. "None of the American generals believed the Reds could build this kind of highway undetected in the jungle. No one knows to this day how they did it. But there it is."

The new road begins on the bank of the Sekong River. Previously, heavy cargoes had been ferried South in barges, a long, complicated, and dangerous trip. Now the river, which is sixty feet wide at Ban Bac, is crossed simply. "It's a mystery to me how the Communists do it," General Ma said. The river is six feet deep, there is no bridge, there are no fords, and yet there are a thousand signs that even heavy trucks have somehow crossed over.

The Laotian general said that he believed the North Vietnamese had dug a tunnel beneath the river's bed. "I know them, I think they're capable of anything." American scouts finally solved the mystery: The Communists had built a bridge with a roadway a few inches under the water's surface that was practically impossible to see from the air.

Lieutenant Chanh flew over the mountain slopes, through ravines and valleys, never higher than fifty yards above the winding trail. Here, coolies of the Vietnamese revolution had drudged away undetected; they had worked tirelessly, in constant danger, without modern equipment, with shovels, pick axes, and wicker baskets. The accomplishments of the work gangs on the Ho Chi Minh Trail eclipse those of the Vietnamese who hacked out highways through the jungles to the battlefield of Dien Bien Phu in 1954 for the sake of "Uncle Ho," General Giap, and their country's "liberation."

When Ban Bac was ten miles behind us we saw explosions rise from a mountain ridge. The second squadron had reached its target. Lieutenant Chanh began circling. I tried to locate the objective but saw nothing except thick woods and, in between, wide and newly built sections of the highway.

Finally we reached Chavane, the last big crossroad on the trail in Laos. Again a large gray field rose up before us —an airfield built by the French and later used by Soviet and North Vietnamese aircraft. Today it is an assembly point for heavy truck convoys to South Viet-Nam.

A mesh of small trails and paths emerges here from the deep jungle and unites with the main routes, which continue on toward Cambodia or end in South Viet-Nam's highlands. Again I saw the tracks of heavy vehicles, the trampled paths of marching columns, bomb craters, charred patches of woods, and debris—signs of previous attacks. Chavane was our main target and it was protected by anti-aircraft and machine guns.

Lieutenant Chanh flew over the field several times at a great height. Then he went into a dive as his rockets left our plane with a deafening hiss. When he leveled off, I looked behind to see the clouds from the rocket's explosion hanging in the air. The missiles had detonated on the edge of the field. Suddenly, I heard yells in my earphones and Lieutenant Chanh began gesticulating and pointing toward the ground. I couldn't understand him, except for one frightening term, "Viet-Cong."

Now I saw the flashes on the ground. The second plane swooped down, then the third. Both were strafed by ground fire. The gunners crouched in a small bunker at the eastern edge of the field. Lieutenant Chanh returned to the attack. His second set of rockets shot down as we raced above the jungle, our air cannons roaring. Smoke rose from the bunker and debris whirled through the air. I realized then that we, too, were being heavily strafed.

After making a wide curve, the pilot flew around behind a range of hills at low altitude. Then we returned to the field, as machine guns blazed away at us. We flew straight toward their muzzles at a speed of at least 250 miles an hour. Tracer bullets streaked around the cockpit, like water drops in the headlight of a car speeding through the night.

A blow shook the craft—the last load of rockets being set off. Once more our plane swept away. Later, we discovered we had been hit four times.

The squadron's next objective was Pakse, a town on the Mekong; our craft refueled there for the return trip to Savannaketh.

We flew across a wide valley bounded by a steep mountain range. Again I saw a section of road. Lieutenant Chanh explained that this stretch of the Ho Chi Minh Trail, too, was first discovered a few days ago, still under construction. "Has the work been stopped?" I asked.

"You don't know the Viet-Cong," he answered. "Now they work at night. There still are other road sections being built. But we don't know where."

If I had not been seated in a Laotian Air Force fighter plane and seen the tropical vegetation below, I might have thought I was flying along an Alpine road. The Ho Chi Minh Trail is built of narrow curves, with sections leading across steep slopes and supported by embankments of wooden planks. The road runs along the edge of ravines, mountain ridges, and through deep valleys. One section, leading across an unusually steep slope, is protected from falling rocks by a wooden roof. Millions of cubic feet of earth had to be moved to carve out the road on the slopes. I could understand the dismay of the U.S. military officials. They had believed they were fighting an army of primitive guerrillas and found out that they faced an organized and resourceful enemy. Scores of thousands of people were working for it, accomplishing great feats— under the most difficult conditions—that would have won admiration in peacetime.

Lieutenant Chanh's voice suddenly came over the earphones. "Attention, we're going down." I saw the other two planes circling a point in the jungle. Their guns began firing again. Whom were we strafing? I asked. "Pathet

Lao," Chanh answered. How could he recognize the enemy? "It was a village. All the villages here are occupied by Communists. We have a standing order to shoot at everything that shows up in Pathet Lao territory."

The T-28 finally landed at Savannaketh. A jeep raced alongside the plane as it taxied down the runway. It reached us as I jumped to the ground. General Ma was the driver. "Have you seen the trail? Now do you believe that it exists?" he asked.

"Yes, I know it does," I said. "But it's not a trail, it's a road—a runway through the jungle." The General grinned with satisfaction.

The Laotian Air Force flies almost daily missions against the jungle road. Americans and South Vietnamese have been bombing it for years. Yet, all attempts to stop the flow of Communist supplies and men through Laos have been little more than harassing operations. Total interdiction or destruction of the trail is impossible.

The obvious question is: Why didn't the Americans long ago engage in massive, annihilating strikes against the Communist supply lines? The answer is that the Americans were not aware of the real extent of the system of trails until recently. They still do not know about all the roads and paths leading south. Besides, every attempt to destroy the jungle trail with conventional weapons involves extraordinary and unsuitable methods.

The total length of the paths, trails and roads, collectively described as the Ho Chi Minh Trail, is greater than 12,500 miles. The trail runs through a territory that stretches from the Chinese frontier to Cambodia. It is impossible to control this enormous, almost unpopulated area for long with ground troops unless whole armies are deployed. Not the Americans, the Laotians, or the South Vietnamese have such forces at their disposal.

Paratroopers could seize sections of the trail, destroy them, or control them for a while. Yet, a few miles from their area of operations, behind the next mountain ridge or through the next ravine, there is possibly another trail running south, and patrolling forces may not even know of its existence.

It is impossible to make combat contact with Communist troops on the trail; an attack force could wander for weeks through the jungle without coming across a single enemy soldier. "It's practically an accident when we meet up with a marching column or discover trucks on the trail," an American Air Force officer said. "The Reds march by night. They're well camouflaged and move in a region that is impossible to keep under watch."

In the winter of 1966, the Americans believed they had the solution; they attacked the "bottlenecks" of the Ho Chi Minh Trail, points where the military highway crosses narrow passes along the mountainous border between North Viet-Nam and Laos. Giant B-52's stationed in Guam flew in massive assault, dropping hundreds of tons of bombs over Mhu-Ghia Pass and other frontier crossings, almost completely destroying large stretches of the trail. The Americans believed they had succeeded in cutting the road, but two days later the Communist columns were rolling again. The attacks were resumed; again the work crews repaired all the damage in a few days, and again the columns rolled south. American fliers had the same experience with other targets along the trail. Finally, General Westmoreland conceded that "There is very little, almost nothing, we can do about the Ho Chi Minh Boulevard."

Washington's decision to force the enemy to its knees by bombing strikes against Hanoi and Haiphong is one result of the lesson taught the U.S. Attempts to destroy the guerrilla communication lines are useless. Despite all U.S. military efforts, reinforcements for the NLF troops keep coming.

The number of men sent south on the Ho Chi Minh Trail during the first war years was relatively small, probably less than 3,000 in 1959 and 1960. These were mainly political functionaries, officers, technicians, intelligence and agitprop specialists who had been trained in the North and now were returning home to South Viet-Nam. Nguyen Cham is a typical Viet-Cong soldier of the first years, who came south down the Ho Chi Minh Trail. He is a native of the Annamite province of Quang Tin. In 1946, he became head of the Viet-Minh youth group in his village; a year later, at fifteen, he was assigned to a guerrilla unit. In 1954, he joined the 20th Independent Battalion of the Viet-Minh and arrived in North Viet-Nam in May, 1955. He soon left his unit and began working in a cooperative farm. The army recalled him in 1960, and he served in the 210th North Vietnamese Infantry Regiment, assigned to smelting work in Nghe An Province—Ho Chi Minh's native province. For a year the Viet-Minh veteran and his comrades, directed by two engineers from Hanoi, poured ore into small, primitive furnaces. Nguyen Cham learned how ores with a relatively high metal content could be treated by simple means; later, he would pass on his knowledge to Viet-Cong soldiers.

In August, 1961, he and thirty-five of his comrades, all South Vietnamese, were transported by truck to the Laotian border. After a nineteen-day march the unit reached Tchepone, then the most important assembly point on the Ho Chi Minh Trail. It had to wait three days until North Vietnamese planes flew in food and equipment. Nguyen Cham and his comrades marched another nineteen days through eastern Laos and crossed the South Vietnamese border in Kontum Province. The Viet-Cong had discovered an ore deposit in Kontum and wanted to exploit it. Nguyen Cham had been chosen to build small furnaces in the jungle and supervise the foundry work. He was finally wounded and taken prisoner in a battle with South Vietnamese Rangers.

In 1962, thousands of South Vietnamese living in the North were recruited and sent back south. Nguyen Thao, a native of Khanh Hoa Province who had joined the Viet-Minh in 1950, was one of them. He was trained as a guerrilla weapons specialist in a secret jungle workshop. Fearing persecution, he fled north after 1954. There he worked in an arms factory, specializing in the rebuilding of American small arms and light guns. He was sent to the town of Ha Dong in December, 1962, where he attended a political training course. Then, he and fourteen other South Vietnamese were told that they must return to the South. The group, which crossed the Laotian frontier in March, 1963, included arms specialists, intelligence technicians, and two chemists. The men reached South Viet-Nam after a two months' march. Nguyen Thao was assigned to a secret arms factory in Quang Ngai Province and supervised a group of fifty workers who produced mines and grenades for the guerrilla army. U.S. troops captured him in 1964.

A thousand trails and paths run through the jungle from North Viet-Nam to guerrilla territory in the South, but most of the men who infiltrated back to their homeland took virtually the same route, the Ho Chi Minh Trail.

Most Viet-Cong guerrillas coming from North Viet-Nam were trained in two places, Xuan Mai, a town near Hanoi, and Thanh Hoa, a town further south. There they passed through a four to six month course before they were taken by truck to Vinh, the largest southern town in Ho Chi Minh's republic. A majority were sent from Vinh to a camp in Dong Ho, near the 17th Parallel, for more training. When they finished, trucks transported them to the Laotian border.

Precise organization and planning are major weapons of the Communist guerrillas; this applies to marches over the jungle trails too. Special units of the North Vietnamese Army and Viet-Cong are stationed along the trail in North Viet-Nam, Laos, and Cambodia. Their task is to supervise and expedite the transports. About 5,000 men are stationed along the highway; they consist of commandos, guards, technicians, mechanic, intelligence and radio specialists. They maintain supply, weapon, and food depots, hospitals, radio stations, and repair shops. The number of labor units has been expanded because of constant bombing of the trails; 30,000 laborers are now on duty repairing damage to the jungle road.

Tchepone long ago ceased to be the trail's main crossroads to Laotian territory. The big assembly areas were broken up into many small, fortified, and camouflaged camps. The columns on the march are channeled from camp to camp. *Montagnards,* who live in the region and know the territory intimately, are stationed in almost every one of them. They act as guides for the troops; but they are only allowed to take them as far as the next camp from where they return to their original camp. They maintain strict silence and are forbidden to give the soldiers the location of the area through which they are passing. Only troop commanders are briefed on the destination. It takes four or five days, at the most, to move from one camp to the next. The troops receive fresh rations and water in each camp and are allowed a brief rest.

Ho Chi Minh's soldiers and the Viet-Cong guerrillas travel in small groups, mainly in units of fifty to sixty. The marches are extremely strenuous and often take weeks or months. Their losses are high. U.S. intelligence estimates that about one fourth of the marching soldiers become casualties: Some fall ill, others are wounded by bombs, and others collapse from exhaustion. What follows is a description of the experiences of one such unit, based upon the diary of its commander.

On September 20, 1965, the last company of the *Groupement* Doan 565 of the 4th Independent Regiment of the North Vietnamese Army left the town of Vinh. Two days later the company commander, Captain Le Huy Linh noted: "We are being transported by truck to the district of Huong Son. An artillery unit of the battalion is with us. We don't know our destination."

September 27. "We are now marching on foot. Corporal Nguyen Xuan Giang thinks we are going to South Viet-Nam. I forbid him to talk about it."

September 29. "It's a very hard march. But we are still not in enemy territory. I don't know what awaits us there.

A commissar accompanying us says that we must, if necessary, change uniforms." (North Vietnamese soldiers often exchange their uniforms for the "black pajamas" of the Viet-Cong. They are instructed to say, if captured, that they are guerrillas, not North Vietnamese regulars.)

October 2. "We have advanced to the Laos border on roads 15, 8, and 12. In one camp we met a company of our army. The men had been supplied with black pajamas. It's going south."

October 3. "Tran Quang Trung, the battalion's political commissar, informs me we're headed for Laos. Reinforcements will join us before we reach the frontier."

October 5. "We have crossed the border. Our company consists of 104 men in four platoons."

October 6. "We have pitched camp on the other side of the border. Two more companies of our battalion have joined us. The 2nd Company came from Ha Thinh, the 3rd Company from Quang Binh. We are now in the region of Kham Mouane [Thakkekh]. We will spend four days receiving instructions on the impending operations."

October 15. "We have reached Ban Khama. They have issued more equipment and rations to us. Every man in the company has received two hand grenades, 100 rounds of rifle ammunition, a poncho, a mosquito net, and eight pounds of rice."

October 22. "Tran Quang Trung leaves. He is going ahead to prepare the way for our march south."

October 27. "We pitched camp in the woods. They say we are going to participate in an offensive against the Laotian Army. I don't believe this rumor."

November 7. "For the first time we made battle contact with the enemy. Laotian troops. They are not very brave. We lost one man, they probably suffered heavy losses."

November 9. "We are in the vicinity of Mahaxay. The Mekong is only 15 miles away. Thailand is on the other side, and so are the Americans. The 3rd Company fought Laotian troops, who quickly retreated. We have met with little resistance."

November 10. "The 2nd Company reports encounter. It lost one man, but destroyed two Laotian artillery guns."

November 14. "The order is given to destroy all papers or leave them in an assembly camp. I don't know whether we can do that. We are marching toward Thakkekh. The Laotian Air Force is giving us a great deal of trouble. Planes overhead constantly. A platoon was hit by a bomb attack and suffered heavy casualties. We are right outside Thakkekh and can't advance another step. Duong Ngoc Dien, a corporal in my 2nd Platoon, discovered a cave, and we took cover in it from the bombs."

November 17. "We are under continuous attack. We have lost four or five men. Four men have managed to escape from the cave."

November 19. "We are being bombarded by artillery, but the Laotians are afraid to move in on us."

November 21. "We're running short of ammunition. Almost no food left. I have a shell fragment in my right leg. The wound hurts."

November 21. "There are still 14 of us, the remnants of an entire company. Hoang Ngoc Nhiem, one of my soldiers, is badly wounded. We're out of ammunition, nothing to eat or drink. It's the thirst that bothers us most. I haven't swallowed a drop of water in four days."

The next day Captain Le Huy Linh surrendered to the Laotians. I talked to him for some time in Vientiane; he told me the story of his march. He assured me that he had had his fill of war and wanted to request asylum in Laos. However, two days later a tunnel was discovered which he and his men had dug under the wall surrounding the jail. They had planned to escape and rejoin their unit.

The job of protecting the Laotian portion of the Ho Chi Minh Trail is shared by the North Vietnamese Army, Viet-Cong guerrillas, and the soldiers of the Pathet Lao. (Pathet Lao forces control about two-thirds of Laos including all of its mountainous northeast). Their main task is to keep the Laotian Government troops in check. It would probably be easy for the Pathet Lao and North Vietnamese to overrun eastern Laos, but they refrain from doing so. As long as the fighting continues in South Viet-Nam, the Communists are interested mainly in keeping open the supply routes, and there is no point in their being tied up in a second theater of war.

Every offensive involving the Mekong River—and with it the Thailand frontier—could precipitate American intervention in Laos. The United States has quietly increased its Laotian contingent recently in order to make clear that American troops would meet a Communist offensive head-on in Laos, the heart of Southeast Asia.

The Vietnamese guerrillas are fighting a war with constantly shifting or no fronts. But in Laos, government troops, North Vietnamese units, and the Pathet Lao occupy fixed positions, with permanent bunkers, often only 100 yards apart. It is a war stabilized for political reasons.

Near Thakkekh, I changed fronts and joined a unit of the Pathet Lao Army. The switch involved days of lonely travel through a mountainous jungle landscape. It was not difficult to leave the Laotian Government lines; it was even easier to contact the soldiers of the Pathet Lao. I was seized by a patrol and taken to a camp near the village of Ban Vieng. The soldiers were courteous, allowed me to take pictures, and sang revolutionary songs in my honor. Since there were no girls around, some of them even donned female costumes to show me their old folk dances.

Laos is in the twilight of what may become the total darkness of a great war, and that is why the Communist rebels are behaving. They have dug into solid bunkers, and so have their countrymen on the other side.

Two Pathet Lao soldiers later brought me far behind the lines of the government troops, right to the gates of Thakkekh. I did not succeed in seeing the Ho Chi Minh Trail, although transports for South Viet-Nam in this area sometimes move along old colonial routes only a few miles from the town.

No Westerner—aside from the pilots who bomb it—has ever seen or been on the Ho Chi Minh Trail except for a French lieutenant whom I shall call Jacques Blanchard. I met him in Vientiane where he was part of a French military advisory group and almost finished with his tour of duty in Southeast Asia. He had been stationed near a military road and knew the Ho Chi Minh Trail was somewhere in the area. "I felt it would make history some day. How could I return to France without having seen it?"

Blanchard went to Pakse in southern Laos, hired several guides, and started out. He told his fellow officers he was off on a hunting trip and would be back in about fifteen days. If he was not, they were to inform his superiors. His equipment consisted of several small bags of rice, a

poncho, canned food, a hammock, and a few hand grenades. "I needed these for fishing, not to defend myself,"
he explained. After marching for two days he knew he
was being trailed; his escorts had vanished.

"They were Pathet Lao, and they kept at a safe distance
behind me. I had some fish and broiled them. I ate one,
left the rest, and continued on. I repeated this several
times. The fourth day I remained seated in my camp until
the Pathet Lao guerrillas came right up to me. They were
friendly when they saw I was not an American. I told
them I wanted to get a look at the Ho Chi Minh Trail,
and their leader said he would take me to a camp in the
jungle where my request might possibly be granted."

That evening Blanchard was in the Pathet Lao camp.
"Not until I was deep inside it did I realize the camp
would accommodate at least 500 men. The bunkers, underground lodgings, and tents were wonderfully camouflaged," he said. A North Vietnamese officer questioned
him briefly and promised to show him a section of road
that was being built.

"We left the next morning, a party of twelve men. We
followed small paths and, after a four-hour march, suddenly came upon another camp. It was not for soldiers,
but workers and peasants building the road. I had never
believed it possible that so many people could work here
in the middle of the wilderness. Hundreds of people
drudged away on the road, with pick axes and small
wheelbarrows, silently and frantically. Sometimes there
were quick commands when a column of porters passed
through carrying heavy loads. The commands and the
clank of tools were the only sounds I heard."

The lieutenant was introduced to several men in a tent

belonging to the squad leader and work supervisors. "Some were Chinese. I've been in the Far East long enough to tell Vietnamese from Chinese at a glance."

Blanchard came across a scene off the main road that astounded him. He saw a column of tall men coming down a narrow jungle path. "At first I thought they, too, were Chinese because they towered over the small Vietnamese. But then I saw they were whites, Americans, captured soldiers who were wheeling heavy loads of earth on bicycles. They were emaciated and exhausted and scarcely looked at me. They were bound by iron chains around their wrists to the bicycle frames. My Vietnamese escort told me they were prisoners paying for their crimes against the Vietnamese people."

Two days later Lieutenant Blanchard was allowed to leave. A week later he was in Vientiane, and five days afterward he left Laos for home. I do not know how accurate his report is, but to my knowledge he is the only European ever to have been on the Ho Chi Minh Trail.

The history of the trail's use tells a good deal about the war itself. About 80 per cent of the supplies for the Communist armies in South Viet-Nam now comes down the Ho Chi Minh Trail. The percentage was much smaller previously when the faster and simpler—but more dangerous—sea route was used. Junks, motorboats, fishing boats, and freighters formerly carried troops and matériel from the North to the delta coast in South Viet-Nam.

On February 16, 1965, an American helicopter pilot spotted a freighter moving along the coast of the central Vietnamese province of Phu Yen. The ship zigzagged in its effort to reach the nearby coast. The American pilot called for air support, and soon planes arrived. The freighter reached the coast but, under bombardment, it ran ashore in the shallow waters.

A regiment of South Vietnamese troops was alerted to inspect the ship. But before it could take it over, it had to fight a hard battle; Viet-Cong guerrillas quickly occupied the wreck and defended it furiously. They finally had to retreat before the superior power of the South Vietnamese.

The ship had left Haiphong at the end of January, 1965, with a cargo of 100 tons of weapons, ammunition, and other military supplies including 1 million cartridges, 2,000 7.95-mm. Mauser rifles, 1,000 75-mm. artillery shells of Chinese make, 1,000 submachine guns, 600 pounds of explosives, and 1,300 pounds of drugs. It was a Chinese ship and had been launched six months earlier; its destination had been a small port on the coast of the Ninh Thuan Province. The cargo would have been sufficient to equip an entire regiment.

Because freighters attract attention, now when the guerrillas transport their supplies by sea, they more frequently use fishing boats and sampans like those that swarm along South Viet-Nam's coast, rivers, and canals. In February, 1966, the crew of an American Coast Guard boat discovered a ton and a half of 75-mm. artillery shells in a sampan navigated by five innocuous looking young men. The cargo was hidden under clumps of bananas. The sampan was seized off the coast of Bac Lieu Province; its crew was found to be North Vietnamese soldiers, who had navigated 750 miles in three weeks, from the North Vietnamese town of Dong Hoi to a point 150 miles south of Saigon. Their destination was to be the Ca Mau peninsula at the southern point of Viet-Nam.

In 1965 and 1966, the guerrillas reduced the transport

of supplies by sea. As American involvement in Viet-Nam became stronger and deeper, the U.S. Coast Guard and airplanes proved too great a risk. Now, more than ever, the main transports roll down the jungle paths of the Ho Chi Minh Trail.

13

The Continuing War

We have only one answer for the American imperialists: to fight, to fight, to keep on fighting.

Nhan Dan, July, 1966

THERE IS NO easy way to close a journalist's report on a war without precedent and without sign of ending. Perhaps I may cite two events that may give some indication of things to come.

In Hanoi, Ho Chi Minh proclaimed partial mobilization on July 14, 1966. The same day, the United States set a new record in the bombing war with 116 attacks. The figure seems outlandish, given the country's economic backwardness and primitive infrastructure. Besides, U.S. officials are the only source of information on the extent of bomb damage in the North. According to their data, up to mid-1966, 800 bridges were destroyed and 800 damaged; the supply routes to Laos along the Ho Chi Minh Trail and those coming south from China were destroyed at more than 2,000 points. The railroad lines from Hanoi and Haiphong to China were disrupted at more than 200 points; 200 trucks were bombed to bits. Bombs wiped out a number of war plants and weapon and food depots. In all, 1,500 missions were flown against North Viet-Nam;

their number had increased by almost 1,000 per cent since February, 1965, and 225,000 tons of bombs were expended in Viet-Nam in that year, while 638,000 tons were "programmed" for 1966. (There were also about 375,000 U.S. soldiers in Viet-Nam at the close of 1966.) Yet, not even 20 per cent of North Viet-Nam's defensive capability and economy was knocked out.

North Viet-Nam is a country engaged in total war. The population of the large cities has been evacuated; the first large relocations began in 1965. A Frenchman who had been teaching in Hanoi told me that trenches had been dug and the people trained in air-raid drills even before the bombings began. Schools and hospitals were moved to the countryside. Later, the universities were closed; high school and university students were assigned to air-defense units, to the militia or army, or sent to work on the land or in war industries.

There have been reports that over 70 per cent of Hanoi's population has been evacuated, with ministries and important administrative agencies scattered to safe, protected villages.

The few Western eyewitnesses who have visited North Viet-Nam in the last few years report that the first bombing attacks created considerable panic, but after a short while the people recovered their sense of discipline. Now, cars mounted with loudspeakers roam the streets daily and announce the positions of the approaching American planes. At the first warning, the people cover their mouths with cloths they have made themselves; they believe—and the government does nothing to disillusion them—that the planes spray poison gas. Civil defense workers with red arm bands guide the people to defense shelters.

"It happens in a ghostlike, silent manner. Life suddenly fades away, cars are parked at the curb, shops close; people disappear from the sidewalks—and in a few minutes soldiers and civil defense workers are patrolling the empty streets. The only sound comes from the loudspeakers announcing the targets and the number of planes shot down," a secretary for the French delegation in Hanoi told me.

The North Vietnamese suffered their greatest losses in lives when the Communist Party leadership, in view of the country's defenselessness against American jets, issued the disastrous slogan, "Rifles against planes." It set off a mass movement that, at times, assumed hysterical proportions. The Communists in the North, as in the South, seriously believed they could shoot down attacking jets with ordinary rifles. The experiment cost hundreds of lives. Not until August and September, 1965, when Soviet anti-aircraft artillery and missiles were put into operation, was the "rifle movement" gradually deflated. It is still in evidence, though; the peasant in a rice paddy shooting his rifle at an attacking jet bomber is one of the widely used clichés of Communist defense propaganda.

The daily report of U.S. aircraft downed is posted in towns, villages, and on the roads. The North Vietnamese claim to have shot down more than 1,200 American planes, an obvious figment of the imagination. Despite anti-aircraft missiles and the latest types of Soviet MiG fighters, North Viet-Nam has yet to find an effective weapon against attacking bomber formations.

The already spartan life of the civilian population has continued to deteriorate. Everything is rationed. The shops are empty. Dummy cartons are displayed in the few shop windows; there is practically nothing to buy. The government has decreed a monthly rice ration of 13 kilograms per person, but this amount is rarely available; most of the time the individual ration comes to no more than 9 kilograms a month.

The people are not starving, but they are hungry. The average earnings of a family of five is about $15. A small can of conserved milk from the U.S.S.R. costs $1.20; a can of fish, 50 cents; a pair of sandals, 60 cents.

The entire country is harnessed to the government's war program. More than 100,000 peasants were mobilized for road construction on the Laotian border and for the Ho Chi Minh system of way stations; many serve as porters for the army of General Giap.

More than 250,000 men and women are enrolled in "voluntary labor brigades" that work day and night shifts to repair bomb damages. Entire divisions are concentrated in the northern provinces between Hanoi and Haiphong and around Vinh, restoring roads and bridges.

The people are urged to ever greater efforts in mass movements. Two million youths signed up in the movement of the "Three Readies"; 800,000 women have promised to double their output because of the "imperialist danger"; more than 200 enterprises made pledges of payless overtime work "in order to guarantee the victory of the nation." But as long as the war lasts, there is no possibility of rebuilding destroyed factories. Nor has the government taken any steps in this direction. However, undamaged industry has been successfully decentralized and relocated in the impenetrable jungles or mountain provinces.

"We live from day to day, not knowing when or where the next bomb will fall," the press attaché of the North

Vietnamese Embassy in Vientiane said. "But we are alive, and as long as we are alive, we can work, and we can fight."

The Western public reads many reports on the extent of the destruction wrought by the bombing war, but it is difficult to gauge the indirect effects of the bombings. There is no way of knowing how long the country can withstand the bombings, or how long the Communists in the North will be able to support their comrades in the South; or whether Ho Chi Minh's government can run the risk of letting the ground war for South Viet-Nam spread to the North.

The growing number of Soviet jet fighters in the North Vietnamese sky, the dispatch of Soviet military specialists, the decisions of the latest conference of the Warsaw Pact states, the offers of aid received by Ho Chi Minh from most Eastern European countries, and, above all, China's rigid attitude, make it probable that North Viet-Nam and the guerrillas in the South can count on greater help from the Communist world in the period ahead. The war in the North, as in the South, will become bloodier. Guerrilla wars—especially the one in Viet-Nam—are upsetting the laws of traditional warfare and economics. The military victory of the guerrillas may now be impossible; but the political defeat of the Viet-Cong may be equally impossible.

The United States may escalate the war further, but it has no guarantee, in the end, of winning it politically. The Communists in North Viet-Nam and their backers in China say that they will continue with the war, whether it lasts another five, ten, or twenty years. Their statements must be taken seriously; after all, guerrilla wars can long lie dormant and then erupt again at a more advantageous moment, under more favorable conditions, for the guerrillas. Prospects for the most rational solution—through political negotiation—remain remote.

Thirty million people have been promised independence, freedom, and their share of the earth's bounty. Meanwhile, they continue to endure the agony of a terrible war. When peace comes, the victors will be neither the United States nor China but the people of Viet-Nam who have managed to survive.